INTRODUCTION TO POLITICAL ECONOMY

MARX, VEBLEN, GALBRAITH, KEYNES, AND THE POLITICAL ECONOMY VIEW

SECOND EDITION

by
Charles Sackrey and Geoffrey Schneider

with Janet Knoedler

ISBN: 1-878585-22-3

The Economic Affairs Bureau publishes *Dollars & Sense*, a bimonthly magazine. *D&S* explains the working of the U.S. and international economies and provides left perspectives on current economic affairs. It is edited and produced by a collective of economists, journalists, and activists who are committed to social justice and economic democracy.

The Economic Affairs Bureau also publishes the following classroom books: *Real World Macro, Real World Micro, Current Economic Issues, Real World Globalization, Real World Banking, The Environment in Crisis,* and *Unlevel Playing Fields: Understanding Wage Inequality and Discrimination.*

Dollars and Sense
Economic Affairs Bureau, Inc.
740 Cambridge St.
Cambridge, MA 02141
Phone: (617) 876-2434
Fax: (617) 876-0008
E-mail: <dollars@dollarsandsense.org>
Website: <www.dollarsandsense.org>

Cover art by: James Schneider
Cover by: Nick Thorkelson

Manufactured by Transcontinental Printing
Printed in Canada

Table of Contents

Preface to the Second Edition

We have written the following essays in order to introduce our readers, we presume mostly students, to the economic thinking of Karl Marx and Thorstein Veblen, to certain unorthodox elements in the thought of John Maynard Keynes, to John Kenneth Galbraith's Theory of Social Balance, to the nature of and implications of social classes in capitalism, and to the efforts of economists and others to build a modern welfare state in Sweden. We are calling this kind of thinking "political economy" to distinguish it from the "mainstream" of economics that dominates instruction in contemporary capitalist societies. In our final essay, we describe and critically analyze mainstream economics from a political economy point of view. Here, we will pause long enough to provide what we consider the most important difference between these two schools of thought by quoting from one textbook that gives attention to them both.[1]

> Political economy…is more concerned [than mainstream economics] with the relationships of the economic system and its institutions to the rest of society and social development. It is sensitive to the influence of non-economic factors such as political and social institutions, morality, and ideology in determining economic events. It thus has a *much broader focus* than [mainstream] economics. (Riddell, Shackelford, and Stamos,

Economics: A Tool for Critically Understanding Society, 5th Edition, 1998. Emphasis supplied.)

A bit of historical background will help to make sense of this quotation. What we are calling political economy was first fully developed in the work of Adam Smith, whose *The Wealth of Nations*, in 1776, contained a fabulously rich combination of theoretical analysis, historical setting, and mountains of details. His book was a work of political economy, in the way we are describing it here, in that he took into account anything and everything that caught his attention, and to read it is to discover the broad outlines, and countless details, of British life in the late 18th century. For most of the next century, people studying the economy, and this included Marx and Veblen, followed Smith's lead in producing broadly cast arguments in which there were no predictable boundaries to the kinds of knowledge that would be brought to bear on the analysis. While Marx and Veblen, and other such political economists, clearly focused attention on economic activity— how people produced their livelihood and how they divided it up—they roamed far and wide in looking for ideas and information that would help them to explain what they saw happening.

However, after the middle of the 19th century, social scientists came to adopt a version of the "scientific method" as their approach, which they borrowed from physical scientists, such as physicists, chemists, and biologists. Successes in these scientific fields starting in the 16th century had gradually recruited many thinkers into taking a scientific approach to their studies, and this was certainly true of economists. By the 20th century, more and more economics came to be expressed in the terms of mathematics and statistics, especially after 1950. Presently the economics profession is dominated, as are the graduate schools that produce professional economists, by economists who tend to exclude from their analyses those things that are not readily measurable or otherwise not appropriate for quantitative model building.

As the discipline has been narrowed in this way, it has pushed to the margin alternative schools of economics, most especially political economy. Political economists who, as Riddell, Shackelford, and Stamos put it, are "sensitive to the influence of non-economic factors such as

---

[1] On this matter of what to call the various schools of economics, the several possibilities mean that we need to define the schools with terms we will use throughout the book. John Kenneth Galbraith, a U.S. political economist, has called the dominating school of economics from Adam Smith until our own time the "central tradition," a usage we will adopt. Concerning schools of thought *within* that tradition, we will draw from a fusion of terms used by Marx, Keynes, and U.S. economist, Paul Samuelson, as follows: we will describe economics from Adam Smith until Keynes' *General Theory*, in 1936, as "classical economics." And, for economists in the central tradition after 1936, we will use the term "mainstream" or "neoclassical." Some kinds of political economy are included in mainstream economics. These are typically an analysis of the relationship between political institutions and economic markets, but done essentially in the terms of mainstream economic models, as we describe them below.

political and social institutions, morality, and ideology in determining economic events," have increasingly found their work shunned by the major economics journals, often because it is considered to be "non-economic." From our view, the most unfortunate consequence of this trend is that the ideas of writers like Marx, and Veblen, or the unorthodox ideas of Keynes and Galbraith, are rarely studied by economists as graduate students, thus less frequently taught by such graduate students when they become professors. Mainstream economists almost never study the social classes that encompass us all and importantly shape who we come to be. And, it would be rare, indeed, for graduate students in the U.S. to learn anything in depth about the Swedish economic "experiment," or even to know its broader outlines. Our readers will discover as we go along that, though mainstream economists have painted themselves into a corner more barren than it need be, others have been more open to the ideas and themes of political economy, including policy makers, scholars, and regular citizens.

We believe that if this book is read alongside the typical mainstream economics textbook, students will end up with a fairly good introduction to both approaches and thus a far richer understanding of capitalist societies than if one such approach is studied without the other one. Also, after our readers go through this book and their textbook, they can judge for themselves which approach, or which combination of approaches, works best to help them understand the economic world in which most will spend a lifetime making a living.

Last, we would like to thank colleagues who read earlier drafts of these essays, all of whom gave us good reasons to rewrite parts of each of them. These helpful critics are: Teresa Amott, Dennis Baumwoll, Lou Casimir, Tom Kinnaman, John Kirkland, Catherine O'Connor, Cadwell Ray,

Eric Ruckh, Paul Susman, and Amy Wolaver. Also, thanks to Ellen Campbell who helped to write and to edit the essay on the modern Swedish economy. And especially to Laurie Dougherty and Alejandro Reuss, we extend our appreciation for editing these essays and in doing so making them a more focused exposition of the arguments we made. And finally, in this project all along we have received a major contribution from Janet Knoedler, who wrote the chapter on Veblen, who wrote a section of our chapter that critiques mainstream economics, and who helped us to imagine and to plan this project.

A BRIEF NOTE TO INSTRUCTORS

We have written these essays to be read independently of each other and in whatever sequence works best for individual courses. Most of these essays would seem to be easily placed; however, where to use the essay where we critique mainstream economics from a political economy point of view, is probably not as easily determined. We wrote and included this essay because we believe it important for readers to understand the nature of political economy in terms of how its basic methodology of studying the world compares to that of the mainstream. Some of us who have taught this book in classes think that the critique essay is best taken up at the end of the course, after students have been exposed to a semester of mainstream models and some political economy. Another possibility would be to begin the course with a discussion of economic methodology, and to contrast the mainstream and political economy approaches throughout the semester. Whatever the sequence, we are hopeful instructors will see fit to take up the essay sometime during the semester.

Chapter I

The Marxist System: An Introduction

Our goal in this essay is to present a coherent summary of Marx's analysis of economic forces in society and how they shaped human lives. We will do that in two parts. The first briefly outlines a theory of historical change that Marx developed with his long-time collaborator, Frederick Engels. In 1845-6, the two wrote a manuscript, *The German Ideology,* that was largely an attack on prominent German philosophers of their time. It was not published during their lives and, as Marx wrote later, he "abandoned it to the gnawing criticism of the mice in his attic." However, when it was published in the Soviet Union in 1932 readers discovered that its first part, probably written by Marx, contained an explanation of historical change that Marx called "the materialist conception of history." We will provide a structural outline of this "conception of history" with a few examples to help the reader learn the basic terminology of the system.

We will then examine how Marx applied his theory of historical change to capitalism. This application is spread over thousands of pages of material that Marx and Engels wrote. However, the single most compact presentation is in *Capital*, volume 1, and the second part of our essay will concentrate attention on the arguments about capitalism in that book. *Capital* is by far Marx's most thorough application of his materialist conception of history: one is actually an example of the other, and by presenting them in sequence we hope to make the "Marxian" view of capitalism less opaque. Marx's analysis of capitalism is an intricate theoretical structure, buttressed by a huge compendium of historical description, that when studied closely can be genuinely breathtaking in its breadth and depth.

We also want readers to see the great divide between Marx's analysis of capitalism and that of most current mainstream economists, who tend to look upon capitalism as a "given system" but exhibit little or no professional interest in the historical process that gave rise to it. They have, as it were, ripped economic analysis from its historical context, ignoring the evolution of the capitalist system. As we tramp our way through the Marxist world we will see how substantial is this difference between his work and that of mainstream economists.

MARXIST SYSTEM, PART I: THE MATERIALIST CONCEPTION OF HISTORY BRIEFLY DEFINED

Marx asks a fundamental question confronting all human societies. What must we do to survive? To live, we must mix our intelligence and our energy—our work—with the basic "materials" of the world we find ourselves in, its soil, water, and air. We must work with what's at hand in order to make this today into tomorrow. In 1878, Frederick Engels summarized his and Marx's theory of historical change in the following way:

The materialist conception of history starts from the principle that production, and with production the exchange of its products, is the basis of every social order; that in every society that has appeared in history the distribution of the products, and with it the division of society into classes or estates, is determined by what is produced and how it is produced, and how the product is exchanged (*Socialism: Utopian and Scientific*, Peking: Foreign Language Press, 1975, p. 74).

This economic organization of society, or the "mode of production" as Marx called it, is therefore the most powerful force in determining the structure of human society. Furthermore, how society is organized to produce necessities—

for example, into serfs and lords in feudalism, or into owners and workers in capitalist societies—constitutes the "class structure" of society. Since virtually all production involves many different people, Marx concentrated on production as a *social* activity and analyzed the class structure that resulted from the organization of production.

Marx's method of analysis is very different from that employed by Adam Smith, who focused on how *individuals* behaved within a beneficent, competitive capitalist society. In contrast, Marx sought to understand the forces that cause the economy to change over time. He believed that change resulted from the struggle between opposing, or "dialectical"—what we might think of as "contradictory" or competing—forces inherent in all societies. Marx found that the social activity of production took many different forms throughout history, with stages of social organization related to techniques of production. He noted that European society passed through a number of different modes of production, including primitive communalism, slavery, and feudalism, on its way to capitalism. He concluded that capitalism is simply the latest in a series of modes of production and that it, too, will yield to some other mode of production in the future.[1]

The pattern of the ownership of the tools and materials generally shapes the system of social classes in a society. The two dominant classes in capitalism are the bourgeoisie and the proletariat. Below, we will discuss their relationship and what generates conflict between them, but for now we can emphasize their different stations with a brief look at how wealth in the U.S. is divided between them. According to Doug Henwood (*Wall Street*, 1997), the richest 10% of the U.S. population owns over 80% of all stocks and almost 90% of all bonds. Since owning the stocks and bonds of companies means owning their "means of

production," the wealth-producing capital of the United States is almost all owned by one tenth of the population. In order to make a living, most of the other 90% must work either for these richest 10%, or their managers, or in the non-profit sector of the economy.

Additionally, for the past two decades, the U.S. working classes have experienced a dramatic decline in income, relative to that of the owners and top managers for whom they work. For example, in 1965, the average CEO's salary was 44 times the average factory worker's wages, but today that ratio is *over 400 to 1*. The changing fortunes of owners and workers in U.S. capitalism are fine examples of what Marx meant by the inherent struggle between workers and capitalists. They also exemplify the inherent contradictions, or "dialectical" pressures, within U.S. capitalism because sustained, relative declines in income for the majority of a society's population tend to produce political upheaval. The interests of Wall Street rarely coincide with the interests of Main Street.

Through his study of history, Marx came to believe that conflict between the classes was the source of most major changes in human society. He summarized this idea in the following passage from *The Communist Manifesto,* written in 1848:

> The history of all hitherto existing society is the history of class struggles. Freeman and slave, patrician and plebeian, lord and serf, guild-master and journeyman, in a word, oppressor and oppressed, stood in constant opposition to one another, carried on an uninterrupted, now hidden, now open fight, a fight that each time ended, either in a revolutionary re-constitution of society at large, or in the common ruin of the contending classes.

Marx's focus on social classes in conflict is central to his analysis of capitalism, and we will take it up again in Part II.

Another principal argument in Marx's materialist conception of history is that every mode of production fundamentally shaped other aspects of society. C. Wright Mills, a sociologist influential in the 1950s and 1960s, wrote in *The Marxists* (1962):

---

[1] In talking about modes of production, Marxists use a few terms that one should know. The *forces of production* include all things needed to produce output: machinery, tools, natural resources, and human effort and human capital (skills and knowledge). By themselves, the machinery, tools, and resources are the *means of production*. Those who own them are the *bourgeoisie,* or *capitalists.* Those who don't own such capital goods, who must live by wage labor, are *proletarians.* The *social relations of production* in capitalism are the ongoing interactions between capitalists and laborers in the workplace, in particular the conditions by which workers will produce enough output to guarantee a profit to capitalists.

Political, religious and legal institutions as well as the ideas, the images, the ideologies by means of which men understand the world in which they live, their place within it, and themselves—all these are reflections of the economic basis of society.

For example, religious beliefs in hunter-gatherer societies usually emphasize the importance of the role of nature and of people within it, and this reflects the importance to survival of the natural environment for that particular mode of production. Concerning religious beliefs, Marx was struck by the influence on economic behavior of the early Protestant religions that began to develop after the revolt by Martin Luther against Catholicism in the early 16th century. These new religions strongly underscored the counsel of the Catholic Church that one should accept one's lot in life and that all would be better in the hereafter. Such a belief, of course, made people more willing to accept the dislocations and deprivations so many experienced in early capitalism. For this reason, Marx described religion as the "opiate of the masses" since he believed that people adopted religious beliefs as the only hope in a world in which "this" life seemed inexorably grim.

Marx also argued that capitalism would eventually tend to demean and devalue all that it pulls under its spreading wings. In 1846, in *On the Jewish Question*, he noted that money could transform all things, until money itself was all that was important in life:

> Money is the jealous god of Israel, in face of which no other god may exist. Money degrades all the gods of man—and turns them into commodities. Money is the universal self-established value of all things. It has, therefore, robbed the whole world—both the world of men and nature—of its specific value. Money is the estranged essence of man's work and man's existence, and this alien essence dominates him, and he worships it.

In Marxist language, alienation derives primarily from a process called "commodification." All things—flesh and blood, inanimate objects, music, poetry, *everything*—ultimately are "for sale" in the capitalist marketplace. We all know countless examples of commodification. Each Christmas, to suggest an obvious one, most of us in Christian countries celebrate the birth of Jesus with an avaricious, competitive, often depressing orgy of consumption of mostly unnecessary products. What was once a simple affair of gift giving to exemplify Christian charity has become in advanced capitalism a gruesome distortion of the original idea. Capitalism, as we all know, incessantly works on all of us to buy things we don't need. However, capitalists pull out all the stops for Christmas. By the time it is over a substantial minority of us need anti-depressants as an antidote to the lack of Christmas joy that millions of advertisements told us the gifts, the cards, and the family gatherings would bring.

Creative output of all kinds is also systematically commodified in capitalist cultures, dragged down into the lowest common denominator of pop culture and/or advertisement culture. About a decade ago, Paul McCartney of the Beatles tried to buy from a record company the rights to many of the popular songs that he wrote with John Lennon. However, McCartney was outbid by another pop icon, Michael Jackson, who then proceeded to sell the rights to some of these songs to advertising firms. The Beatles song "Revolution," written in response to the political turmoil of the 1960s, was put in the service of selling laundry detergent. Beatles fans might call this sacrilege, but to a Marxist this kind of commodification is the end road for cultural products in capitalism. "Public" radio stations that increasingly depend upon corporate funds to stay alive, the "Tostitos" Fiesta Bowl, and the Nike swoosh on the uniforms of college athletes exemplify how things that were not once part of the cash nexus have become commodities.

To Marx, the most costly form of commodification occurs when capitalists buy labor power in labor markets. This commodity, labor power, is the irreplaceable aspect of capitalist production because without hired laborers to produce the output capitalism cannot exist. Even in this age of high technology, labor costs still make up two-thirds of the costs of production for firms, indicating how essential labor remains in the production process. When a capitalist buys labor time, however, he or she must treat that labor power like any other input, meaning it must be bought as cheaply as possible and drained of its last ounce of usefulness for profit making. The fact that labor power is brought to the market by a human being is, of course, often a problem. Human beings, unlike sheets of plywood and computer chips, have imagination, and wishes and plans and dreams— perhaps even to challenge the boss! While imagination and dreams and independence of mind can make for productive workers, such traits can also be problematic for the capitalist who is trying to maximize profits. Who wants an imaginative dreamer—who thinks for himself or herself—on the assembly line, or as a secretary, or in the mind-numbing jobs in retails sales and custodial work that are the fastest growing niches in the economy?

Because workers are interested in many things other than their jobs and, in fact, many workers hate their jobs, capitalists face the complicated problem of focusing their employees' attention on the work at hand. The modern capitalist workplace—particularly in the United States—is usually a dictatorship, where all the rules are made by the bosses and followed by all workers who want to keep their jobs. Capitalists want ordered work from the conforming, non-complaining bearer of the crucial labor power. They want a "thing," rather than a human being. This is the commodification of labor – a linchpin of Marxist analysis.

Globalization, a major social transformation now engulfing everybody, everywhere, provides a good example of the materialist conception of history, particularly its dialectical and contradictory nature. Globalization is the ultimate expression of the free market system, as capitalism expands inexorably around the world in search of new markets and cheap, desperate labor. Marx described this search for desperate labor power in his often-flamboyant style by suggesting that, "The worshipful capitalists will never want for fresh exploitable flesh and blood, and will let the dead bury their dead." For capitalists, globalization can be immensely profitable as they search the globe for the cheapest labor and resources to minimize their costs of production. Capitalists can also increase the scale of both production and profits by adding customers from the furthest reaches of the world.

However, capitalists do not act alone. As often as not their behavior produces countervailing responses and unintended consequences. As an example, globalization in recent decades has contributed to the decline of the real wages of the working class in the United States. U.S. laborers cannot, for example, compete with Egyptian teenagers making 29 cents per hour, hundreds of millions of Chinese laborers making a few cents more, and other low wage workers in other developing nations. But as U.S. workers lose jobs and income to these foreign workers, the capacity to buy back all the output they are producing diminishes. Marx saw clearly that low wages in capitalism would mean the system could produce more than could be sold, with the result an international crisis of "underconsumption." Furthermore, the increasing inequality generated by globalization tends further to destabilize the political institutions of developing societies. As recent rioting in Indonesia and other developing countries demonstrates, workers in such countries will not accept low wages and limited human rights forever. In the Marxian view, out of this new set of conflicts generated by globalization will arise new societies, which we now can only imagine vaguely, but which will be driven into being by the very historical processes put in motion by the spread of capitalism.

To sum up Marx's theory of history: he believed that in order to survive, people must construct economic systems—modes of production—and that in all societies these modes principally determine the way people behave. Capitalism, now the dominant mode of production in the world, is no exception to this rule, and we have looked at a few of the ways this system shapes our lives. Marx argues that capitalism is a system of social classes that are in conflict and that the "cash nexus," as Marx once referred to capitalism, will in the end make commodities of all things and all people.

How, then, does capitalism actually work, such that it makes us into what we are, and especially into commodities? To this point, we have only hinted at the answer to this question, and now we turn our attention to the broader and deeper answer developed in *Capital*.

MARXIST SYSTEM PART II: MARX'S CRITIQUE OF THE CAPITALIST MODE OF PRODUCTION IN *CAPITAL*

After Marx and Frederick Engels developed their materialist conception of history, sporadically between 1845 and 1857, Marx began work on a longer project to describe and to explain the "laws of motion" of capitalism. The overall structure of that explanation had been presented with great compactness in the first part of the *Communist Manifesto,* but its dozen or so pages gave only a fleeting glance at what would be the complete story. The expanded version was published in 1867 in the first volume of what was to be a multi-volume project, and Marx gave it the title *Capital: A Critical Analysis of Capitalist Production.* The book was published first in German, and later editions in French (1872) and English (1886) made his critique available to most parts of the industrialized world. Marx was emphatic that the purpose of this book, and of all his analysis, was not just "to understand the world, but to change it," as he had put it in 1845.

The first volume of *Capital* was the only one published during Marx's life. Volumes II and III were prepared by Engels from Marx's notes, and volume IV, more a massive compendium of economic ideas than an extension of his critique, was edited by a German Marxist, Karl Kautsky, between 1905 and 1910. We will focus almost entirely on volume I because in it Marx presents his most fundamental arguments about capitalism, especially the relationship between the owners/managers of capital and wage earners who work for them.[2] By focusing on *Capital,* we do not want to leave the impression that it is a compact statement of all that Marx wrote, for his other voluminous writings have influenced virtually every aspect of modern thought in the social sciences and the humanities. Nonetheless, as an argument about how the production system of capitalism comes to be and how it functions, as well as the crucial implications of those functions, *Capital* works well on its own.

Despite the wide influence of *Capital* for over a century, few people outside of universities have the time or inclination to read the book. Inside U.S. universities, new interest in Marx emerged in the 1960s and 1970s, and then waned until quite recently. This lack of access to an ordered and protracted discussion of *Capital,* however, does not mean we need to remain ignorant of the basic ideas put forth there. Indeed, the central ones are quite easy to understand when they are placed in a modern context, using the experiences common to people who live in capitalist culture. It is our purpose here to take up the major themes in Marx's critique of capitalism in precisely that kind of context. And we will begin our analysis by elaborating, in Marx's often-dramatic presentation of capitalist culture, on the principal players we alluded to briefly above.

The Players on the Capitalist Field, I: Owners/Managers and their Competition

As we stated earlier, Marx argued that most people engaged in economic activity in the capitalist mode of production would fall into one of two major groups. First, there are the capitalists and their managers, or what Marx called the "bourgeoisie." Their identifying trait is that they own or manage the capital equipment of society, the buildings, furniture, materials, and everything else needed to produce commodities (goods and services) for sale. Like the classical economists before him, such as Adam Smith and David Ricardo, and the mainstream economists in our time, Marx believed these capitalists have the single goal to maximize and to accumulate profits from their investments in machines, materials, and labor power. And, like all the others, he had a high regard for the power of this capitalist accumulation process to accomplish gigantic tasks. As early as 1848, in the *Communist Manifesto,* Marx wrote this oft-quoted passage:

> [The capitalist class] during its rule of barely one hundred years, has created more massive and more colossal productive forces than have all preceding generations together.... It has accomplished wonders far surpassing Egyptian pyramids, Roman aqueducts, and Gothic cathedrals; it has conducted expeditions that put in the shade all former exoduses of nations and crusades.

Few in our own capitalist age would disagree with this claim, though others might use less florid language to make it. Marx says elsewhere in the

---

[2] Unless otherwise indicated, all references to *Capital,* are to v. 1., International Publishers, 1967.

Manifesto that capitalists can be depended upon constantly "to revolutionize the means of production," by which he meant that the owning/managing class will never stop imagining ways to make their production more efficient and therefore less costly. A new technique, a new "revolution in the means of production," will give the individual capitalist the power to make extra profits until the inevitable occurs and competitors adopt the same technique, or perhaps even better ones. Less industrial societies will have their "walls battered down by cheap commodities," as Marx put it in the *Manifesto*, for no mode of production can compete with capitalism in its capacity to drive down costs and shape the world after its own image. The globalization of capitalism that is now restructuring the world economy is a process Marx saw with uncanny accuracy in 1848, as reading the *Manifesto* will demonstrate.

For Marx, when the capitalist brings together land, labor, and capital, he or she produces a volatile mix, with conflict an inevitable outcome. This view that struggle preeminently characterizes the capitalist workplace puts him at odds with Adam Smith and others in the classical school, and with mainstream economists. It is, of course, not lost on mainstream economists that owners often have conflicts with their workers. Yet, anything beyond a perfunctory mention of the relationship between labor and capital, or what Marx called the social relations of production, is left outside the province of mainstream economics. From his different perch, Marx saw market competition compelling owners to see their workers as two-sided creatures. On the one hand, workers are crucial for production. On the other, they are unpredictable and resistant to change and authority. They are given to slowdowns if not monitored carefully, and, if united, they possess the collective power to demand higher wages and different working conditions or to halt production altogether. This threat means that workers must be controlled continually, their rebellions squelched at their inceptions.

Marx concluded that this world of hostile workers and hungry competitors would ultimately corrupt even the most saintly capitalist. It doesn't matter whether he or she is a Christian, Muslim, or Jew; is friendly or mean-spirited; is Asian, Latin American, or what you will. Ultimately, the forces of competition would entice the most well-intentioned capitalist to close the factory, reduce wages when possible, break the law, buy the politicians, adulterate the product, and so on. Whereas mainstream economists see competition as the "invisible hand" that gives capitalism great moral authority over other economic systems, Marx saw competition as an unrelenting pressure that threatens to drag all capitalists down to the moral level of the most unscrupulous ones. As an example, one that Marx emphasized in *Capital*, without laws against child labor, *some* capitalists will hire children if doing so will lower costs, and the advantage thereby gained will force competitors downward into a squalid moral abyss. This imperative to follow the least scrupled leader

produces the assaults of the capitalist class on their customers, on their workers, and on the environment that one can find described daily in any newspaper.

In his assessment of the great power of competition to shape the actions of capitalists, Marx wrote this in chapter 10, on "The Working Day":

To the out-cry as to the physical and mental degradation, the premature death, the torture of over-work, [capital] answers: Ought these to trouble us since they increase our profits? But looking at things as a whole, all this does not, indeed, depend on the good or ill will of the individual capitalist. Free competition brings out the inherent laws of capitalist production, in the shape of external coercive laws having power over every individual capitalist (p. 257).

And, regarding the effects of competition on capitalist morality, toward the end of *Capital*, in chapter 31, Marx quotes approvingly from a contemporary British writer this appraisal:

With adequate profit, capital is very bold. A certain 10% [profit] will ensure its employment anywhere; 20% certain will produce eagerness; 50%, positive audacity; 100% will make it ready to trample on all human laws; 300%, and there is not a crime at which it will scruple, nor a risk it will not run, even to the chance of its owner being hanged (p. 760).

Marx's description of the owners differs dramatically from the mainstream version, where the capitalist basks triumphantly on a heroic pedestal as a risk taker who brings together the factors of production, land, labor, and capital. To paraphrase Marx's view of that version, "Mr. Capital and Mr. Labor combine with Madam Land (as he actually did put it) to produce the best of all possible worlds for them all."

The Players on the Capitalist Field, II: The Workers

Estranged Labor. The importance Marx gave to the oppression of workers under capitalism emerged early in his thinking. In 1844, Marx wrote a long manuscript, clearly intended to be a book, that provided a structural overview of his thinking about "economics" at the time. The notes lay undiscovered for almost a century, yet when they were published in English in the 1950s as the *Economic and Philosophic Manuscripts*, they created great interest among Marxist scholars, who found a modern-sounding and compelling view

about how capitalist wage labor limits human freedom.

In particular, the *Manuscripts* contained a section called "Estranged Labor," in which Marx described what, for him, were the fundamental conditions of labor under capitalism and why he found them so appalling. This theme—workers in capitalism are alienated from their work, their fellow employees, and themselves—is preeminent in Marx and in all those who followed in his steps. Alienation stems, in the first instance, from historical processes starting in the 14th century in England that gradually separated (alienated) workers from the land and tools with which as peasants they had forged a living. Eventually their survival depended on being hired as wage laborers. The most famous passage from "Estranged Labor" about working conditions in capitalism states:

First…labor is external to the worker, i.e., it does not belong to his essential being;…in his work, therefore, he does not affirm himself but denies himself, does not feel content but unhappy, does not develop freely his physical and mental energy but mortifies his body and ruins his mind. The worker therefore only feels himself outside his work, and in his work feels outside himself. He is at home when he is not working, and when he is working he is not at home. His labor is therefore not voluntary, but coerced; it is forced labor. It is therefore not the satisfaction of a need; it is merely a means to satisfy needs external to it. Its alien character emerges clearly in the fact that as soon as no physical or other compulsion exists, labor is shunned like the plague. External labor, labor in which man alienates himself, is a labor of self-sacrifice, of mortification. Lastly, the external character of labor for the worker appears in the fact that it is not his own, but someone else's, that it does not belong to him, that in it he belongs, not to himself, but to another. Just as in religion the spontaneous activity of the human imagination, of the human brain and the human heart, operates independently of the individual—that is, operates on him as an alien, divine or diabolical activity—in the same way the worker's activity is not his spontaneous activity. It belongs to another; it is the loss of his self.

We don't need to add much to this long quotation because in it Marx speaks plainly enough for himself. His conclusion that "lost labor" is a "lost self" perhaps says it all. Soon after writing the *Manuscripts*, Marx would enter into his long collaboration with Frederick Engels, and they would turn out thousands of pages in the form of essays, books, newspaper articles, and letters about capitalism. An ongoing burden of these pages was to explain to workers the nature of the system that oppressed them and to urge them to rise up against it. The collaborators asked how, if imaginative and creative work were not possible for workers in capitalism, could the system be defended?

Divided Labor. In *Capital*, Marx had a good deal more to say about the causes of estranged labor, and his analysis was more in the language of classical economics and less in the philosophical language that characterized his earlier writing. In three key chapters of the book (13-15), Marx outlines the evolution of what 19th century economists called the "division of labor" (what we call "specialization"). Marx saw that central to the estrangement of factory labor was the fact that it was profitable for the owners to break all tasks down into smaller and smaller individual units of work. As Marx put it, in describing the division of labor in manufacturing:

> Some crippling of body and mind is inseparable even from division of labor in society as a whole. Since, however, manufacture carries this social separation of branches of labor much further, and also, by its peculiar division, attacks the individual at the very roots of his life, it is the first to afford the materials for, and to give a start to, industrial pathology (p. 363).

He then quotes from a French economist of the time, who wrote that:

> To subdivide a man is to execute him, if he deserves the sentence, to assassinate him if he does not…. The subdivision of

labor is the assassination of a people (p. 363).

The words are a bit different here than in the *Manuscripts* in 1844, but the argument is the same: *the capitalist mode of production strips the souls from working people.*[3]

Stripped of their souls or not, who are these workers in the Marxist system if we take a look at them in less general terms? Who is truly a worker, and who is not? Are supervisors workers? Are medical doctors? How about teachers in public schools, or in private schools? These are important questions, not answered sufficiently by Marx's habit of putting everyone into two warring groups, capitalists and workers. Yet, his two-part class system is not as superficial as it might seem. Consider U.S. society, where most of us work for wages or for salaries in positions where the following conditions prevail: we do not control what we produce, how it is produced, or how it is priced; we have nothing to say about whether our workplace will be open tomorrow; we must take the wage offered us, even if it is not enough to live on (unless we can easily get another job or are part of a union that will collectively fight for higher pay). And, our labor is "divided" as a matter of course, and it will be sub-divided into ever-smaller tasks as long as it is profitable for the owners to do so. If these are the conditions of your job, you are a worker in the Marxian version of the capitalist world. On the other hand, if you do have some control over these matters, you are a capitalist, or a high ranking official in a capitalist firm; that is, you are in the capitalist class. But the control that owners have over workers does not come easy, as we shall now see.

Controlled Labor. With the development of manufacturing (used in this context to mean, "things made by hand") in 17th and 18th century England, and with the industrialization that followed, production moved from families to factories. To be sure, small farmers or cottage industry producers had never had much control over the prices paid them by large merchants.

---

[3] Adam Smith had also noticed the negative effects of the division of labor on workers. In *Capital*, Marx quotes from Smith's *The Wealth of Nations* that divided labor can "make the worker as stupid and as ignorant as it is possible for a human creature to become." To appreciate the argument both make, one only has to imagine performing the same operation hundreds, or thousands, of times per day for decades.

However, because factory workers toiled for owners rather than for their own immediate benefit, their efforts had to be monitored carefully. From this process evolved the need for a new kind of worker—managers and supervisors—to keep other workers doing increasingly alienating work. The division of labor, Marx put it, gradually separated "the hand from the brain" in capitalist workshops by generating ever more tasks demanding simple, repetitive motions but not much thinking. Marx often compared the factory system to the way military officers keep the ranks in order. As he put it in *Capital*, when production begins, the capitalist:

> …hands over the work of direct and constant supervision of the individual workmen, and groups of workmen, to a special kind of wage-laborer. An industrial army of workmen, under the command of a capitalist, requires, like a real army, officers (managers), and sergeants (foremen, overlookers), who, while the work is being done, command in the name of the capitalist (p. 332).

To Marx, the increasing complexity of production in capitalist systems demands ever more complex and sophisticated ways to keep workers on jobs they typically do only in order to pay their bills.

What people involved in capitalist firms want from the experience varies with their relationship to the firm: do they own, manage, or supervise the work, or do they do it themselves for wages? The owners want brisk, timely, committed work, done as quickly as possible consistent with high quality output. They want workers to be there promptly in the morning, to stay as long as they are supposed to, and longer if possible, and so on. Workers, though, compelled to make a living, would prefer a friendly, flexible environment, over which they have some measure of control. Thus, workers keep their noses to the grindstone only when forced to do so by managers, supervisors, electronic monitors, spies, or whatever else the owners can use to compel them to greater productivity.

In brief, then, the major players on the capitalist field are capitalists hustling profits and workers hustling a wage or salary. We have described the two classes in the way that Marx

chose to describe them, as "in relation to each other." By this he meant that the term "capitalist" refers to someone who hires "wage laborers," that neither can exist without the other. Their relationship to each other produces the central dramatic action of the capitalist mode of production. Like all good dramatic action, this one is a waxing and waning struggle, and, in this case, what is being fought over is what Marx called "surplus value."

Surplus Value

For Marx, the origin of profit in capitalism is surplus value, and the difference between Marx and the mainstream on the origin of profits is essentially two-fold. First, Marx's capitalist world is one in which the present is the tip of a vast iceberg of history. And, second, even when he reaches similar conclusions as mainstream economists about certain aspects of capitalism—such as the drive to maximize profits—Marx is usually looking at them from a different perspective. To appreciate how this difference works out, as we describe Marx's theory of profits in capitalism we should keep in mind the following (quite typical) version from a popular mainstream principles textbook:

> Profit is what entrepreneurs earn for undertaking the risks and uncertainties of enterprise. It is distinct from the wages or salary entrepreneurs may receive for providing managerial skills. The entrepreneurs associated with modern corporations are its many stockholders, who assume all corporate risk and uncertainty, which generate for the stockholders their profit (or losses). Corporate managers earn salaries (Fred Gottheil, *Principles of Economics*, South-Western, 1999).

Let's look at Marx's alternative tale about how profits emerge in capitalism. He defined surplus value simply as the difference between the value of what a worker produces and what he or she is paid (and we shall present a simple example shortly). In his analysis Marx adopted what he calls "socially necessary labor time" as his standard of value for products exchanged in the market. The exchange value of a good or service is determined by the average number of hours of labor time that went into its production. The issue of what gave products their value had been debated by social theorists before Marx, including most prominently among economists, Adam Smith and David Ricardo, both of whom had also developed a version of the "labor theory of value."

Marx's own version of this theory is much more closely argued, and he uses the first several chapters of *Capital* to work out its internal consistencies and logical implications. In these chapters, Marx assumed that value, as he defined it, would in the long run determine (more or less) market prices. In volume III of *Capital*, at least in the version Engels fashioned from Marx's notes, Marx attempted to prove that the labor theory of value could be used as a basis for determining market prices. However, many critics have not been persuaded, and the debate continues. Fortunately for us, the framework Marx establishes about value is useful in analyzing capitalism, and this is true whether value determines prices, as Marx argued, or not. In the example below we will work with the market prices of labor, materials, capital equipment, and products, rather than their embodied "socially necessary labor time." And, as we shall see, doing so does no harm to the analysis.

The idea of surplus value is easy for anyone who has worked for wages, or for a salary to understand. Take for example, a young woman, a recent graduate from college who is offered $26,000 dollars a year to work for a capitalist company. What can we surmise about this transaction? The former student will likely be taking such a job because she is making an important transition in life and will soon pay the bills heretofore paid by her parents. She will probably have surveyed the possibilities and taken the best job available, given all her needs. What we know for certain is that the owner will be looking for one thing from the work of the student, and that thing is profit. In a nutshell, then, our new worker will be expected to produce something over $26,000 of new value, net of the cost of any materials used while doing it. Pure and simple. Our ex-student knows the rules, too, we can be sure. She knows that if she does not produce an amount of value greater than what she is paid, she will unceremoniously be ushered out the door.

None of this would be news to anyone raised in a capitalist society, though mainstream economists choose to look at it differently. Of course, they know that workers are hired to make profits for a firm, yet as we have said their work most typically avoids analysis of the historical processes by which that distribution was shaped. However, for Marx central issues concern how this distribution of income and power came to be and how it shapes profit making now. His answer is a detailed historical description of how the land and tools necessary for production were stripped from peasants and artisans, making it mandatory that they work for wages in order to survive. Under capitalism, when the entrepreneur and the worker arrive at the workplace to seek their fortunes, the principal rule that emerged from this historical (rather than natural, or divine) process is that one must work to produce surplus value for the other. In his analysis of the working day, to which we now turn, Marx explained profits in capitalism in a way that provokes a number of interesting questions of the type that mainstream economists long ago stopped asking.

The Working Day

At the beginning of his great historical essay called "The Working Day" (chapter 10 of *Capital*), Marx breaks down the day into two parts, a very simple model but one with complex implications. He asks the reader to look at the day of the typical employee as comprised of two parts, as follows:

A------------------B and B------------------C

The first of these parts, A—B is the part of the day it takes for the worker to produce enough output (again, net of any material costs) to pay for his or her wage. We can more clearly exemplify this if we extend the example we began earlier with our recent graduate making $26,000 a year. We have chosen that apparently random number on purpose because it allows us to draw a simple example to make the point. Such an annual salary would come to $500 a week, or $100 a day. This means that, on average, *each day* this worker must add extra value to the firm's output of more than $100 in order to justify continued employment.

To extend the example, let's assume that this employee adds value to the firm's output of $160 a day or, assuming the typical eight-hour day, $20 an hour. Already, we can see that the employee is making surplus value (profit) for the owner, because the $160 of added value is more than the

$100 daily salary. As we take one step further into this analysis, we move away from the depoliticized firm of the mainstream and into the world seen in Marxist terms. That step is simply to say this: if the employee is adding $20 per hour of extra value, she will have produced enough extra value to pay for her wage during the first five hours of the day. Given the eight-hour workday in our example, that means for the last three hours our ex-student will be producing surplus value for the capitalist, the only reason why she was given the job in the first place. Marx called the first five hours of this day "necessary labor" and the remaining three hours "surplus labor" to differentiate the part of the day the worker was working for the wage, and the part of the day spent toiling to produce the owner's profits.

Marx focused the whole center section of *Capital*, several hundred pages, on these last three hours, or the B—C part of the day. He does so because this is the part that provides the capitalist surplus value, the quest for which gives the system its single most distinguishing trait. Marx does not, in his theorizing anyway, pass judgment on the process by which surplus value arises in capitalism. As we have already learned, the capitalist is only doing what is necessary to survive, and the worker is doing the same thing. The nature of the working day, in Marx's view, is but another way to look at the experience of most people who live in capitalist culture, because most of them do, in that view, work to produce surplus value for someone else. What did Marx make of this particular configuration of the day? The answer is "just about everything" in his system, and here we will take up the most important things.

Extending the working day. To begin with, we can ask ourselves a simple question: what are the ways the owner of our firm, or any firm, can increase the B—C part of the day? One immediate way would be simply to extend the length of the working day. Marx called surplus value generated this way "absolute surplus value," to distinguish it from "relative surplus value," which we will take up soon. If our recent graduate worked say, 10 hours a day, rather than 8, this would generate roughly another $40 of surplus value for the firm. The rub, of course, is that the owner cannot do that in most modern capitalist countries, because it is illegal, without paying an extra premium for "overtime" hours.

Marx describes the political realities of the length of the working day this way:

> But when the transaction was concluded, [the worker] discovered that he was no 'free agent', that the period of time for which he is *free* to sell his labor-power is the period of time for which he is *forced* to sell it, that in fact the vampire will not let go 'while there remains a single muscle, sinew or drop of blood to be exploited'. For 'protection' against the serpent of their agonies, the workers have to put their heads together and, as a class, compel the passing of a law, an all-powerful social barrier by which they can be prevented from selling themselves and their families into slavery and death by voluntary contract with capital. In the place of the pompous catalogue of the 'inalienable rights of man' there steps the modest Magna Carta of the legally limited working day, which at last makes clear 'when the time which the worker sells is ended, and when his own begins' (p. 416, emphasis added).

Some of the more compelling periods of U.S. and British history, and of that of all capitalist societies, describe the battle waged over the length of the working day. When Marx was writing *Capital* in the 1860s, both British and U.S. laborers were engaged in a protracted and often bloody battle with owners over the conditions of work in virtually every industry. To Marx, this struggle over the length of the working day is an inevitable outcome of the capitalist mode of production, and focusing on the B—C part of the day will make it obvious why this is the case. Both parties, owner and worker, have diametrically opposed needs: the former has strong incentives to work the worker as long as possible, while the latter will (typically) do anything to make the workday shorter.

Laws concerning the workday, along with a tangled forest of others that have sprung from the same soil, exist in all advanced capitalist countries. In the early part of this century in the U.S., company violence against workers, including the use of the militia against them, and sorry working conditions produced a reform movement led by working people and their allies that continues to unfold. The unending political battles in the U.S for the past sixty years over workplace safety, social security, unemployment compensation, minimum wages, welfare, federal trade, monetary and fiscal policy (to name only a suggestive list of issues) attest to this fact.

Once the length of the working day is fixed, the essential nature of the "contested terrain," as economist Richard Edwards described the workplace, does not change. Surplus value remains the goal of owners and high wages and good (if not easy) work conditions the goal of workers. What's a poor owner to do? Consider again the working day, A-----B-----C. If "A----C" is limited by law to represent eight hours in total, and the owner wants the part of the day in which the workers produce surplus value, B----C, to be as long as possible, what are ways to expand that part of the day? The answer must be to restructure work so that the laborer pays for the wage earlier in the day; or, in terms of the diagram, to restructure work so that "B moves to the left." Marx called profits made by such changes *relative* surplus value, and distinguished them from greater profits made simply by lengthening the working day.

Technological displacement of workers. Marx was quite explicit in one example concerning relative surplus value. The hunger for surplus value and market competition force owners *always* to replace their workers with machines when it is profitable do to so. Making workers more productive with better, faster machines means that they pay for their wage earlier in the day. Marx took up the issue of machinery at great length in chapter 15 of *Capital*. Although his argument concerns British *industrial* capitalism in the 19th century, his language remains operative. He says at one point:

> …a machine immediately becomes a competitor of the workman himself. The self-expansion of capital by means of machinery is thenceforward directly proportional to the number of the workpeople, whose means of livelihood have been destroyed by that machinery. The whole system of capitalist production is based on the fact that the workman sells his labor-power as a commodity. Division of labor specializes this labor power, by reducing it to skill in handling a particular tool. So soon as the handling

of this tool becomes the work of a machine, then….the workman becomes unsaleable…. That portion of the working-class thus by machinery rendered superfluous, either goes to the wall in the unequal contest of the [other outmoded industries] or else floods all the more easily accessible branches of industry, swamps the labor-market, and sinks the price of labor power...(pp. 405-406).

Of course, this is the natural process by which technological unemployment occurs in capitalism. As an example from our own capitalist world, assume a capitalist firm that can make 1,000 units of a commodity at an average price of $1.00, with a process that uses one machine and 100 workers. Then, a supplier drops by with news about a new machine which will allow the owner to produce the same 1,000 units but with only 50 workers and at a cost of $.80 per unit. Will the capitalist fire fifty of his workers? Of course he or she will.

In the two preceding chapters, 13 and 14, Marx had demonstrated, as he had in the *Communist Manifesto*, a genuine appreciation for the ability of the bourgeoisie to develop technology rapidly enough to transform the world with a theretofore unprecedented breadth and speed. He remained committed to the idea that machines could, in a mode of production designed for "free men," deliver people from the drudgery that has been the lot of most of them throughout human history. Yet, with the emergence of a system whose central dynamic is the production of surplus value, the machine becomes the agent of the worker's displacement and, more horribly, it leads to workers being crushed among its moving wheels. Selected quotations from the chapter will make his point. On the moral imperatives of capitalism and the machines, Marx wrote:

> In so far as machinery dispenses with muscular power, it becomes a means of employing laborers of slight muscular strength….The labor of women and children was, therefore, the first thing sought for by the capitalist who used machinery (p. 372).

and:

> …[M]achinery sweeps away every moral and natural restriction on the length of

the working day. Hence, too, the economic paradox, that the most powerful instrument for shortening labor-time, becomes the most unfailing means for placing every moment of the laborer's time and that of his family, at the disposal of the capitalist for the purpose of expanding the value of his capital (p. 385).

Concerning dangers of the factory, Marx had this to say:

[In the factory] every organ of sense is injured in an equal degree by artificial elevation of the temperature, by the dust laden atmosphere, by the deafening noise, not to mention danger to life and limb among the thickly crowded machinery, which, with the regularity of the seasons, issues its list of the killed and wounded in the industrial battle (p. 401).

On this last point, Marx was, as we have said, writing about industrial capital rather than U.S. capitalism today (with its 70 per cent of the workforce in the services industries), but we should not presume his comments about safety are outdated. In 1995 for example, 5,300 people were killed on the job in the United States and another 3.9 *million* received disabling injuries, meaning that the mechanized capitalist workplace remains a threat to life and limb. For those workers who remain on the job, *and* ambulatory, what else can the owner do to get them to pay for their wage earlier in the day?

<u>Cutting Wages.</u> Let's assume that the student from our earlier example is toiling away for $26,000 a year in a consulting firm with one hundred workers. Assume further that the owner decides to cut wages for all of them. Doing so would increase surplus value by moving the "B" part of the work day to the left, if we assume productivity doesn't change, because at a lower wage workers will provide enough extra value to pay for their wage earlier in the day. Will the workers accept these wage cuts like good soldiers? It depends, of course, and Marx made it clear he believed this battle over wages, like that over all the other conditions of work, would wax and wane. As an excellent example of this

FREDERICK ENGELS, 1868

ongoing struggle between capital and labor over wages, workers held their own against their bosses in the U.S. for about twenty-five years after World War II. During this period, real wages (that is, wages after accounting for inflation) rose regularly because of steadily rising productivity, and because there was an informal "accord" between major firms and their workers (itself one reason productivity was rising). This accord reflected that with roughly one-third of the work force unionized, including virtually all of the big industries, labor unions had genuine collective power at the workplace and on the national political scene. However, for several reasons, including a declining manufacturing sector, globalization, and the intentional strategies of major capitalists to reduce the rate of unionization, labor's power relative to its bosses began to decline in the early 1970s. Since then, the rate of unionization has fallen by about a half—it is less than 15% of the workforce—and real wages for an hour's work are now lower for most workers than they were in 1970. The current generation of "bottom line" employers is no more cold-blooded than their counterparts from, say, 20 years, or 120 years ago. The difference is that the weakened political power of workers allows the cold-bloodedness, ever lurking in capitalism, to come to the surface. To put it another way, if we ask when employers try to lower the wages of their employees, the answer comes quickly to any of us: whenever they can get away with it.

<u>Speeding up the workplace.</u> Consider again our student and her ninety-nine fellow workers in the hypothetical capitalist firm. Let's say these workers toil for a company providing consulting services to other firms. Maybe fifty of these workers use computers to keep information flowing through the office, or to keep tabs on costs, or what have you; maybe the other fifty are outside the office consulting, drumming up customers, or hanging out when they can get away with it. How could the owner speed up the work of these hundred employees? Or, formulaically, how can he or she make them more productive and, by doing so, enlarge the B—C part of the workday? The owner could monitor the work of those fifty on the computers, rank them according to their speed, and publicize the rankings. Or, the

owner might devise ways to speed up the efforts of the outside workers by increasing the number of contacts they must make, or by transferring to them some of the computer work usually done in the office. When, we ask again, will the owners/managers speed up the work of employees? The answer, again, is: whenever they can get away with it. Further, given the nature of work in most capitalist firms, we can also predict when workers will goof off: whenever they can get away with it!

Moving the production somewhere else. Another major method by which owners try to enlarge the B—C part of the day is to seek out lower wages somewhere else. Most of the shoes worn by Americans used to be made in mills in New England, produced by family-owned firms which dominated local economies but nonetheless provided relatively high wages and a good measure of security. Now, only a few such shoe mills continue to exist in New England. First, the plants were moved to the southern U.S. because wages were lower there and, stemming from the same conditions that generate low wages, there was a relative hostility to organized labor. But, before long, producers were moving their mills further south to places like the Dominican Republic, because the wages were even lower there; then, the move was to Taiwan and South Korea. This quest for the lowest wages reached its nadir when the Nike Corporation moved its production to Indonesia, where, in the early 1990s, it hired young women to make its shoes for 14 cents an hour.

To sum up briefly his arguments about "relative surplus value," Marx showed that confining the length of the working day to a maximum number of hours did not change the essential dynamic of the capitalist mode of production. However, it mandated that capitalists, in order to maximize surplus value, would, using Marx's term, have to "intensify" labor, by cutting wages, speeding up work, replacing workers with machines, or marching around the globe in search of low wage workers.

The Industrial Reserve Army

For his arguments in chapters 10, 15, and 25 of *Capital*, Marx drew from dozens of reports of Parliamentary investigations in order to chronicle the debauched circumstances endured by so much of the working class in Britain. His principal guide

into this territory was Frederick Engels, whose book *The Condition of the Working Class in England* (1845) had early on helped to draw Marx's attention away from philosophy and toward political economy. In chapter 25, Marx theorized about these conditions, paying particular attention to the nature of what we call "unemployment" and why it occurs with regularity in capitalism. What, in part, distinguishes Marx's treatment from current ones, is the content and tone of the language he uses. Marx called those without jobs in capitalism "the industrial reserve army." His words conjure complex images in our minds and present a far richer notion about workers without jobs than the abstract mainstream term "unemployment." Consider the implications of Marx's term. First, again he uses a military metaphor, reminding us that those without jobs are foot soldiers in some capitalist's army and, like their counterparts in the real army, utterly at the mercy of the "generals" directing the struggle. More important, however, is the key word "reserve" in Marx's definition because in his system it carries crucial political and economic implications.

The unemployed in Marx's system are "in reserve" in the sense that they provide an absolutely key role in allowing the capitalist to make surplus value. Consider an economic recession, where production and employment spiral down together, the decline in each bringing about further declines in the other. The first workers to get the axe will be the last hired, or the least skilled, least educated, least desirable for whatever reason. If the contraction is great enough, those losing jobs will be a bit more educated and experienced.

We all know this, but Marx adds the emphasis that these people must take their lumps, if not in silence, at least without posing a political threat to everyone else. Clearly, capitalism cannot work if owners are denied their right to fire or lay off workers. Nor will it last for very long if those who are tossed into the street arm themselves and revolt or otherwise pose a threat to the capitalists' efforts to amass surplus value. Capitalism *absolutely depends upon* a class of people at the bottom who can be fired without explanation and sent off to fend for themselves but who also are not able to organize a resistance to the system that has tossed them out. Capitalism also needs these, and any other unemployed workers, graciously to blame their lot on themselves, rather than blame a production system that makes their unemployment necessary and predictable. The reserve army also holds down wages because those who remain working know they can easily be replaced if they make demands on their employers.

Consider, also, the other side of the business cycle. When the economy starts expanding it won't grow for long unless there are people "in reserve" who can be absorbed back into the system. And, naturally, the hope is that those in reserve will not have made themselves into a real "army" in the meantime. Throughout *Capital*, Marx fulminates and rages, in between the lines of his dense theoretical arguments, about the lot of workers in capitalism. It deeply provoked his moral outrage. Yet in mainstream economics the morality of unemployment typically is looked upon as a short-term failure of the system or a long-term failure of hopeless individuals. The relationship between joblessness and the political system is also generally ignored because, as is usual in mainstream economics, politics and questions of power are cavalierly ignored. The "army" of unemployed also points to the fact of social classes in capitalism, about which Marx had much to say.

Social Classes

One of the more intriguing aspects of life in U.S. society is that those who shape opinions, including many professors, have long denied the existence of social classes. Instead of concepts such as "working class" or "ruling classes," we have substituted entirely different kinds of ideas and metaphors, such as "social status" or the "melting pot." The "American Dream" is a solid anchor to this mythical understanding of ourselves, and in this dreamland any lad or lassie can, by trying hard enough, make it to the top. Those who actually have done so are paraded through our media and our history books as proof of typical experiences, though they are really not that at all. Research debunks the myth with a crashing finality by showing that, while there is a great fluidity to American life, most upward mobility is across only one class line. This means that many people born in working class families get to go to college and end up as low-end professionals or in comparable occupations. And, of course, a few go all the way "to the top," at

least in terms of the money and power they accumulate. But, most end up where they started, and the best way to get to the top is to be born to parents already there.

Marx wrote often about social class, both theoretically and through his accounts of key events of his times. However, his theory is quite undeveloped, and he never abandoned what he argued early on in the *Manifesto* that society is ultimately divided into the two great camps of the bourgeoisie and the proletariat. In his system other classes were fated to extinction. "Petit bourgeoisie" is Marx's term for owners of small firms, intellectuals, and all others who did not hire wage laborers. He also referred to those truly outside the production system as the "lumpenproletariat," a term very close to the current idea of the "underclass." Marx believed that smaller firms would ultimately fail to compete with big firms and the petit bourgeoisie would be "hurled into the proletariat" along with all those intellectuals who did not end up as apologists for capitalism. This is yet another reason that he thought that basic to capitalism was its tendency to become two great warring camps of owners and their workers.

If we think of Marx's model of social classes as made up of "those who control" production and "those who don't" we might better grasp his idea of what the terms "capitalist" and "proletariat" meant to him, and have come to mean to contemporary Marxists. The complexity of the modern world has led latter-day Marxists to construct variations on Marx's themes about social class, mostly by adding classes that don't fit very neatly into any of Marx's categories. For instance, Pat Walker's *Between Capital and Labor* (1978) describes a "professional managerial class" made up of professionals such as doctors, lawyers, academics, and others who have some control over their working environment but who do not typically hire wage laborers and earn surplus value. Other scholars have, in this same vein, tried to account for these "in between" classes. In their accounting for professionals, these theorists are not abandoning the Marxist framework but are trying to modernize it so that it remains a viable paradigm in which to think about capitalism.

Implicit in Marx's discussion about social class is the quite limited number of prescribed roles that can be played out in particular modes of production. As an example, presume that a youngster reads captivating books that make him or her want to be a shining knight, or a provincial duchess, or a hardy English yeoman, or a plains Indian warrior, or a pioneering woman ready to prove herself when pushed up against the rough elements of the weather (not to mention patriarchy), or the fair-minded leader of a workers' council in a democratic, socialist country. It is not possible to play these, or any number of other roles, if one resides in modern capitalism because you can only be an owner, a worker, a government servant, or inhabit some other such slot as those slots are shaped by capitalism. And, once inside your role, you must play it to the hilt to survive: as an owner you must worship the bottom line, and as a worker you must obey the owner. This does not mean, of course, you have no agency—no free will—but as Marx put it so very well:

> Men make their own history, but they do not make it just as they please: they do not make it under circumstances chosen by themselves, but under circumstances directly encountered, given and transmitted from the past. The tradition of all the dead generations weighs like a nightmare on the brain of the living (*The 18th Brumaire of Louis Napoleon*, 1852)

By placing people in social classes in terms of "their relationship to the means of production," Marx introduced new language in the terms of a larger, powerful theoretical framework. But discussions of social class continue to ignore Marx at a cost. As one economist, Teresa Amott, put it recently:

> …No matter how far from *Capital* the debate [about social class in capitalism] has strayed, Marx's original conceptions continue to define the shape and logic of the argument. In fact, one could argue that the burden of twentieth century thought on class has been the task of rehabilitation, elaboration, deconstruction, and contestation of Marx's original construction of class, that to criticize Marxist concepts of class, one must stand in the space that Marx cleared (Michael Payne, *et. al.* editors, *A Dictionary of Cultural and Critical Theory*, 1996).

As Amott argues, though Marx did not himself give the same kind of full theoretical treatment to social class than did many other writers, he established the framework for a discussion about social classes in capitalism that continues into our day. How could there not be social classes in our society when even small children know that the people who own or control the businesses also own houses, cars, food, clothes, and all the rest, that are better than those of the people who work for them? (We take up social classes in much greater detail, including a brief review of Marx's arguments about them, in a separate chapter below.)

Other Economic Arguments about Capitalism

Capital is a book of about seven hundred pages, and in it Marx wrote about many, many aspects of capitalism. We have taken up those arguments that dominate the book *and* which remain mostly germane, even eye opening, to readers in our own day. We have ignored some of his arguments because they do not have a great deal to say about our own world. Still other claims Marx made do not merit much explanation in this kind of review, because they are now so commonplace. However, we will mention two of the latter because they have a particular importance to *Capital* and might help one to see the book better as a whole. We will also say a few words about Marx's theory of revolution.

Booms and Busts. In mainstream economics, John Maynard Keynes is generally considered to have founded the modern study of the business cycle in the mid-1930s. However, the history of economic thought is now rarely taught in graduate schools, and thus economists usually do not know that others, including Marx, had developed complex and persuasive theories of the business cycle long before Keynes produced his own system. The problem is that Marx scattered arguments about the instability of capitalism throughout all four volumes of Capital, and few readers have taken the time to compile and assess his claims. One of his arguments, made in volume III and quite modern, indeed, is this:

> The ultimate reason for all real crises [recessions/depressions] always remains the poverty and restricted consumption of the masses as opposed to the drive of capitalist production to [produce as much

output as possible] (Vintage edition, p. 484).

This idea is now central to all modern mainstream theories, and interestingly, it is an insight into capitalist processes that is gathering considerable current attention. Many economists, including prominent ones in the United States, are beginning to fear that the increasing inequality in the distribution of world income is creating just such a "restricted consumption of the masses." Such economists suspect that consequent underconsumption could bring the world economy into a serious depression.

In the second and third volumes of *Capital*, Marx developed other intriguing theories of the business cycle. One of them, his argument that profit rates in capitalism would gradually decline over the long run and extinguish the fire in the belly of the system, has simply not come to be. Profit rates seem more closely tied to the short term business cycle, and each time Marx's theory is resuscitated in the face of longer term declining profits, they seem to start going up again. Another of Marx's explanations for the business cycle is a clear precursor to Keynes, and in it Marx argues that there is interdependency between the investment and consumption sectors of a capitalist economy. He shows, with a fine logical consistency in volume II, that over- or under-production in one of these can produce a "realization" crisis, or what we call a recession or depression. It is only because British economists, who with Keynes developed modern macroeconomics, were not reading Marx that they did not see that much of their own work only extended what he had already written about.

Concentration and Centralization. Marx was the first major social theorist to predict that capitalism would lead to a growing centralization and concentration of power in the hands of a few capitalists. Marx meant by this language what we call horizontal, vertical, and conglomerate mergers (a firm merging, respectively, with one of its competitors, one of its suppliers, or one from a completely different industry). In the middle chapters of *Capital*, Marx explains in great detail how the technological imperative of capitalism would produce ever more costly machinery and buildings, and ever more complex and centralized systems of finance, to the point that in time the economy would be dominated by a few big multinational firms. His arguments on these matters are more interesting for their prescience than as new information. Marx also tied the concentration of capital to the eventual collapse of capitalism, as discussed below, because he thought that as monopolies grew in power they would gradually cause more and more workers, and the owners of small firms, to be "hurled" into a proletariat undergoing increasing immiseration.

Such a process has been clearly underway for many small business people in most capitalist societies. Consider the effect of the immense chain of Wal-Mart stores. The gathering monopolization of retail sales by such giant firms has made it ever more difficult for main street merchants to compete with them. Wal-Mart gains its advantage over its smaller competitors in two principal ways: its huge stores spread the overhead for each sale over hundreds of thousands of products in the typical store. And, Wal-Mart now purchases directly almost one quarter of the total output of another giant, Proctor & Gamble, giving it the market leverage to buy its inventory at volume prices considerably lower than those charged to smaller retail outlets. Direct purchases such as these immediately wipe out whole strata of small wholesalers and put at risk all retailers who compete with the giants. Millions of small business owners, particularly those who are not highly educated or do not have professional skills, face a future that might hurl them into jobs with low pay and where they will have no control over their work. As another example, if you owned a Mobil or an Exxon gasoline station, would you not wince at the news that these two giants have now merged and plan to "consolidate?"

The Theory of Revolution. In one rhetorical outburst in the next-to-last chapter of *Capital*, Marx predicted that capitalism was ultimately doomed and that it was but a matter of time before the capitalist "expropriators were expropriated"(p. 715). Marx argued that the booms and busts would get more and more tumultuous, each one leaving a greater and greater trail of debris—small firms driven from the field, workers ever greater misery—and the tumult eventually would lead to an overthrow of the capitalist class. That this has not happened is a testament to the resilience of capitalism, and its great capacity to adapt over time to technological and political changes. Marx, too, in his last years, was aware of this adaptability, and in particular he thought that in democratic capitalist societies workers might restructure the system and make it more civilized without overthrowing it. To some degree, this is what happened in the capitalist welfare states in Northern Europe, as we shall see in the essay below on Sweden. Whether, however, the workers of the world will ultimately "unite" and overthrow their oppressors remains to be seen. One estimate of the current level of worldwide unemployment is 150 *million*, and we can only expect these numbers to grow as industrialization in developing countries drives more rural people to cities looking for wage labor. At what level of world unemployment, we might ask, might Marx's prediction about revolutionary upheaval come true? It remains to be seen.

The Moral Standing of Capitalism

In the last six chapters of *Capital*, Marx took up a question for which throughout the book he has only implied an answer: where does accumulated capital originate? The substance of his answer is generalized in chapter 31, in which he says:

> The discovery of gold and silver in America, the extirpation, enslavement and entombment in mines of the aboriginal population, the beginning of the conquest and looting of the East Indies, the turn of Africa into a warren for the commercial hunting of black-skins, signalized the rosy dawn of the era of capitalist production (p. 751).

These examples follow two chapters on the enclosure movements, particularly in Britain starting in the sixteenth century and continuing up to Marx's time, whereby the crown joined with land barons and the church to drive most of the agricultural work force—the peasants and the yoemanry of Britain—off the land and into the cities as vagabonds or wage laborers.[4] These, and

---

[4] This "enclosure movement" in England meant that land in villages traditionally set aside in "commons"--groups of plots farmed by individual families--were by Parliamentary acts taken over by large landowners or by the British Crown. In eliminating the commons, these enclosures thus made it impossible for most rural families to sustain themselves on the land. This was, of course, the first step in the process by which such rural families found themselves headed to cities and into the factories of the emerging class of capitalist owners.

similar brutalities, led Marx to argue that capital originated in plunder and violence, that it had been seized, first by the nobility and by the Church, then by the emerging capitalist class, from the whole population. Because wealth and power are passed down from generation to generation, this early pillaging remained the foundation of the distribution of wealth and power in Marx's time. Later on in the chapter, Marx unburdened himself of this verbal thunder:

> If money, according to Augier [a Frenchman writing in 1842] "comes into the world with a congenital blood-stain on one cheek," capital comes dripping from head to foot, from every pore, with blood and dirt (p. 760).

In these last six chapters, Marx is making two interconnected claims. The first is that capitalism was born in pillage and murder, and the second that it is a system of unremitting oppression and violence against working people. Do these claims have any merit as descriptions of modern capitalism? Was U.S. capitalism built on violence and plunder? Does it remain oppressive to the majority of the people who live in it? The answer, of course, depends on whom you ask. The story of the United States is subject to countless versions, and some of them differ dramatically concerning these questions. Were John D. Rockefeller and J.P. Morgan "robber-baron" criminals, as some historians have concluded? Or, was their inexorable drive to accumulate profits— constantly to revolutionize the means of production—the force that brought modern, industrial capitalism into being? Or were they both, as seems to be Marx's position? For those who adopt the benign meritocratic view of capitalism, its inequalities of opportunity and outcome can be justified with the claim that it is, and always has been, an open system in which all who genuinely make the effort can make the grade (and even rise to the top). This view is, without question, the dominating one in our times.

Others, though, see things quite differently from the currently dominant view. They argue that central to modern capitalism are owners and managers who *by definition* live off surplus value produced by someone else; who *must* create mindless tasks for most of their workers; who *must* withhold loyalty to their workers; and who *must* fire, or replace, or even harm their workers' health, if doing so will increase their surplus value; who *must* ever monitor their workers' efforts to keep them on jobs which many hate; and so on.

This is a language of force and oppression, and to a Marxist it is also the language of plunder and pillage. The surplus value—stolen from the workers only because the capitalists control the productive system—is the means by which these owners build their fortunes, amass their political power, and dominate the capitalist world. Last, and more specifically, for all the cheap products the capitalist class has helped to bring into the world, it also has a long history of doing damage to everything in its path. Consider, for a moment, tobacco executives who claim their product doesn't kill their customers, or Phil Knight of Nike refusing to accept responsibility for the wretched conditions of the workers who make the shoes that make him a billionaire, or the countless chemical companies that have left in their wake toxic fields for children to play on. Are such characters on the modern capitalist stage any different from the "blood sucking werewolves" of Marx's world? Like everything else, it depends on your point of view.

CONCLUSIONS

This second part of our essay has been confined to trying to put into an unforbidding language the basic ideas about capitalism that Marx advanced in the first volume of *Capital*. He was a prodigious writer and thinker about the economy, and the remaining volumes of *Capital*, along with the arguments in many other of his and Engels' writings, contain a further elaboration of their ideas, many of them in powerful, sometimes elegant, language.

This introduction is meant to urge readers to look for themselves into Marx's writings. As suggested earlier, if one wants to take on *Capital*, or some of Marx's other more demanding texts, the best way to do so is in a college course or in a reading group. On the other hand, much of what Marx and Engels wrote is quite accessible, as the reader will see if he or she browses through a selection of these works. Our readers should give Marx another chance and not listen to those who claim from the rooftops that "Marx is dead!" That is, quite frankly, a claim that could only be made by someone who has never read his works.

Chapter II

Thorstein Veblen on the Predatory Nature of Contemporary Capitalism[*]

INTRODUCTION

Thorstein Veblen is another of the radical economists whose theories of the economy diverge significantly from the standard neoclassical (i.e., mainstream) analysis that is offered in the economics textbooks that you will otherwise read. Veblen's system of analysis has some similarities to that of Marx. Veblen treats the modern American economy as dominated by business interests and inherently prone to cyclical crises, rather than resembling the mythical perfectly competitive world created by Adam Smith. Veblen makes conscious use of learning from the other social sciences in order to analyze the factor that he thought to be most important for understanding the economy—economic and social change.

Before we proceed, let's dismiss one of the common complaints about Veblen, and that is his unique writing style. Critics, and even many admirers, of Veblen characterize much of his writing as "mordant irony," dismissing his work as humorous satire. As one example, a famous quote from Veblen examines the role of habit in human thought processes:

> The patriotic spirit, or tie of nationalism, is evidently of the nature of habit . . . More particularly is it a matter of habit what particular national establishment a given human subject will become attached to on reaching what is called "years of discretion" and so becoming a patriotic citizen. 'The analogy of the clam may not be convincing, but it may at least serve to suggest what may be the share played by habituation in the matter of national attachment. The young clam,

THORSTEIN VEBLEN
1920

after having passed the free-swimming phase of his life, as well as the period of attachment to the person of a carp or similar fish, drops to the bottom and attaches himself loosely in the place and station in life to which he has been led; and he loyally sticks to his particular patch of oose (sic) and sand through good fortune and evil. It is, under Providence, something of a fortuitous matter where the given clam shall find a resting place for the sole of his feet, but it is also, after all, "his own, his native land" etc. It lies in the nature of a clam to attach himself after this fashion, loosely, to the bottom where he finds a living, and he would not be a "good clam and true" if he failed to do so; but the particular spot for which he forms this attachment is not of the essence of the case. At least, so they say. 'It may be, as good men appear to believe or know, that all men of sound, or at least those of average, mind will necessarily be of a patriotic temper' (*The Nature of the Peace*, Transactions Press 1998, pp. 134-135).

Veblen's writing was often characterized by such subtle sarcasm, but the sarcasm masked the cogent and important analysis contained therein. To quote his most famous student, Wesley Clair Mitchell, "there [was] always an aura of playfulness about his attitude toward his own work in marked contrast to the deadly seriousness of most economists" (Quoted in John Kenneth Galbraith's "Introduction" to *Theory of the Leisure Class*, p. v.). The humor sometimes employed by Veblen may have softened his message somewhat; as John Kenneth Galbraith put it in his introduction to a 1973 reissue of *The Theory of the Leisure Class*: "That Marx was an enemy whose venom was to be returned in kind, capitalists did not doubt. But not Veblen. The American rich never quite understood what he was about—or what he was doing to them."

But, as we will see, famous Veblenian phrases such as "conspicuous consumption," "leisure class," and "captains of industry," were in fact theoretical concepts of the same central importance to his system of analysis as are concepts such as self-interest and profit

---

[*] This chapter was written by Janet Knoedler

maximization to the neoclassical analysis. To understand the importance of conspicuous consumption or to see the role played by the captains of industry, we will situate those terms below within his system of analysis.

THE ROOTS OF VEBLEN'S UNDERSTANDING OF THE ECONOMY

Veblen was a careful observer of the changes taking place in the United States economy at the beginning of the twentieth century and an innovating economist who specialized in studying economic change. Many of Veblen's views of the economy were conditioned by his father's experience as a late nineteenth century farmer in Minnesota contending with the changing economy of the post-Civil War United States. In the early 1870s, Midwestern farmers had taken advantage of new agricultural technologies to improve wheat processing and, in turn, to expand their production. As you will learn when you study the operations of markets, a bumper crop causes a rightward shift in the supply curve that tends to lower prices, a good thing for consumers, but not necessarily for farmers. Lower prices led to falling incomes and economic misfortune for many farmers. Farmers attributed their financial woes to the groups who seemed to be prospering. To quote Joseph Dorfman, biographer of Veblen, farmers reacted with a "wave of bitterness against the business interests . . . from the country-store trader and banker to the railroad company" (Dorfman, *Thorstein Veblen and His America*, p. 14). Fellow Minnesotan and chief lecturer for the Grange, Ignatius Donnelly, lamented in 1873: "Could the ordinary man retain his economic independence, or must he become the wage slave of the possessor of great wealth?" (Dorfman, p. 16).

Midwestern farmers believed themselves to be victimized by several groups of villains: the railroad tycoons who raised their rates and made it costlier for them to ship their produce to the East, the bankers who advanced them loans and then demanded payment even when falling prices destroyed the farmers' profits, the jobbers or wholesalers who bought the farmers' produce at low prices and resold these products at higher prices. To the typical farmer, it appeared that he was doing all the productive work and losing money while the railroads, middlemen and

financiers were profiting at his expense. Yet the decisions of the railroads, middlemen and financiers, at a remove from the farmers and workers, dictated the economic fortunes of the actual production workers. Below we will explore this distinction between what Veblen called industrial and pecuniary activities in more depth. (This same clash of monetary and real values is found in Marx.)

Veblen also examined other such conflicts, believing them to be central to his analysis of the pace and direction of economic change. The conflict between scientific or "matter-of-fact" thinking and superstitious or animistic thinking explained the often slow pace of change in our increasingly technological society. Veblen believed firmly that past-binding thinking locked society into habitual ways of thinking and being. Even today we can find examples, ranging from the Serbian-American who recently said that he would not purchase a "convenient appliance called a Dirt Devil because he does not want anything called a devil in his house," to the persistent gender and racial stereotypes that hinder women and minorities from rising to the top of corporate hierarchies or earning the same average salaries as their white male counterparts (Rankovic, Catherine, "Reflections of a Serbian-American," *Progressive*, June 1999, p. 26). In the same way, the conflict between what Veblen once referred to as "imbecile institutions" (his term for past-binding behavior) and the logic of the machine process, his metaphor for modern production techniques, could also impede technology's path and even alter its beneficent consequences. In one obvious example, the modern school year in the United States still includes a three month summer break, even though that summer break no longer serves its original purpose—to free children to work on family farms during the busy summer months. As a result, U.S. children attend school on average some two fewer months during the year than Japanese children.

VEBLEN'S EVOLUTIONARY ANALYSIS

Veblen (not unlike many early economists) was first trained in philosophy, so he took great pains to examine the philosophical foundations of the received economics of his day. He found that those foundations were outmoded for understanding the kind of economics emerging in the twentieth century. Mainstream economics then (and now) relied on the philosophical underpinnings of natural law that swept most social science thinking in the late eighteenth century, when Adam Smith wrote *The Wealth of Nations*. Smith and other early classical economists were influenced by the work of Isaac Newton, and they described the social world in the same terms then used to describe the physical world. The physical universe was seen as an immense clock set into motion by a divine Clockmaker, and the social universe was seen to be similarly well organized and mechanically ordered. Just as the Newtonian laws of physics kept the physical world operating in orderly fashion, the "natural" economic laws of self-interest would keep the competitive actions of human beings from colliding with each other. The natural order of the social universe was believed to be a system of free markets, with humans free to consume and to work as they pleased, controlled, if not by the Divine Clockmaker, then by his close counterpart the invisible hand (the metaphor used to describe the impersonal market forces perceived by Adam Smith and his followers to regulate the economy), but certainly by no earthly (government) regulators.

The Newtonian world-view led economists to see a world that was for the most part fixed and immutable. To quote David Hamilton, these early economists assumed that "the social order of their day was the natural product of sufficient reason and therefore fixed" (Hamilton, *Evolutionary Economics*, p. 22). Most economic historians agree that Adam Smith's England resembled the microeconomic model of perfect competition (even though great joint stock companies dominated much of England's international trade).[1] Hence Smith could justifiably construct a model of a perfectly competitive economy, where many small producers competed and self-interest alone sufficed to maintain social order and to produce the greatest economic welfare. Influenced by natural law philosophical thinking, Smith also assumed that the economic world had reached its ideal form with the flourishing of competition in late eighteenth century England. Analysis of change was deemed irrelevant, because the "classical" economists believed they were describing the archetypal economic system that would henceforth prevail always and everywhere. In such a world, analysis of economic change was restricted to the temporary—and unnatural—movements away from competitive market equilibrium. The main question to be answered, then, was: When demand rises for one product or falls for another product, how will the market reach a new equilibrium price and quantity?

Veblen argued that an evolutionary model was more useful for understanding the economy. Writing one hundred years after Smith, and observing the economic changes that had so concerned Marx, Veblen, like Marx, declared that the social universe was not fixed and immutable. Indeed, during the period that Veblen wrote most of his major works, 1898 to about 1923, the evidence abounded that economic and social change was a permanent feature of the economy. New technologies allowed for mass production of goods and services, transforming industries that may have once conformed more closely to the model of atomistic competition developed by Adam Smith, into industries now dominated by a few large multinational firms. Moreover, a huge wave of mergers and acquisitions at the turn of the century created huge national and multinational business firms that dominated their industries and transformed the nature of competition. The economists who clung to Smith's theories and applied them to the greatly changed economy of the late nineteenth century, assumed that the natural order of the world (in the form of placid price competition) would quickly restore Adam Smith's ideal economy. According to Veblen, neoclassical economists came to conceive of

> … the sole motive force concerned in the industrial process [as] . . . the self-regarding motive of pecuniary gain… Whether the end and outcome is an invidious gain for the individual (in

[1] Robert Heilbroner, "The Wonderful World of Adam Smith," *in The Worldly Philosophers*. Smith devoted considerable effort in *Wealth of Nations* to a critique of monopolies, so much so that many interpreters of the book see it as a polemic attack on the existing government policies as well as an exposition of classical economic theory. Smith believed that the great joint stock companies such as the British East India Company were products of the mercantilist policies that had granted these companies monopolies over the trade between England and certain parts of the world (cf. Canterbery, *The Literate Economist*, p. 49, as well as the *Wealth of Nations* itself).

contrast with or at the cost of his neighbors), or an enhancement of the facility of human life on the whole, is altogether a by-question… The serviceability of the given line of activity, for the life purposes of the community or for one's neighbors, 'is not of the essence of this contract' (Veblen, *Place of Science in Modern Civilization*, p. 139).

AN EXAMPLE OF BUSINESS SABOTAGE

It is not placid Smithian price competition that has characterized the modern industrial economy. The effort of John D. Rockefeller, in the 1865-1890 period to smash his competition, is an exemplar of the Veblen's version of competition. By 1869, at the age of 30, Rockefeller was already a major oil refiner in Cleveland (the early center of the oil refining industry in the United States). John D. Rockefeller came up with the idea of negotiating lower shipping rates from several key railroads to gain a competitive advantage over rival oil refiners. At the time, most of the markets for refined oil were on the eastern seaboard of the United States and thus transportation represented a major cost for oil refiners. Using his clout as Cleveland's largest refiner and therefore as an important bulk shipper of oil, Rockefeller secured preferential rates for shipping his oil. (Recall that the railroads during this same period were raising the rates charged to farmers.) This gave him an enormous cost advantage over smaller competitors who could not guarantee bulk shipments to the railroads. Rockefeller believed that he was simply exploiting his "economies of scale," but critics at the time argued that he was instead using his "special power to compel railroad-freight concessions" (Ron Chernow, *Titan*, p. 114).

In 1872, Rockefeller devised an even more ambitious scheme, innocuously named the "South Improvement Company," or SIC. Under SIC, all refiners who joined their operations with his would receive up to a 50% rebate from the railroads on their shipping costs, not only for their own oil but for all oil shipped by rail, including oil shipped by their competitors.[2] The SIC included most of the major refiners and all the major eastern railroads, in effect, forming a double cartel. The SIC in turn guaranteed the major railroads a steady flow of oil shipments. To quote Ron Chernow, "the railroads acquired a vested interest in the creation of a giant oil monopoly that would lower their costs, boost their profits, and generally simplify their lives" (Chernow, p. 113). The provision that the SIC refiners would receive rebates for oil shipped by their competitors has been described by one Rockefeller biographer as "an instrument of competitive cruelty unparalleled in industry" (Chernow, p. 136). In fact, the SIC oil refiners would now have a huge advantage over their smaller independent rivals; "the harder their competitors worked, the more money Rockefeller and associates would make" Dillard, *The Economic Development of the North Atlantic Community*, Prentice-Hall, 1967, p. 410). Moreover, this same provision in the SIC agreement would give SIC members precise pricing and shipping information about their competitors, permitting the SIC oil cartel to undercut their rivals at every turn.

While it is true that this SIC contract violated no actual law (this was two decades before the first federal antitrust laws were passed), rumors leaked out about the "scheme of gigantic combination among certain railroads and refiners to control the purchase and shipment of crude and refined oil from [western Pennsylvania]" (Chernow, p. 138). A firestorm swept the local newspapers in the affected regions; the railroads abandoned the agreement; and the Pennsylvania legislature canceled the SIC's charter in 1872. So the SIC never actually went into effect. However, during the six weeks in early 1872 that the SIC rumors were spreading, the remaining competition realized that if they didn't sell out, they would be driven out of the industry. 22 of the 26 remaining Cleveland refiners sold their operations to Rockefeller during that six week period, most of them later acknowledging the implicit SIC club

---

[2] Ron Chernow discusses this in depth in his biography of Rockefeller (*Titan*, 1998). The opportunity for railroads to get large and steady shipments of oil lowered their own costs, so the rebates were a way of sharing those benefits with the shippers; as Rockefeller himself said, "It was a large, regular volume of business such as had not hitherto been given to the roads in question" (Chernow, 113). Rockefeller was further aided by the fact that railroads like the Erie and the New York Central were very interested in promoting Cleveland as an oil-refining center, in order to boost the shipments through their own railway networks.

held over their heads by Rockefeller.[3] This was not the friendly competition between small local blacksmiths that drove prices down, as described by Adam Smith. Instead, Veblen recognized that the very nature of competition had changed and he used words like "sabotage" to describe the brutal tactics of Rockefeller and the other robber barons.

VEBLEN AND EVOLUTION

Writing in an age where a Darwinian model of evolution was being adopted in the physical and other social sciences, Veblen adopted an evolutionary model to explain the cumulative causation[4] and constant change that he observed in the American economy. However, Veblen's use of the Darwinian approach did not mean that Veblen believed in survival of the fittest, despite the fact that Veblen actually studied under William Graham Sumner, one of the architects of social Darwinism. Veblen took from Darwin, and Sumner, a different scientific method, "which studies humanity in its process of continuous adaptation to both its social and natural environment and which sees the conditions of human existence as subject to ceaseless change" (Tilman, *Veblen Treasury*, p. xxvi). It is not survival of the fittest that is relevant to understanding economic and social change, but rather the simple fact of evolution itself. For example, the practice of men wearing ties—a non-utilitarian adornment with which most men who move in professional circles still torture themselves—for important social or professional occasions, dates to an era where men used their ties or cravats to wipe their faces while eating. Over time, ties evolved into the quintessential symbol of the gentleman of

---

[3] Chernow, *Titan*, pp. 143 ff. See also Dillard, Ch. 23 and Porter, *The Rise of Big Business*, Ch. 3. Rockefeller also used less brutal tactics to compete. He was the first oil refiner to build his own pipelines for shipping oil, to set up his own marketing operations, and to reduce his costs further and further. At the same time, by owning his own pipelines and setting up marketing operations, he closed off the distribution markets from the wholesalers and railroads in favor of his own divisions, thus centralizing even more power over the national oil refining market in the hands of the Standard Oil Trust. Chandler, *Visible Hand*, Ch. 10.

[4] Cumulative causation is contrasted to simple cause and effect, where action a results in reaction b, end of story. Cumulative causation suggests that reaction b may become a cause of reaction c, and in turn reaction c may be a cause of reaction d, and on and on infinitum.

business, even though the modern businessman would no sooner wipe his face on an expensive silk tie than he would appear in public with a cheerful checked napkin wrapped around his neck.

THE LEISURE CLASS

To understand why Veblen, and other heterodox economists after him, saw analysis of economic change from an evolutionary approach as crucial to understanding the dynamics of any economic system, we will look at his most important economic ideas in their appropriate context. Let's begin with his concept of the "leisure class," which he singled out as "an economic factor in modern life" in his most famous book, *The Theory of the Leisure Class* (all cites are from 1973 Houghton-Mifflin Co. edition). In that volume he set forth many of the basic concepts of his analytical system, and made explicit use of his evolutionary understanding of the modern economy. The book was written as the excesses of the Gilded Age of the late nineteenth century began to reveal themselves in the lavish entertainments and opulent mansions enjoyed by the wealthy capitalists of the era. However, Veblen began his analysis, not with these wealthy robber barons, but with the feudal cultures of Japan and medieval Europe, because he believed that modern economic behavior had evolved slowly from those beginnings, and that any analysis had to unearth the long historical roots of our modern institutions (Lerner, Introduction, *Portable Veblen*, p. 22).

A common theme ran through economic history: "Wherever the institution of private property is found, even in slightly developed form, the economic process bears the character of a struggle between men for the possession of goods" (*The Theory of the Leisure Class*, p. 34). The word "struggle" conveys Veblen's view of competition—not merely placid price competition of the sort described by Smith, but the "slash and burn" competition more common in our modern business landscape. Veblen also recognized that property had held a dual role throughout history, one economic, one symbolic.

In that struggle for subsistence, according to Veblen, there has always been a "warrior" or "leisure class" and a "menial" or "productive class" (this taxonomy is similar to the class distinctions made by Marx). The leisure class first emerged in early hunter-gatherer societies. Veblen defined this group as the class of persons exempt from menial labor and for whom the "honorable employments" of hunting were reserved (*The Theory of the Leisure Class*, p. 21). In these early cultures, the gender division of labor between men and women was strictly observed: the men hunting for food, the women gathering and farming and preparing the food. Both sets of activities were, of course, equally indispensable to economic survival, but not equally honored.[5] The hunters constituted the first leisure class: "in [the hunter's] own eyes, he is not a laborer, and he is not to be classed with the women in this respect; nor is his work to be classed with the women's drudgery, as labor or industry" (*The Theory of the Leisure Class*, p. 23).

Over time, the *leisure class* came to include the entire class of persons who were exempt from the more routine and menial tasks necessary for economic survival; the leisure class was not exempt from work of any kind, but was exempt from menial labor. These invidious distinctions between different lines of work have persisted over time, Veblen insisted, meaning that our modern understanding of methods of making a living is rooted in our deep anthropological past. While a modern industrial economy no longer depends on a class of hunters to provide a large portion of society's means of subsistence, the higher honor accorded those engaged in "predatory" pursuits has endured, and the low repute accorded those engaged in actual productive work has also continued. The modern day robber barons were, in Veblen's analysis, the economic descendants of the warring nobles of medieval Europe or the warrior class of Japan, struggling not against nature or against other clans for control over land and property, but against other robber barons for control of their industries. You can see similar struggles today. The U.S. government's antitrust trial against Microsoft exposed Bill Gates' ruthless tactics to increase use of Microsoft's Internet Explorer, such as forcing computer manufacturers to install IE on their computers or withholding Windows from

manufacturers, such as IBM, building operating systems that might compete with Windows.

In the Veblenian system, therefore, the modern leisure class would consist of those whose ownership of wealth and whose control of the means of production permits them to engage in the same kind of relentless competition and predatory activity carried out by their barbarian forefathers, and more importantly, to be exempt from the menial jobs occupied by ordinary workers. Modern leisure activities would include high finance, corporate law, management, and other activities undertaken by those concerned mainly with "conversion of goods and persons to [their] own ends, and a callous disregard of the feelings and wishes of others, and of the remoter effects of his actions" (Dorfman, p. 184). The modern menial class would thus consist of those who are not owners of property and thus must work for wages or salaries for someone else.

For Veblen, the leisure class was, by definition, also the wealthy class, and that too has historical precedents. In ancient cultures, wealth came to be equated with social status: as Veblen argued, "possession of wealth confers honor" (*The Theory of the Leisure Class*, p. 35). Initially, wealth consisted of the booty dragged back from wars with neighboring clans or nations; the items seized, be they treasures or slaves, were the spoils of battle and served therefore as a very public sign of physical prowess. Possession of wealth came over time to represent "a trophy of successes scored in the game of ownership carried on between the members of the group" (*The Theory of the Leisure Class*, pp. 36-37). Over time, mere possession of wealth came to confer reputability on the possessor, as if the wealth itself signified the superior strength of the leader of the household. By the late nineteenth century, robber barons such as Rockefeller, Vanderbilt, and Morgan were considered both successful and honorable largely because they were wealthy, despite their destructive and often dishonorable business practices. Moreover, ownership of property came over time to be seen as the indication of the prowess of the owner, and thus "it becomes indispensable to accumulate, to acquire property, in order to retain one's good name" (*The Theory of the Leisure Class*, p. 37). Wealth thus equated to esteem, humans strive to emulate and to surpass the wealth of their neighbors: "A certain standard of wealth in one

---

[5] In an example of his irony Veblen notes that "it may even be that the men's work contributes as much to the food supply and the other necessary consumption of the group." *The Theory of the Leisure Class*, p. 23.

case, and of prowess in the other, is a necessary condition of reputability, and anything in excess of this normal amount is meritorious" (*The Theory of the Leisure Class*, p. 38).

CONSPICUOUS CONSUMPTION

Of course, mere possession of wealth does not confer upon the possessor this honorific position in society unless the rest of society perceives that the wealthy are indeed wealthy, so the wealthy must engage in "conspicuous consumption." Conspicuous consumption was an important element of Veblen's understanding of human behavior. To quote Veblen at length on this point:

> The quasi-peaceable gentleman of leisure [by which Veblen means the modern robber baron 'descended' from the early warrior], then, not only consumes of the staff of life beyond the minimum required for subsistence and physical efficiency, but his consumption also undergoes a specialization as regards the quality of the goods consumed. He consumes freely and of the best, in food, drink, narcotics, shelter, services, ornaments, apparel, weapons and accoutrements, amusements, amulets, and idols or divinities. . . . Since the consumption of these more excellent goods is an evidence to wealth, it becomes honorific; and conversely, the failure to consume in due quantity and quality becomes a mark of inferiority and demerit (*The Theory of the Leisure Class*, p. 64).

Conspicuous consumption is how the wealthy demonstrate their wealth, and thus their success in war or in business, by purchasing the finest houses, autos, suits and shoes—all visible and public signs of financial success—to gain respect and admiration from their peers and subordinates. Today, the BMW parked outside the office, the Armani suit for everyday wear, and the Coach bag slung casually across a shoulder, tell the casual onlooker that the bearer is a successful (i.e., wealthy) person. Veblen referred to this as "conspicuous waste" because, "in order to effectually mend the consumer's good fame, [a conspicuous expenditure] must be an expenditure

of superfluities" (*The Theory of the Leisure Class*, p. 77). Those expenditures are "traceable to the habit of making an invidious pecuniary comparison"—to demonstrate the level of income and wealth held by the conspicuous consumer (*The Theory of the Leisure Class*, p. 79).

In other words, the Lexus owner would be as ably transported around town by a Chrysler Neon, or the Range Rover owner would have his or her needs just as efficiently and dependably met by a Chevy truck. The point of making an expensive purchase is precisely to demonstrate to those who can not afford the Lexus or the Range Rover the superior social status of the conspicuous consumer. Juliet Schor confirms that this motive still dominates in our modern era in her recent book, *The Overspent American*. The ubiquitous "visible logo"—be it the Nike swoosh, the Hilfiger label, or even the Starbucks name on a disposable paper cup—tells observers that the purchaser has bought the real deal (Schor, *Overspent American*, p. 46). One nationwide poll of women revealed that half of the respondents participated in status buying, with 80% of the respondents—a percentage that would not have surprised Veblen at all—admitting that purchases were more often based on the designer label than on the intrinsic quality of the goods. Robert Frank recounts how some "nouveau" millionaires in both Silicon Valley and suburban Chicago have demolished large modern homes, valued in the hundreds of thousands of dollars, so they could build much larger homes on the same sites to suit their elevated social status. As one new executive for America Online declared, the "scraper" that he razed "was definitely livable. I just wanted something bigger" (Frank, *Luxury Fever*, pp. 28-39).

PECUNIARY EMULATION

Mainstream economic theory has long taught that consumers make purchases based on rational assessment of the intrinsic utility of the item in question. Veblen rejected that analysis as overly simplistic, in one of his most famous paragraphs:

> The hedonistic conception of man is that of a lightning calculator of pleasures and pains, who oscillates like a homogeneous globule of desire of happiness under the impulse of stimuli that shift him about the

area, but leave him intact. He has neither antecedent or consequent... Self-imposed in elemental space, he spins symmetrically about his own spiritual axis, until the parallelogram of forces bears down upon him, whereupon he follows the line of the resultant. When the force of the impact is spent, he comes to rest, a self-contained globule of desire as before (Veblen, "Why is Economics not an Evolutionary Science," in *The Place of Science in Modern Civilization*, New Brunswick, New Jersey: Transaction Publishers, 1990, p. 75).

The mainstream theory of consumer choice reduces all of the complex processes and influences involved in human consumption to a simple and overtly rational choice. Consumer tastes and preferences are taken as "given," with the relative price being the main factor that causes consumers to buy more (or less) of some commodity, such as shoes or cigarettes. The mainstream preconception is that the product in question generates utility, i.e., that the smoker derives utility from consumption of his or her cigarette, with no further questions asked. Veblen recognized that this approach ignored the considerable and important influences on consumption exercised by advertising, peer pressure, the symbolic nature of commodities in a capitalist culture, and many other external influences.

In particular, Veblen argued that mainstream economics ignored a powerful motive for consumption, the motive of pecuniary emulation: "Goods are produced and consumed as a means to the fuller unfolding of human life . . . . But the human proclivity to emulation has seized upon consumption of goods as a means to our invidious comparison" (*The Theory of the Leisure Class*, p. 94). In this context, consumption decisions are driven by the need to fit in with our peers or, in popular parlance, to keep up with the Joneses. Again, to quote Veblen at length:

the standard of expenditure which commonly guides our efforts is not the average, ordinary expenditure already achieved; it is an ideal of consumption that lies just beyond our reach... The motive is emulation—the stimulus of an

invidious comparison which prompts us to outdo those with whom we are in the habit of classing ourselves...each class envies and emulates the class next above it in the social scale, while it rarely compares itself with those below or with those who are considerably in advance (*The Theory of the Leisure Class*, p. 81).

Veblen thought that this "propensity for emulation," as he termed it, was among the strongest of economic motives. To quote a more recent proponent of this theory, economist Robert Frank, "Concern about relative position is a deep-rooted and ineradicable element of human nature" (Quoted in Cassidy, "No Satisfaction," The *New Yorker*, January 25, 1999, p. 90).

Veblen's argument that conspicuous consumption and pecuniary emulation are the driving forces behind much of the consumption we observe in capitalism is persuasive but not necessarily pejorative. Human beings are social beings and we cannot help but to emulate much of the behavior of those around us, in fact, to try to outdo others (Lerner, p. 24). Pecuniary emulation, as Veblen called it because we emulate the spending habits of others, takes place in a context of capitalism. In capitalism, social status is heavily tied to income and wealth, and is demonstrated visibly by the accoutrements of wealth—fancy clothes, luxury cars, and stately houses. To maintain our status in our desired communities, we endlessly strive to "keep up with the Joneses." Imagine for a minute the businessperson who arrived at an important meeting in a polyester suit, wearing coke-bottle glasses and carrying papers in a shopping bag rather than in an expensive leather briefcase. Would he or she be given the same attention at that meeting, or receive important promotions? Similarly, the student who wanted to join the most popular sorority on campus, but showed up for rush events in sweatpants and a bowling shirt would most likely be hastened out the door. While both individuals might have much of substance to contribute, their outward appearance would send a signal to their potential peers that they just wouldn't fit in.

MARGINAL PRODUCTIVITY

Another tenet of neoclassical economics that Veblen disputed was the theory of marginal productivity. This theory, that the wage earned by any given worker would naturally tend to be equivalent to the marginal productivity of that worker, was articulated by Veblen's own former professor, John Bates Clark. Marginal productivity theory is still a central element of mainstream labor economics; it is used, for example, to explain the high salaries of professional athletes (they receive high salaries because they sell tickets and advertisements) or why it would be inefficient to interfere with market processes by raising the minimum wage. At the time Veblen began to write his *Theory of Business Enterprise*, many economists considered the high incomes received by the robber barons to be simply their fair returns, the hard-earned fruits of their intense and stressful labors. As entrepreneurs, they organized the production process, and their earnings were the equivalent of their contributions to the firm, just as the factory worker or the shop clerk earned his or her wage in proportion to the productivity that they contributed to the firm. In recent years, marginal productivity theory has been used to justify the enormous and growing pay gap between CEOs and workers—a gap that now exceeds 400 to 1— and to justify the growing inequality of income. This argument claims that top management has increasingly had to make tough decisions (thus earning the millions of dollars that they are paid) or that good managers are a scarce commodity and it is simply the working of supply-and-demand that elevates executive salaries.

Veblen argued for a different taxonomy to compare the work of the robber barons to that of ordinary workers. Within the modern firm emerging at the turn of the century, Veblen saw two basic groups of workers—those who made goods (those engaged in industrial activities, as he called them) and those who made money (those engaged in pecuniary activities). This is not quite the same as the breakdown between the owners of property and the property-less described by Marx, for Veblen includes in those engaged in pecuniary employments many who hold no property at all— for example, people working in advertising, middle managers, corporate lawyers—i.e., the modern-day businessman or businesswoman.

Veblen argued that the work of the typical business person was directed at making the product of their firm vendible—i.e., marketing and selling the product. Thus they were engaged in buying and selling, negotiating and contriving, merging and financing, but not actually involved in producing the product in question.

For Veblen, this distinction between the work of those involved directly in the productive process and those he called undertakers who perform administrative or managerial or financial work became a central part of his understanding of the modern economy. Moreover, he argued that the businesspersons—the captains of industry as he later called them or the financiers, the lawyers, the CEO's and others at the top ranks of Wall Street or corporations today—were chiefly concerned with the distribution of wealth (and the fattening of their own wallets) rather than with ensuring that needed goods and services were made available to consumers. To quote Veblen, their concern was with the "exchange values of goods and . . . the vendibility of the items with which they are concerned, and on the necessities, solvency, cupidity, or gullibility of the persons whose actions may affect the transaction contemplated" (Quoted in Dorfman, p. 193).

By contrast, actual production was carried out by those engaged in "industrial pursuits"—e.g., engineers, craftsmen, assembly line workers. These workers were, in Veblen's view, actively furthering the "material interests of the community," or more precisely, "adapting the material means of life, and the processes of valuation constantly involved in the work run on the availability of goods and on the material serviceability of the contrivances, materials, persons, or mechanical expedients employed" (Dorfman, p. 192-3). Taken to its logical conclusion, this dichotomy suggests that profit-seeking businesspersons can be as interested in marketing products in clever and creative ways as they are in improving the actual product. As an example, consider the following: in recent years, Nike has spent more to hire Michael Jordan to hawk its shoes than it has paid to its entire Indonesian work force to produce the Air Jordans. Nike contracts out most of the production work for its shoe lines, relying on labor-intensive production technologies and low-cost labor, leaving Nike as little more than a large marketing company.

Veblen analyzed the changes in business firms since the halcyon days of Adam Smith in the same evolutionary terms he used to explore the evolution of consumption. In the early stages of manufacturing, dating back to the British Industrial Revolution and even before, the typical owner-entrepreneur was also a producer, who often manufactured or at least handled the goods that he sold. The master who crafted horseshoes, for example, might spend a portion of his day checking bank statements and logging orders, but would also work side by side with his journeymen and apprentices making the actual product. To quote Veblen here, this early "captain of industry" "was business manager of the venture as well as foreman of the works, and not infrequently he was the designer and master-builder of the equipment, of which he was also the responsible owner" (*Absentee Ownership*, p. 103). As firms became larger and the management of those firms required more and more of the owner-manager's time, "industry and business gradually split apart" (*Absentee Ownership*, p. 106). The captain of industry—originally "a cross between a business man and an industrial expert"—became removed from the shop floor and did not deal with matters of production, spending more and more of his time engaged in financial management of the firm (*Enigneers and the Price System*, p.59). He became a "captain of finance," rather than a captain of industry, far removed from the production lines. As his daily occupation changed, so did his interest as he became less interested in production and more interested in profit. To quote Joseph Dorfman, Veblen's biographer:

> The modern captain is not interested in the permanent efficiency of the industrial system or of any plant, but in the control of a segment of the system for the strategic purpose of influencing the security market for the flotation of securities, the maneuvering of a coalition or any other well known method of manipulation . . . . The modern captain does not create opportunities for increasing industrial efficiency, but only watches for opportunities to put his competitors in an uncomfortable position; cut-throat competition, rate wars, duplication, misdirection, wasted efforts and delay of improvements long after they are advisable are the price the community pays (Dorfman, pp. 125-126).

In a later, famous quote, Veblen described this watchful waiting carried out by modern businessmen as being similar to the activities of toads sitting on a country road:

> Doubtless this form of words, 'watchful waiting,' will have been employed in the first instance to describe the frame of mind of a toad who has reached years of discretion and has found his appointed place along some frequented run where many flies and spiders pass and repass on their way to complete that destiny to which it has pleased an all-seeing and merciful Providence to call them; but by an easy turn of speech it has also been found suitable to describe the safe and sane strategy of that mature order of captains of industry who are governed by sound business principles. There is a certain bland sufficiency spread across the face of such a toad so circumstanced, while his comely personal bulk gives assurance of a pyramidal stability of principles (*Absentee Ownership*, pp. 109-110 of the 1997 Transaction Publishers edition).

INDUSTRIAL SABOTAGE

During the same period that Veblen wrote, most of the firms that were soon to become important American corporations began to employ modern mass production technologies which relied increasingly on the use of knowledgeable engineers and trained personnel to keep the production lines running (Porter, *Rise of Big Business*). One feature of mass production— what Veblen referred to as the "machine process"—was the need for standardized production processes and interchangeable parts. For Ford's assembly line to run smoothly and efficiently, every part had to be made precisely to the same specifications, so that an individual worker could simply insert the widget into the gizmo as it rolled across the work station. Interchangeable parts eliminated the need for hand crafting of each automobile from top to bottom and greatly improved both the quantity and quality of output. Parts suppliers—firms supplying the steel chassis, the nuts and bolts, the frames and engines—were also required to meet exacting specifications. Production became less and less a matter of individual discretion and craftsmanship and more and more a matter of technological expertise and mechanization. The mass production that accompanied the Second Industrial Revolution in late nineteenth century

America created both huge productivity gains and great economic growth (Ratner, Soltow, and Sylla, *The Evolution of the American Economy*, Ch. 12). Indeed, American dominance in the machine tools industry (the industry that promoted mechanization of many previously hand crafted tasks) and its early use of industrial research to develop new products and better manufacturing processes, led to new technologies, large production and distribution facilities, and the emergence of the big business that we know today.

In Veblen's analysis, these vastly superior machine technologies and the greatly improved capacity remained under the control of the captains of finance, always with an eye toward greater profits rather than toward greater productivity. Productive capacities were great, indeed, but Veblen believed that the captains of industry prevented industrial capacity from becoming even greater. Observing the great merger movement that occurred at the turn of the century, where nearly 3,000 firms disappeared into mergers with larger rivals, Veblen argued that businesspersons were taking control of large segments of the nation's industrial apparatus in order to carry out "industrial sabotage." He defined industrial sabotage as a "conscientious withdrawal of efficiency," or more fully, as "any degree of obstruction, diversion, or withholding of any of the available industrial forces, with a view to the special gain of any nation or any investor, unavoidably brings on a dislocation of the system; which involves a disproportionate lowering of its working efficiency and therefore a disproportionate loss to the whole; and therefore a net loss to all its parts" (*Engineers and the Price System*, p. 73).

This was sabotage in Veblen's view because an industrial system that was increasingly interconnected, needed rapid and reliable flow of goods and services from one industrial sector to another—steel to the auto and rail industries, raw materials to the chemicals producers, railways transporting disposable food stuffs—and needed to be free of all obstructions to those necessary intersectoral flows. However, businesspersons could often profit from disrupting those flows or at least by holding up supplies in order to secure higher prices and more lucrative profits. (Recall the earlier example of Microsoft withholding its Windows software from IBM. According to

testimony at trial, Microsoft waited until the last possible moment to make a deal with IBM for its Windows O/S, and then raised the price by nearly 900 percent. This, of course, placed IBM machines at a huge disadvantage with its PC competitors.)

By sabotage, Veblen did not mean that the captains crept by dark of night into the factories that they controlled and meddled with the machines. He took a broader view of sabotage, one grounded in the notion that modern production technologies would allow humankind to produce sufficient goods and services to alleviate all poverty and human want. However, Veblen believed that modern business practices subverted these possibilities by prizing profit over production, thus restricting total output far below its potential levels. Both Marx and Veblen acknowledged the enormous productive capacity of modern technology. But they also agreed that modern capitalism placed pecuniary values above all others, such that greed, corruption, and invidious consumption eroded the productive potential of modern industry, generating instead enormous inequality and universal dissatisfaction with the goods already possessed. Both believed that if pecuniary values could somehow be displaced and the common welfare honored, that enormous productivity could be harnessed for all peoples. It is a utopian view of an economy, surely, but one that has merit. In fact, the 1997 UN *Human Development Report* argued that we would need to redistribute no more than one percent of global income to eradicate poverty in the world. In other words, we have the material means to provide a decent living for each and every person on the planet. The question is, how to permit sufficient output of the needed goods and services, ranging from basic foodstuffs to good schools, to be produced, and how to arrange for distribution of these goods and services so that the basic needs of all peoples on the planet are met.

Veblen's analysis of sabotage resonated with Marx's analysis of the reserve army of the unemployed, and the relentless drive of the bourgeoisie to keep wages low and profits high. Veblen adds to that arsenal of the businessperson the use of mergers and buy-outs, and all other business tactics that are used mainly to garner profits rather than to benefit consumers or workers. To quote Veblen, "in no such community that is organized on the price system…can the industrial system be allowed to work at full capacity for any appreciable interval of time, on pain of business stagnation and consequent privation for all classes and conditions of men. The requirements of profitable business will not tolerate it" (*Engineers and the Price System*, p. 43). In other words, it is imperative for business interests that industrial capacity be kept below its potential. Otherwise supply would increase too rapidly, prices would fall, and profits would suffer. Veblen elaborated on this point, arguing that even in periods of high profits, business interests would act to make those high profits even higher: "it is considered doubtful whether an increased production, such as to employ more workmen and supply the goods needed by the community, would result in an increased net aggregate income for the vested interests which control these industries. A reasonable profit always means, in effect, the largest possible profit" (*Engineers and the Price System*, p. 45).

In more pedestrian terms, Veblen also believed that businesspersons engaged in sabotage when they chose to rely on obsolete but profitable methods of production rather than to move to more modern and innovative production techniques or to produce products that would better serve the consumer. In a famous example, J.P. Morgan, a captain of finance par excellence at the time Veblen wrote, gathered hundreds of previously competing steel producers into a new large firm, U.S. Steel, that dominated all segments of the steel industry. Having thus removed most of the relevant competition by merging with them, U.S. Steel then slowed its pace of innovation to a crawl, setting the stage for a pattern of sluggish innovation and noncompetitive behavior that persisted for the rest of the century, and left the Japanese to take over the world steel market. One has only to ponder the story of the American automobile industry during the second half of the twentieth century or the dismal performance of corporate giants such as GM and IBM in the 1980s during the decades when those companies were relatively free from international or technological competition, to see what Veblen meant. It was not internal lobbying by GM engineers that prompted GM to develop more fuel efficient cars, but the gradual erosion of GM's market share and the superior cars made by foreign competitors that finally prompted some

changes (Adams and Brock, *Structure of American Industry*, 1995, pp. 65-92 Knoedler, *BHR*, p.1993).

CONCLUSION

In sum, Veblen saw that the economy itself was constantly evolving and strove to understand the nature of economic and social change. At the same time, he understood that our anthropological roots influenced our modern economy in important if unrecognized ways and that the often predatory nature of competition, the prevalence of pecuniary standards of success, and the failure to use modern technologies to alleviate human want and misery were all symptoms of a capitalist economy that placed pecuniary values above all others. As a consequence the economy no longer functioned primarily to provision all its inhabitants. Veblen is remembered today mostly for his colorful analysis of the leisure class, but his criticism of business interests, his understanding of the importance of economic change in economic analysis, and his belief that the economy could be used to alleviate all the genuine needs of all human beings, remain his important if ignored contributions to the discipline of economics.[6]

Veblen's writings not only contain trenchant critiques of the received economics of his day, but also offer alternative forms of analysis that would lead economists to different conclusions. Veblen was quite critical of the view that human beings were merely self-interested beings. He held an affirmative view of human nature, and argued what really promoted human welfare was not self-interest, but rather the instinct of workmanship and the parental bent. The parental bent extended beyond concern for one's own children, and, according to Veblen, was a culturally instilled proclivity to provide for the next generation and to contribute to the common good. The instinct of workmanship was the human proclivity to improve things, to make things work, to be both creative and efficient. We can only imagine how different mainstream economics might be if it had started from these alternative premises.

---

[6] He is often accused of moving into an activist stance with his book, *Engineers and the Price System*, where he advocated for the engineers and others of an industrial state of mind to take over the nation's industrial apparatus and reorganize it to provision the entire economy.

Chapter III

John Kenneth Galbraith
And The Theory of Social Balance

The ideas of John Kenneth Galbraith, so well known around the world from his many books and articles, and his more than half-century in U.S. public life, are surprisingly little known inside the mainstream of economics. Economist Ron Stanfield has called Galbraith "the most famous economist of the last half-century." Nonetheless, Stanfield notes, "he also represents a very obscure American institutionalist tradition. This paradox I cannot resolve for the reader... The Galbraithian Paradox puzzles me."[1]

Neither will we try explaining the marginal effect Galbraith has had on his own discipline, despite his wide renown. Instead, we will shift that question to our readers. After you read this essay, and perhaps more of Galbraith's work, ask yourself why you are unlikely to hear his ideas in a mainstream economics course. But, for now, who is this economist whose influence in the world is so oddly distributed?

I. The Myriad Worlds of John Kenneth Galbraith

Galbraith has said that Keynes, Marx and Veblen were the economists who most influenced his own thinking. We shall see that, like Marx and Veblen, Galbraith worked mostly outside the confines of mainstream economics. Now in his early nineties and still writing and giving interviews, Galbraith has been a prominent social critic or public servant for an astonishing *six* decades. He taught economics for forty years, mostly at Harvard University, starting in the 1930s. During the first two years of the Second World War, Galbraith led the federal Office of Price Administration, a position that gave him the immense power to determine which U.S. companies could raise which prices. He was an ambassador to India during the John F. Kennedy administration in the early 1960s. He wrote speeches for, and advised, prominent Democrats including Adlai Stevenson, the party's presidential candidate in 1952 and 1956, Presidents Kennedy and Lyndon Johnson, and Eugene McCarthy, a U.S. Senator who challenged Johnson for the Democratic presidential nomination in 1968.

Mostly, however, Galbraith is known for books and writings covering an immensely broad range of genres and issues. He has written terse theoretical works, articles about economics for *Fortune Magazine* (between 1942 and 1947), twenty highly readable books analyzing the economics and politics of modern capitalist societies, three memoirs, and two novels. He co-authored a book on Indian painting, wrote and narrated a thirteen-part PBS series on the history of economic ideas, and produced countless shorter pieces for academic journals and the press. All his analytical books have typically focused attention on three matters: (1) the operations and effects on economic and political life of the giant corporations that dominate the world economy; (2) the failure of mainstream economics to incorporate adequately the effects of these large firms into its analyses of capitalism; and (3) the issue of whether the central value in mainstream economics – that "more is better than less" – is a reasonable guide to social policy.

An especially prominent feature of Galbraith's writing and political activities is that he puts them forward as an unapologetic liberal, always arguing from the perspective that public policy needs to countervail the immense powers of huge corporations and, more generally, that an unregulated capitalist economy is chaos in-the-making. This open advocacy for a broad-reaching government sector separates him from mainstream economics, whose practitioners put forward the pretense of being "scientific," despite their typical belief that capitalist economies work best with minimal "government intervention," and that more is better than less. We will say more on this contradiction shortly.

In the first two decades of Galbraith's prominence as a writer, until about the late 1970s, mainstream economists frequently responded in print, or at conferences, to his critique of their own explanations of the economic order. However, since then, as most of them have retreated into a much narrower theoretical world than the one that engages Galbraith, they have increasingly ignored him. Thus, the irony that

---

[1] James Ron Stanfield, *John Kenneth Galbraith*, St. Martin's Press, 1996. We have focused in this chapter on Galbraith's theory of social balance rather than on a larger slice of his work because we believe it is his most important contribution to modern social analysis. Also, his books are readily accessible to any adult reader, and there are numerous readable overviews of Galbraith's writing, such as the one cited here.

Galbraith's ideas are known and respected worldwide but largely ignored by most of the members of his own profession. Yet political economists, and many others outside the academic world, continue to find much of his work – above all his theory of social balance – relevant and important. To that interesting set of ideas, we now turn.

II. The Theory of Social Balance Described

In his 1958 book *The Affluent Society*, Galbraith argued that the slavish commitment of people in advanced capitalist societies to private goods at the expense of public services – such as schools, roads, efficient government, clean air and water, beautiful cities – could bring them to ruin. He called this analysis of private and public spending the "theory of social balance," and he stated its essential meaning in a well-known passage, as follows:

> The family which takes its mauve and cerise, air-conditioned, power-steered, and power-braked automobile out for a tour passes through cities that are badly paved, made hideous by litter, blighted buildings, billboards and posts for wires that should long since have been put underground. They pass on into a countryside that has been rendered largely invisible by commercial art. . . .They picnic on exquisitely packaged food from a portable icebox by a polluted stream and go on to spend the night at a park which is a menace to public health and morals. Just before dozing off on an air mattress, beneath a nylon tent, amid the stench of decaying refuse, they may reflect vaguely on the curious unevenness of their blessings. Is this, indeed, the American genius?[2]

What is the larger, structural, context of this florid, in some ways angry and frustrated, statement? Here is how Galbraith describes that larger structure:

> [The] disparity between our flow of private and public goods and services is no matter of subjective judgment. On the contrary, it is the source of the most extensive comment, which only stops short of the direct contrast being made here. In the years following World War II, the papers of any major city – those of New York were an excellent example – told daily of the shortages and shortcomings in the elementary municipal and metropolitan services. The schools were old and overcrowded. The police force was under strength and underpaid. The parks and playgrounds were insufficient. Streets and empty lots were filthy, and the sanitation staff was under-equipped and in need of men. Access to the city by those who work there was uncertain and painful and becoming more so. Internal transportation was overcrowded, unhealthful, and dirty. So was the air. Parking on the streets had to be prohibited, and there was no space elsewhere. (p. 252)

And, a bit later in his text, Galbraith argues that:

> .... Every increase in the consumption of private goods will normally mean some facilitation or protective step by the [public sector]. [If] these [public] services are not forthcoming, the consequences will be in some degree ill. It will be convenient to have a term which suggests a satisfactory relationship between the supply of privately produced goods and services and those of the state, and we may call it *social balance*.
>
> The problem of social balance is ubiquitous, and frequently it is obtrusive.... An increase in the consumption of automobiles requires a facilitating supply of streets, highways, traffic control, and parking space. The protective services of the police and the highway patrols must also be available, as must those of the hospitals. Although the need for balance here is extraordinarily clear, our use of privately produced vehicles has, on occasion, gone far out of line with the supply of the related public services. The result has been hideous road congestion, an annual massacre of impressive proportions, and chronic colitis in the cities. (p. 255, *our italics*)

Galbraith went on to cite other examples, the particularly prophetic one that there was delinquency everywhere because the growing absence of parents – more of them working to feed their consumption habits – meant that children, "in effect, become the charge of the community for an appreciable part of the time. [And] if the services of the community do not keep pace, this will be another source of disorder." These and other examples together embodied the theory that consumer oriented societies will inevitably produce "private opulence and public squalor," as Galbraith put in one of his more memorable phrases. Why does this happen?

---

[2] Houghton Mifflin, 1958, College Edition, p. 253. Unless indicated otherwise, all quotes from *The Affluent Society* are from this Edition.

III. The Dependence Effect

We begin with the "private opulence," whereby individuals shower themselves with more goods than are good for them and for society. How does this come about? Galbraith's answer focuses importantly on what he called the "Dependence Effect," explained as follows:

> As a society becomes increasingly affluent, wants are increasingly created by the process by which they are satisfied. This may operate passively. Increases in consumption, the counterpart of increases in production, act by suggestion or emulation to create wants. Or producers may proceed actively to create wants through advertising and salesmanship. *Wants thus come to depend on output. In technical terms it can no longer be assumed that welfare is greater at an all-around higher level of production than at a lower one. It may be the same.* The higher level of production has, merely, a higher level of want creation necessitating a higher level of want satisfaction. There will be frequent occasion to refer to the way wants depend on the process by which they are satisfied. It will be convenient to call it the *Dependence Effect*. (p. 158, *our italics*)

The point here is that in high consumption societies, wants come to depend on output, and for two major reasons that we now turn to.

Veblen's Pecuniary Emulation, Revisited

The first reason wants come "to depend on output" is that increases in output will generate spreading consumer envy wherever new products, or multiple units of other products, come to rest in a private household or driveway, become the latest fashion styles, or otherwise gain the attention of consumers. As we discussed in another essay in this volume, social critic Thorstein Veblen called this process "pecuniary emulation" and considered it a consequence of our desire to mimic the habits of those with a higher social ranking. This is an easy idea to remember because now everyone calls it "keeping up with the Joneses," and of course because we all do it. For instance, ten years ago university students would not be bothered by lack of access to "Power Point," or to a CD player, both now regarded by a growing number as utterly essential. Similarly, most U.S. households now view air-conditioning and dishwashers, once "luxuries," as necessities.

The Dependence Effect and the Advertising Blitz

The second cause of the Dependence Effect is the enormous and corrosive influence of advertising, or, as Galbraith puts it more gently, "...producers may proceed actively to create wants through advertising and salesmanship." Modern U.S. society is abuzz, ever more loudly, with the noise of advertising. Indeed, as we point out in our chapter on economic methodology, one estimate is that adults in our society are bombarded with over 3,000 ads per day.[3] For an idea of the level of this intensity, consider a few quotes from an article that appeared last year in the *Washington Post*[4]:

> As the U.S. economy continues to roar and traditional commercial spots on television, radio and even billboards are booked and/or too expensive, companies are seeking ever more novel places to promote their goods and services. Parking meters, elevators, restaurant restrooms, portable toilets, golf course locker rooms – plus the handles of golf clubs and baseball bats – have all become eligible targets....
>
> A combination of factors is spurring advertising's aggressive movement into virtually every facet of daily life. The healthy economy continues to give companies both money and incentive to advertise. Yet, at the same time, many advertisers believe the traditional means of advertising have become less effective....particularly [in reaching] 20- to 30-year-olds.

This article provides a number of intriguing examples of places where advertising is, literally, penetrating the collective consciousness: television monitors that run short loops of programming in gasoline stations, convenience stores, elevators, and train platforms; and ads on cocktail napkins and glasses at bars, in restrooms above urinals and inside stall walls, on turnpike coupons and portable toilets, and on ATMs. Other bright ideas, so far rejected by producers, have been to place stickers on melons advertising bras and on bananas advertising condoms.

No less frenzied, and likely more deleterious, is the increasing number of ads aimed at children. *Business Week*, hardly a chronicle of social criticism, discussed this trend in a 1997 article.[5] Kid-centered ad campaigns, it argued:

---

[3] This estimate was given by Sut Jhally, who narrates a documentary film, "Advertising and the End of the World," by the Media Education Foundation. This film provides compelling evidence that Galbraith's 1958 theory of social balance was genuinely prophetic.

[4] Caroline E. Mayer, "It's becoming a mad ad world." The quotes here are from a version of this article in *Manchester Guardian Weekly*, June 1-7, 2000.

[5] David Leonhardt and Kathleen Kerwin, "Hey Kid, Buy This!" *Business Week*, 6-30-97.

... represent a quantitative and qualitative change in the marketing aimed at children.... [V]irtually no space is free of logos. And traditional ads have more venues than ever, with a gaggle of new magazines, dozens of Web sites, and entire TV channels aimed at kids. From 1993 to 1996, alone, advertising in kid-specific media grew more than 50%, to $1.5 billion, according to Competitive Media Reporting.

The cumulative effect of initiating our children into a consumerist ethos at an ever earlier age may be profound. As kids drink in the world around them, many of their cultural encounters – from books to movies to TV– have become little more than sales pitches devoid of any moral beyond a plea for a purchase.... Instead of transmitting a sense of who we are and what we hold important, today's marketing-driven culture is instilling in them the sense that little exists without a sales pitch attached and that self-worth is something you buy at a shopping mall.

A Slight Digression: The Dependence Effect and Mainstream Economics

A discussion of the corporate creation of demand inside the heads of toddlers is a good place to digress briefly and relate Galbraith's concept of the Dependence Effect to mainstream economics. In fact, the idea is a straightforward challenge to the central article of faith in mainstream economics that more output always makes people better off. Mainstream *micro*-economists typically presume that, given the resource base, firms in competitive markets will produce the greatest possible output for "rational" consumers, who will be best off by getting the most products at the cheapest prices and will choose these products according to their pre-determined "preferences." In *macro*-economics, the central article of faith is that a growing GDP is good and grand (despite what it might be doing to the forests, lakes, streams, mountains, and seas that will be maimed a bit with each increase in output).

This idea that more output automatically produces more welfare became the national religion – and is now becoming a world religion – by virtue of what Galbraith termed the "growth lobby." Conservative political leaders are members of the lobby because a growing economy provides greater revenue, profits, and economic power for the big firms that are their principal supporters, hefty defense budgets that most conservatives support, and (especially important) because growth affirms the conservative's central idea that capitalism is the best of all possible economic systems. Liberal politicians join the lobby because they, too, get generous support from corporations, and because more output also means more taxes for more public services. Further, until recently, they had adopted

Keynesian growth policies as the best way to create employment for, and increase the incomes of, the lower classes in capitalist societies. Politicians from both these camps also get crucial support from mainstream economists who use complex models to make their case, models put forward as "science" but that always carrying the crucial assumption that more is better than less. The fact that millions of their listeners are captive audiences of college students in their formative years helps to inculcate each generation with the religion.

Yet, despite the overwhelming adoption of the mainstream notion that more output means higher standards of living, in *The Affluent Society* Galbraith raised a question that continues to be fresh and challenging: How much extra welfare do we get from an additional 1% of GDP if it represents goods we did not know about last year (or even last week), *and* if their production and consumption spoil the environment in which we use them? We will not pursue this Galbraithian critique here except to suggest that, however astute, his critique turned out to have very little impact on mainstream thinking.

The Dependence Effect and the Big Firms

Why are the big firms compelled to continue turning up the volume of advertising? To begin with, in industries dominated by a few firms (what economists call "oligopolies"), price competition is generally replaced by product differentiation as the major way that firms distinguish their own output. This dimension makes it mandatory that, for example, consumers see Post Toasties as altogether different from Wheaties. In the global economy, increasingly companies seek customers everywhere, and so must scream out their slogans loudly enough to be heard all over the planet. This feature of capitalism has not been lost on any economist who has studied it, whether in or out of the mainstream. What Galbraith and other political economists add to the mix is how this process is increasingly orchestrated by gigantic firms operating on a world scale.

In another of his major works, *The New Industrial State* (*NIS*), where Galbraith gave careful attention to these big firms that dominate the modern economic and political life, he called them the "planning system." He argued that the big firms themselves are under the control of a host of professionals – technicians, engineers, production, distribution, and sales executives, accountants, lawyers, economists, and others – whom Galbraith called the "technostructure." Circling around these mammoth suns are millions of smaller planets, the more or less competitive firms that make up the rest of the economy, and in some ways fit the description given them in mainstream micro-economics. Galbraith noted the broadly *anti-democratic* influence of the planning system on government at every level, with the big firms spending whatever it takes to get government officials to do their bidding. So it is, too, with their necessarily growing influence abroad: as the tentacles of the companies they control reach ever further into an ever more globalized world, the technostructure broadens its influence on the activities of people everywhere.[6]

The argument about big firms in *NIS* is, of course, thoroughly compatible with the theory of social balance. Most centrally, in order to shape consumer wants these big firms can afford a well-paid cadre of skilled artists, designers, marketing specialists, psychologists, and others, to design and to impose their message. As examples of the scale of this sales effort, in 2000 the two largest corporate advertisers in the U.S., Proctor & Gamble and General Motors (GM), each spent over $2.5 *billion* for ads,[7] and the top twenty spent over $20 billion to try to cajole you, me, and the rest of the population to buy their products.

In a later book, *The Anatomy of Power,*[8] Galbraith developed a useful structural model to describe how corporations, or any modern organizations, wield power in the contemporary world. Organizations accumulate and use two different kinds of power, according to Galbraith, "compensatory" and "conditioned," to get their will done. Regarding firms, the first of these is simply paying for things, particularly labor power and materials. The second, *conditioned* power, is the ability of the large corporations to use persuasion through public relations and advertising to affect the views of the citizenry, and lobbying to affect the views of politicians, about the general beneficence of corporate activity. Of course, compensatory and conditioned power comes together in the capitalist firm's "power of the sack," its ability to hire and fire workers at will. This immense power means that those who work for capitalist firms – most of us – are conditioned to think the corporate way, at least in public … or else. The now omnipresent laissez-faire ideology attests to the power of the capitalist class to "condition" the rest of us to believe along

with a General Motors CEO, Charles Wilson, who stated in the 1950s that "What's good for General Motors is good for America."

Big firms must condition consumers with ad campaigns because the bigger the corporation the greater are the stakes of not selling its output. Consider, for example, a company like GM. Assume, for instance, it produces 10,000 cars a week that cost $10,000 each to produce, a total expenditure of $100 million to buy labor, materials, other inputs, and to pay interest on the loans borrowed to finance capital expansions. Those costs of $100 million explain why consumer demand for these cars *must* be created.[9] And, that is why GM is the nation's second-largest advertiser. Smaller firms also need to advertise, and from their perspectives the stakes are the same: convince the public to buy the output or fold the tent. However, the smaller the firm the fewer funds it has available for advertising, another reason why the larger firms end up dominating, absorbing, or driving out of business their smaller rivals.

To Galbraith, then, the effects of pecuniary emulation, along with the unceasing imperative that the dominating firms sell their products, constitute what he calls the "Dependence Effect." Consumers develop a dependence bordering on addiction for the products generated by these firms. Of course, we should remember that all this producing, advertising, and emulating mostly takes place in the *private* sphere of the economy, and this growing private sector inevitably creates a need for goods in the *public* sphere. But, according to the theory of social balance, the supply of goods forthcoming in the public sector will always lag behind, leaving pollution, congestion, poor schooling, and all the rest in its wake. Why is that true, according to Galbraith?

III. The Public Sector as the "Inferior Sector"

In *The Affluent Society,* Galbraith makes the following argument for why the public sector inevitably lags behind the production and consumption of private goods:

> [The consumer] is subject to the forces of advertising and emulation by which

---

[6] Some of Galbraith's critics have argued that he overestimated the power of the technostructure to direct the operations of the giant firms and that globalization has shifted some of its power to high-profile CEOs and, especially, investment banking firms. While no doubt there is merit to these criticisms, they are actually not particularly relevant to the theory of social balance. Suffice it say that the world economy is under the sway of giant firms, getting more giant-like as we write, thoroughly committed to maximizing profits, and their effects on social balance are the same whether they are themselves dominated by owners, the technostructure, financial interests, or all three.

[7] These numbers are taken from *Advertising Age,* 9/2000, which each September publishes a list of the 200 largest advertisers in the U.S.

[8] Houghton-Mifflin, 1982. This book, as in the case with so many of Galbraith's works, is highly recommended for those who seek to understand our economic order. We can only mention its argument in passing because to give it the credit its many insights merit we would need to go considerably beyond the limits of a short chapter. The bright side of this situation is that *The Anatomy of Power* is another of Galbraith's most clearly written books.

[9] A further complication for producers in this regard is that if the average consumer decides to save more income this year than last year, some companies will lose customers no matter the intensity of their advertising efforts. This is the familiar "underconsumption" problem in capitalism that our readers will take up in the chapter on J.M. Keynes, or in any discussion of macroeconomics.

production creates its own demand. Advertising operates exclusively, and emulation mainly, on behalf of privately produced goods and services. Since management and emulative effects operate on behalf of private production, public services will have an inherent tendency to lag behind. Automobile demand which is expensively synthesized will inevitably have a much larger claim on income than parks or public health or even roads where no such influence operates. The engines of mass communication, in their highest state of development, assail the eyes and ears of the community on behalf of more beer but not of more schools....

The competition is especially unequal for new products and services. Every corner of the public psyche is canvassed by some of the nation's most talented citizens to see if the desire for some merchantable product can be cultivated. No similar process operates on behalf of the nonmerchantable services of the state.... The scientist or engineer or advertising man who devotes himself to developing a new carburetor, cleanser, or depilatory for which the public recognizes no need and will feel none until an advertising campaign arouses it, is one of the valued members of the our society. A politician or a public servant who dreams up a new public service is a wastrel. Few public offenses are more reprehensible. (pp. 260-1)

And, later Galbraith adds this:

In this discussion [about the proper role of government] a certain mystique was attributed to the satisfaction of privately supplied wants. A community decision to have a new school means that the individual surrenders the necessary amount, willy-nilly, in his taxes. But if he is left with that income, he is a free man. He can decide between a better car or a television set. This was advanced with some solemnity as an argument for the TV set. The difficulty is that this argument leaves the community with no way of preferring the school. All private wants, where the individual can choose, are inherently superior to all public desires which must be paid for by taxation and with an inevitable component of compulsion.... (p. 268)

In sum, a social imbalance arises from an increase in the production and consumption of private goods that is not matched by the public services required by their use and

where "all private wants . . . are inherently superior to all public desires...." The tendency becomes an imperative in capitalist societies that are dominated by giant firms because of their great need to sell their products and because of the enormous sums of money they use to market them. Last of all, it leads down the road to "private opulence and public squalor." Is this a "good" theory, in that it might help us to understand and improve our own world? We turn now to that question.

IV. Assessing the Theory of Social Balance: Galbraith's View

In a special edition of *The Affluent Society* published in 1998 to commemorate the fiftieth anniversary of its publication, Galbraith made very few changes, letting the book stand on its own. In an "Introduction" to this edition, he wrote the following:

On two matters this book was right, and before its time.... [One of them is that] forty years ago I stressed the compelling difference between public and private living standards. We had expensive radio and television and poor schools, clean houses and filthy streets, weak public services combined with deep concern for what the government spent. Public outlays were a bad and burdensome thing; affluent private expenditure was an economically constructive force.

My case is still strong. The government does spend money readily on weaponry of questionable need and on what has come to be called corporate welfare. Otherwise there is still persistent and powerful pressure for restraint on public outlay. In consequence, we are now more than ever affluent in our private consumption; the inadequacy of our schools, libraries, public recreation facilities, health care, even law enforcement, is a matter of daily comment. The private sector of our economy has gained enormously in role and reward and therewith in political voice and strength. No similar political support is accorded the public sector, the weaponry and corporate welfare as ever apart. In civilized performance it has lagged even further behind the private sector, as it is now called....

So, Galbraith agrees with Galbraith, and for someone as self-confident as he has always been that cannot be a surprise. What's the evidence for his continuing advocacy of his theory of social balance? The first part of our response to this question concerns the public's attitude about government, and the second part concerns a substantial body of evidence from *real* scientists, rather than from economists, that Galbraith was right all along. We take these up in turn.

V. The Public Sector as Enemy of the People: 1958 and Now

In 1958, close to the end of *TAS*, Galbraith expressed hopes for a better social balance coming from a growing "New Class" of mostly educated people. He believed that this "new class" would see the problem clearly and fight politically for adequate public services and against the overpowering need of the giant firms to blind us with ads and bury us with products. This hope led him to call for broader and deeper education, as "our hope for survival, security, and contentment." (p. 355) For myriad reasons, particularly a complex restructuring of the U.S. economic and political system and the abiding mistrust of government that has characterized most of our nation's history – reasons far too complex to take up here – this anti-government mood has persisted and has actually deepened since the late 1950s. Galbraith's hopes for a "new class" to bring us to our senses, in his terms, were dashed utterly.

So ingrained now is the sentiment against government in the U.S. that for about two decades it has been virtually *impossible* in the U.S. to get elected to public office by campaigning for higher taxes, at any level of government. The push to demonize government received great momentum with the election of Ronald Reagan in 1980, who championed tax cuts for the wealthy and a rollback of federal regulations of the economy. He, and the events of the time, succeeded in legitimating to a large segment of the population the dream of a return to the "good old days" before the New Deal social welfare programs of the 1930s. By 1999, according to a Gallup poll, only about a third of the public had solid confidence in the federal government and almost a third had "little or no" confidence.[10]

In part reflecting this deeply ingrained suspicion of government, in 2000 U.S. citizens, with a mighty push from the U.S. Supreme Court, put into the White House George W. Bush. Bush campaigned on a promise to limit government "interference" in the economy, and his major initial efforts were to reduce taxes, especially for rich people, and to declare war on environmental regulations,

particularly those concerning the oil, mining, and utility industries. The public protest to the Bush economic policies was muted, but with the attacks on September 11, 2001 on New York and the Pentagon, there is a gathering body of criticism about our reflexive antagonism to government. At this point (December 2001), the public is clamoring for more federal government action regarding national security, and corporations are clamoring for more tax breaks. The friendly ear that the Bush administration has lent to corporations in this regard, and especially his and others' claim that these proposals to cut business taxes are part of an overall plan for "national security," is fooling few outside the White House. Perhaps the public's view about less government is changing and citizens will press for a broader government presence in our lives. However, aside from expanding the government's roles in national security, the federal government remains controlled by people who beat loudly the drums for laissez-faire.

What can we say about this failure of Galbraith's theory to influence public policy and spending patterns in both the public and private sectors? Most fundamentally, we would say that the failure of an idea (or the typical complex of ideas that makes up a theory) to influence public opinion or policy does not mean that it is *wrong*. The "theory" that blacks, Native Americans, and women are less capable than white men in organizing and directing social life has been, to use Galbraith's term, "conditioned" by those in power – mostly white men – throughout most of our history. The social policies that emerged from this mistaken idea about human capabilities have been enormously costly to us as a society, particularly to most black people, Native Americans, and women. In other words, the truth of the matter – that the ability for leadership is determined by things other than one's sex and skin color – was a dormant one, bound to be discovered, but still ignored for centuries. In an analogous sense, we believe that Galbraith's theory of social balance is also a dormant truth about our form of capitalism, one bound to be discovered. We shall now explain why we think that to be the case.

The Social Balance and Public Services

In a recent collection of essays written about Galbraith's ideas,[11] Robert Reich, a professor of public policy and Bill Clinton's Secretary of Labor from 1992-1996, wrote a brief lament about public services forty years after *The Affluent Society* was published. As a liberal, he provided a familiar litany about their decline:

> [By] some estimates, two thirds of our
> elementary and secondary schools are in

---

[10] These figures are from Saxon-Harold, Susan, K. E., Murray, Weitzman, and the Gallup Organization, Inc., *Giving and Volunteering in the United States*, 1999 Edition, Washington, D.C., 1999.

[11] Helen Sasson, ed., *Between Friends: Pespectives on John Kenneth Galbraith*, Houghton-Mifflin, 1999, p. 89.

disrepair, and too few of them are providing our children with adequate education. Comfortable movement along public roadways and over bridges now requires the most sophisticated of automobile shock absorbers. Public recreational facilities are fast disappearing. More than one in five of the nation's children lives in poverty – lacking adequate housing, clothing, and nutrition. An ever-growing number of and percentage of Americans have no access to health care. Publicly supported basic research is on the wane. After rising through the 1960s and 1970s, federal investments in education, infrastructure, and research as shares of GDP have continued to fall over the last three administrations. They represented…sixteen per cent in 1998, lower than at any time since 1962.

Like many other liberals, in the Galbraithian sense that a broader and more efficient public sector will allow us better to enjoy our private riches, Reich sees freedoms lost in bad schooling, poverty, and sick kids without recourse to good health care. It is not simply the inability to choose health care that is costly to freedom, but freedom also implies the ability to choose a society where one's own health is protected because *everyone else* has ready access to quality health care. Particularly troubling is that in the "affluent society" all this squalor is unnecessary, as in Reich's estimate that two-thirds of all public schools are in disrepair while almost all of us are buying things we don't need.

An inherent problem with our views about the need for, and the quality of, government services is that none of us can actually *prove* our case. While a liberal might see a crumbling transportation system (exemplified by a recent report from the state of Pennsylvania that about one-third of all its bridges needs repairs), conservatives might see a wondrous system of highways available to all, and the freedom to drive anywhere as one of the great benefits of our kind of society. Nevertheless, as we have seen from the introduction to a recent edition of *The Affluent Society*, Galbraith continues to see certain elements of social imbalance about which, in the terms of his argument, there can be little ambiguity. As an example, consider first one involving the ongoing culprit, the private automobile, as described in *Parade Magazine* (2/25/2001):

> Most auto accidents occur while we're driving to and from work, not late at night. And, that's not encouraging, because key commuter arteries are getting worse around the nation. In the last 30 years, there has been a 131% increase in vehicle miles traveled, while our highway capacity has grown by only 5.7%.... For example, planners in the '70s recommended building 14 new highways in

the Washington, D.C. region to accommodate future demand. Because of public resistance, only two of the 14 were built, and now the area trails only L.A. for highway congestion despite being No. 2 in use of public transportation.

What characterizes this situation as a social imbalance is not, as *Parade Magazine* would have it, that there are too few roads in the D.C. area and elsewhere, because building more highways will simply attract more cars. And, an imbalance will continue to exist until a mass transportation system emerges in Washington that will begin substituting train riders on public transportation for drivers in private vehicles.

Our second example concerns food. A recent article in the *New York Times* (3-18-2001) claims that people in the U.S. are twice as likely now as just seven years ago to get sick from eating contaminated food. A particular problem concerns imported foods, and as a pristine example of the social imbalance, here is why:

> With imported foods, the FDA [Federal Food and Drug Administration] is at a particular disadvantage. In the last four years alone, the number of foreign food items increased by 50 percent, from 2.7 million items in 1997 to 4.1 million last year. The responsibility of examining that avalanche falls to a cadre of just 113 federal food inspectors, and the force has grown by only 3 workers since 1997. As a result, the FDA *inspects less than 1 percent* of all imported foods, according to the General Accounting Office. (*Our emphasis*)

This gridlock in the nation's capital and the tidal wave of uninspected foreign foods seem clear enough evidence of a social imbalance, and it is unclear how the anti-government majority might explain such squalor in public services as a net addition to personal freedom. Yet, even with such examples as these, conservatives and liberals are likely never to agree about the overall quality of public services; that is, Galbraith and his followers still don't have the smoking gun of proof that our public services are "squalid." The best we can offer is for our readers to test the theory of social balance, as it relates to public services, by looking closely at the cities and towns where they live. Are the malls, the cars, the homes, the driveways, and the lawns usually cared for better than the schools, roads, hospitals, and the children of the poor?

VI. The Social Balance and the Environment

Increasingly, scientists are concluding that environmental degradation threatens us all, rich and poor alike, and our different views in this regard cannot so readily be dismissed as a matter of judgment. Further, governments are typically responsible for trying to protect the environment. In the U.S. that effort is a complex matrix of federal, state, and local regulations defining what any of us, and especially firms, can emit into the air and water. There are other aspects of the environment, in particular its aesthetic qualities and how it nurtures all living things, for which the government is also ultimately responsible. Who, for instance, would trust the habitats for birds or for other beasts to, say, Exxon or Dow Chemical Company? Yet, despite this matrix of laws, parts of which all capitalists resist as "intrusions in free enterprise," there is an enormous and growing body of evidence that high levels of production and consumption in the developed world, and the lack of adequate environmental controls in much of the developing world, threaten the planet.

To state our case in the most general terms, we will cite first the voices of the heads of the two most prestigious scientific associations in the world, Sir Michael Atiyah, president of the Royal Society of London, and Dr. Frank Press, president of the U.S. National Academy of Sciences. In a 1992 joint statement, "Population Growth, Resource Consumption and a Sustainable World," they wrote that:

> [I]f population growth and patterns of human activities remain unchanged ... science and technology may not be able to prevent either irreversible degradation of the environment or continued poverty for much of the world.... The future of our planet is in the balance.... Sustainable development can be achieved, but only if irreversible degradation of the environment can be halted in time. The next 30 years may be crucial.[12]

What do these two eminent scientists mean by these sweeping, frightening comments?

Below we provide examples that we find compelling in terms of the theory of social balance. We chose these examples both for their dramatic effect and moral implications, and because we find them to be information all citizens should consider carefully. Our best advice to our readers is to extend their consideration of these claims by moving from our sources to a broader reading.

Children (1)

As a beginning, consider comments by biologist Sandra Steingraber, concerning breast milk:

> *Of all human food, breast milk is now the most contaminated.* Because it is one rung up on the food chain higher than the food we adults eat, the trace amounts of toxic residues carried into mothers' bodies become even more concentrated in the milk their breasts produce. To be specific, it's about 10 to 100 times more contaminated with dioxins [described below] than the next highest level of stuff on the human food chain, which are animal-derived fats in dairy, meat, eggs, and fish. This is why a breast-fed infant receives its so-called 'safe' lifetime limit of dioxin in the first six months of drinking breast milk. Study after study also shows that the concentration of carcinogens in human breast milk declines steadily as nursing continues. Thus the protective effect of breast feeding on the mother appears to be a direct result of downloading a lifelong burden of carcinogens from her breasts into the tiny body of her infant.... [A principle source of dioxin], Polyvinyl Chloride (PVC), ... is found in medical products, toys, food packaging, and vinyl siding. [Frequently, these products] are shoveled into incinerators [that] are de facto laboratories for dioxin manufacture, and PVC is the main ingredient in this process. The dioxin created by the burning of PVC drifts from the stacks of these incinerators, attaches to dust particles in the atmosphere, and eventually sifts down to Earth as either dry deposition or in rain drops. This deposition then coats crops and other plants, which are eaten by cows, chickens, and hogs. Or, alternatively, it's rained into rivers and lakes and insinuates itself into the flesh of fish. As a breast-feeding mother, I take these molecules into my body and distill them in my breast tissue.... [And through other biologic processes] this milk springs from grape-like lobes and flows down long tubules into the nipple, which is a kind of sieve, and into the

---

[12] The world press, to which this report was promulgated in 1992, virtually ignored it. The report was reprinted in the following newsletter: *Rachel's Environment and Health Weekly*, #699, 9-23-99. This newsletter is an exceptionally valuable resource for ongoing reports concerning environmental pollution and it is written for the general public. Its editor is Peter Montague, an environmental chemist, and each issue heavily documents his own sources so that those interested can read beyond his analysis. The newsletter is typically referred to as *Rachel's*, and we depend upon it heavily in this part of our essay. You can receive the newsletter free and online by sending an email to: listserve@rachel.org, with the words, SUBSCRIBE RACHEL-WEEKLY [YOUR NAME] in the message.

back of the throat of the breast-feeder. My daughter."[13]

Dioxin, increasingly seen by many scientists as an expanding threat to living things, is a product of both incineration and some other industrial processes. It does not degrade easily, is cumulative, and is stored in fat cells in the body. And, because we live in a world in which dioxin is now widely distributed in the water, the soil, and in our bodies, we are accumulating it constantly. The federal Agency for Toxic Substances and Disease Registry in Atlanta concluded that the typical dioxin accumulation in people in the U.S. is presently between three and six times what it believes to be a "safe" level.[14]

On the matter of chemicals in women's breast milk, Canadian scientists Frances Labreche and Mark Goldberg, along with many scientists all over the world, have been working to determine if there is a causal relationship between such chemicals and the widening incidence of breast cancer. Central to this research, as they point out, is the astounding fact that the breasts of *all women in industrialized countries* harbor at least eighteen different chemicals that come from the production of industrial and consumption products, several of them known carcinogens in certain concentrations. It is hard to fathom this kind of information if you are a not a scientist in the field, but it remains nonetheless an extraordinary comment on the insidious nature of modern industrial production.

The known deleterious effects on living creatures from so many industrial chemicals makes it striking that we allow the production and distribution of roughly 3,000 of these industrial chemicals without their having ever been subjected to analysis by the EPA to determine their toxicity to living things. The two barriers to our knowing, of course, are the considerable funds the EPA would have to expend to find out, and the ongoing resistance of the chemical industry to "outside interference" by government.

---

[13] Sandra Steingraber, "Why the Precautionary Principle? A Meditation on Polyvinyl Chloride (PVC) and the Breasts of Mothers," *Rachel's*, # 658, 7-8-99. (Italics supplied)

[14] For the evidence, ranging from a recent EPA "reassessment" of the effects of dioxin, to an enormous array of other sources, see *Rachel's* #640, 3-4-99. For virtually unlimited information, simply search under "dioxin" on the Web. As a hint of what you will find, dioxin exposure has been shown to be related to the following health disorders in humans: cancer; chloracne, a skin disease that can cause acne-like sores all over the body, sometimes lasting for years; decreased testosterone in blood of dioxin-exposed males; a variety of disorders in the development of human reproductive organs; and diabetes. In animals exposed to certain levels of dioxins, the following results have occurred: endometreitis, learning disabilities and immune system toxicity in monkeys; decreased sperm production in rats (and during the last 50 years, sperm production of men through the industrialized world has dropped 50%).

Children (2)

As a second example regarding children, consider the food they eat. The *New York Times* (2/19/1999)[15] reported that:

Using U.S. Department of Agriculture statistics based on 27,000 food samples from 1994 to 1997, *Consumer Reports* (the magazine of the Consumer Union) looked at foods children are mostly likely to eat. *Almost all the foods tested for pesticide residues were within legal limits, but were frequently well above the levels the EPA says are safe for young children.* According to the Consumer Union *Report*, even one serving of some fruits and vegetables can exceed safe daily limits for young children.... Methyl parathion [the pesticide ingredient] accounts for most of the total toxicity on the foods that were analyzed, particularly peaches, frozen and canned green beans, pears and apples. *Last year EPA said that methyl parathion posed an 'unacceptable risk' but that it had not taken any action to ban it or reduce its use.* Organophosphates [such as methyl parathion] are neurological poisons and work the same on humans as they do on insects. *(Our emphasis)*

The *New York Times* also reported (9/29/97) that an increase in the incidence of cancer among children nation-wide, "may be tied to new chemicals in the environment." The *Times* stated that between 1973 and 1994 one form of leukemia had risen 27% among children, and brain cancer had risen nearly 40%.

Children (3)

New York Times columnist Bob Herbert wrote this about a report from the American Lung Association on ground level ozone:

A series of well-documented scientific and medical studies have linked [ground level] ozone and particular matter [from such sources as truck exhausts, gasoline powered lawn mowers, and unpaved roads] to decreases in lung function and other forms of respiratory distress in children and adults, to increases in emergency-room visits and hospital admissions and to increases in mortality. According to the American Lung Association, children playing outdoors in

---

[15] For more on this matter, see *Rachel's*, #660, 7-22-99, which is also the origin of this quote.

ozone levels 33% percent below the current standard have experienced as much as a 20% loss of lung function. The problem is worsened by the fact that ozone levels tend to be highest on warm, sunny days – the very days on which kids are most likely to be playing outside.[16]

The national organization Environmental Defense, whose Web site is an exceptionally valuable source of information about pollution in the U.S., reported on an "asthma epidemic," most of whose victims will be children, with a headline that read, "Asthma Cases Are Projected To Double by 2020, Hitting 1 in 5 Families." Environmental Defense summarized the report this way:

> The nation is in the grip of a rapidly growing asthma epidemic whose victims will more than double by 2020, according to a recently released study by the Pew Environmental Health Commission at the Johns Hopkins School of Public Health. Asthma is a chronic disease whose causes are largely unknown, but genetic predisposition *and environmental triggers* in both indoor and outdoor air are known contributors to asthma's developmental severity. The Johns Hopkins researchers concluded that new cases of asthma among Americans are increasing so rapidly that by the time another generation of children is born, asthma will strike 29 million Americans.[17] *(Our emphasis)*

The point of these examples involving children is that, to the extent that the scientific assessments are true, they are woeful examples of the failure of government to provide a crucial public good – clean air and water – that would protect the welfare of the most vulnerable and most innocent among us. This damaging, unchecked pollution comes, of course, from the production and consumption of goods and services. And, it is our pleasure from them that blinds us to Galbraith's point that we quoted earlier:

> Advertising operates exclusively, and emulation mainly, on behalf of privately produced goods and services.... [And] every increase in the consumption of private goods will normally mean some facilitation or protective step by the [public sector]. [If] these [public] services are not forthcoming, the consequences will be in some degree ill.

Children are the "ill" in this case, a social imbalance of the grimmest form.

---

[16] *Bad Air Day*, Op Ed Page, 2-10-97.
[17] For greater details of this study, see the Web site for The Pew Environmental Health Commission.

Fish
According to Peter Montague:

> The world's fishing fleet has doubled since 1970. New fishing gear (global positioning system receivers, fish finders, and new kinds of trawls and nets) have made it possible to sweep the oceans like a vacuum cleaner, sucking up nearly everything that lives. A recent report from the Marine Conservation Biology Institute in Redmond, Washington, says modern fishing is comparable to forest clear cutting – except that the wreckage caused by modern "factory trawlers" is hidden from view. As a result of new fishing technologies, 13 of the world's 17 major fisheries are depleted or in steep decline. For fish and for fishing, the future looks grim.

Because the shallow fishing beds are being exhausted, fishing companies are using military technology to develop ways to fish as deep as a mile. Tyson's, the chicken giant, has expanded into fishing and its several huge ships sink nylon nets that sweep the ocean's bottom to gather up to 400 tons of fish at a time. Unwanted creatures, like seals, sea lions, and fish with no markets, are called "bycatch" and are ground up and thrown back into the sea. This grinding amounted to almost 4 billion pounds of fish in 1997, in the northeast Atlantic alone. Deep-sea fishing threatens a gradual depletion of the bottom dwelling species, as well as the loss of much of the other life at the ocean's bottom that sustains all above it. How *incredible* that, within a few decades, we humans would eat the fish at such a rate that they might face extinction! Other studies, of New York Coastal waters, have found as many as 40% of shellfish infected with viruses with human origins.

Apparently, many of us share with the fish the perils of swimming in the ocean. The *New York Times* (1/4/99) reported on a study showing that *almost 25%* of people who swim, windsurf, or boat in the water along Florida beaches pick up viruses from 1.6 million septic tanks releasing sewage into Florida's coastal waters. The viral diseases included ear, eye, throat, respiratory and gastrointestinal infections, along with more serious ailments like heart disease, meningitis and hepatitis.[18] And, how *bizarre* – there is no better word

---

[18] Key references here on fish depletion are, Timothy Egan, "U.S. Fishing Fleet Trawling Coastal Water Without Fish," *New York Times* (3-7-94); Daniel Pauly and others, "Fishing Down Marine Food Webs," *Science*, Vol. 279 (2-6-98); Nigel Williams, "Overfishing Disrupts Entire Ecoostystems," *Science*, V. 279 (2-6-98). For Peter Montague's analyses of these sources, and of many others, see: *Rachel's* #587 (2-26-98) and # 659 (7-15-99).

– that for health's sake we should give up frolicking on Florida's beaches because we refuse to pay the taxes necessary for sewage treatment plants. Is there a more insightful explanation for these kinds of anomalies than the theory of social balance?

Ruining The Whole Planet: Global Warming

Last, in this exemplary tip of a huge iceberg, there is the problem of global warming, perhaps the direst threat of them all over the long haul. It is caused by the "greenhouse effect" of sunlight striking the planet, turning into heat, and then being trapped by "greenhouse" gases. These gases, primarily water vapor, carbon dioxide, and methane, allow the sunlight in, but do not allow all the resulting heat to escape, thus causing "global warming." After a few years of trying to deny the problem, a growing number of major corporations now admit that it is real and it is really threatening. Bette Hileman, writing in the American Chemical Society's *Chemical and Engineering News*,[19] gives the details this way:

> The Earth's average temperature has been rising for at least 100 years, but in recent decades the rate of increase has speeded up. Eleven of the past 16 years have been the hottest of the century. The average global temperature in 1998 was higher than it had been at any other time during the previous 1000 years. The polar regions of the planet are heating up much more rapidly than the average. The carbon dioxide is thrown into the air mainly by burning fossil fuels, deforestation, and methane from growing cattle and rice, and landfilling garbage. Increasingly, the carbon dioxide comes from vehicular pollution, and with 5% of the world's population, we in the U.S. are responsible for about 20% of the whole world's production. If left unattended, global warming will cause immense relocations in the developed world and be absolutely catastrophic for billions of people in developing countries, particularly from flooding, crop loss, and violent weather.

Other indications of global warming are changes in the weather. Annual rain and snow fall over the continental U.S. has increased about 10% during the last century, increasingly in the form of big storms. As an example, days with rainfalls of over two inches in the U.S. have also increased by about 10% during the past century, trends shared by Canada, Japan, Russia, China, and Australia. Intense storms over the North Atlantic and North Pacific have doubled during the past century. And, Britain's

Hadley Centre for Climate Change, using billions of calculations from the world's largest supercomputer in Berskshire, concluded, among other horrific predictions, that current trends of emissions from burning fossil fuels (mostly by vehicles), "will turn parts of the Amazon rain forest ... into deserts by 2050, threatening the world with an unstoppable greenhouse effect."[20]

Global warming, and our collective reaction to it, reflects well all that Galbraith has written about social balance. As we stated above, the public's longstanding lack of confidence in government helped in 2000 to elect George W. Bush, who campaigned in large part against government and for the expansion of all aspects of the private sector (via lower taxes and fewer regulations). Bush's first decision concerning the environment was to go back on a campaign promise to press for reducing the emissions of coal burning utilities that are, along with vehicle emissions, a principal cause of global warming. A companion to this decision was his administration's abandonment of the international treaty on global warming known as the "Kyoto Protocol," despite the fact that our 5% of the world's population is responsible for emitting 20% of its carbon dioxide (the principal pollutant leading to global warming). This policy on global warming, which has stunned and enraged most of the rest of the developed world, is part of an overall administration plan that Bush has stated must not include any environmental regulations that would "weaken the American economy."[21] Soon after his pronouncements on global warming, Bush decided to ignore the advice of the American Academy of Sciences, and his own EPA, to lower by a factor of ten the acceptable level of arsenic in drinking water. In these two cases, it is clear that the president was responding, not unwillingly, to immense pressure from a handful of oil, gas, and mining corporations. The Bush administration's vision of our future will lead it to give the private sector every advantage to expand, relative to the public sector. No doubt, if Galbraith is the sort to have nightmares, George W. Bush will be an actor in his worst ones.

Thus, in the end, the ultimate irony is that the one public good that we most desperately need, the protection of the environment, is in many of its dimensions not available to any of us, regardless of our income, status, or location. Even the richest of the rich in our society have children breathing fouled urban air and eating peaches, apples and pears whose sweetness disguises the bitter poisons many of them harbor inside. One is left with such questions as this one: How hot does the planet have to get before we begin to see the hottest consumer products as a problem for all of us rather than a solution for those who buy them?

---

[19] Bette Hileman, "Case Grows for Climate Change," *Chemical and Engineering News* (8-9-99), 16-23. This article, and several others on global warming, is analyzed in *Rachel's*, #664, 8-19-99.

[20] Paul Brown, "Greenhouse Effect Worse than Feared," *Manchester Guardian Weekly*, (11-9-98).

[21] As quoted in the *New York Times*, 4/1/2001, p. 3.

Conclusion

We conclude this essay on Galbraith's theory of social balance by saying that we believe it an indispensable guide to understanding the kind of capitalism that has developed in the United States. In his theory, and in his other works, Galbraith points to the unyielding and growing power of corporations to shape our wants, even to the point of taking the lowest road of them all – trying to shape toddlers into insatiable consumers. A central marker of this growing corporate influence in our lives is that the number of messages we must endure, urging us to buy private goods, has increased to *thousands per day*. While we hear this cacophony of corporate pleas that we buy consumer goods, these same voices tell us little about the desirability of public goods except that the government sector is too big, too inefficient, and that our very freedom depends upon its being reduced even more. Joining the corporate choir are the voices of politicians, most in office only because of corporate donations. This perplexing, perhaps insoluble, problem confirms Galbraith's claim, emerging first in the work of Karl Marx, that the corporate capitalist class largely fashions the actions of government. For us, the most compelling evidence leading us to see Galbraith's theory as crucial in explaining our world is that growing production and consumption levels in the U.S. have already led to the contamination of breast milk suckled by our children, the sickening of some of these children and some of the rest of us from a spewing of chemicals most of which have health effects we know nothing about, and the filling of the atmosphere with enough carbon dioxide to render the planet, in the long run, uninhabitable.

Along the way in this essay, we have mentioned, but not developed, the other side of the story, the conservative critique of Galbraith's theory. In this critique, the bedrock presumption is that government is at best a necessary evil; that with every reduction in taxes and public services, our freedom is expanded; that the booming economy during the last two decades proves the case, if nothing else does; that dominance by the U.S. of world economic and political affairs attests mightily to the powers unleashed in the absence of an intruding, inefficient government; and that the alleged squalor in public services seen by liberals like Galbraith is caused by a blindness about what constitutes true freedom and liberty.

Each of us, of course, ultimately will judge which of these two assessments best describes the world we experience. Are we a freer people as our economy expands; is more always better than less? Are we always better off when taxes come down and public services are cut? If your community has more cars in family garages, are you likely to enjoy more "consumer welfare" than if you and your neighbors had fewer cars but your city had ambient air that was healthy for you, or for your children? Is their a richer and deeper meaning to "freedom" and "liberty" than the ability to buy anything you want, no matter the consequences to your neighbors, the world community, and the planet itself? Or, as Galbraith would have it, are we in a lemming-like march to the abyss, done in by a love affair with consumer goods?

Chapter IV

John Maynard Keynes

INTRODUCTION

Human beings are both weak and strong, and of their several frailties none is more complex than their ability to believe strongly in things that are clearly not true. We all fall prey to this folly. For examples, in the fifteenth century there were those who warned Columbus that the earth was flat. And today, mainstream economists pretend that social classes do not exist in U.S. capitalism. It can be quite costly to trudge forward into the cold and piercing winds of life on the basis of wrong ideas, and especially so if we are experts with an audience.

One such costly idea was held for almost two centuries by the classical school of economics and, like so much of modern thinking about the economy, this one started with Adam Smith. The idea was simple enough: capitalist economies cannot experience *long term* "gluts," producing more output than customers could buy because of natural, internal forces that automatically end overproduction before it becomes a recession or depression. Yet, despite being at odds with the downturns that occurred with awful regularity in all capitalist economies, this classical theory held sway in economic thinking roughly from the late eighteenth century until the middle of the Great Depression in the 1930s. And, it was John Maynard Keynes who dealt it a crushing blow in a 1936 book, *The General Theory of Employment, Interest, and Money* (sometimes called the *General Theory*). This book swept away much of the debris of classical thinking about business cycles, and what to do about them.

To the economist in the classical school, the self-regulating character of capitalism meant that the government's role in the economy could be limited. Adam Smith, also a principal source of this idea, wrote his famous treatise *The Wealth of Nations* in 1776 primarily as a tract against the "mercantilist" thinking of his time. The mercantilists believed in government economic policies that would foster favorable trading conditions with other nations. This required a mosaic of government rules and regulations, including favoring monopolies in crucial trading industries. Under mercantilism, the state was an instrument for the benefit of a few industries and individuals, often to the detriment of everyone else. Smith and the biggest fans of his ideas, members of the emerging capitalist class in Britain and France, believed that unregulated capitalism would, in contrast, benefit all groups in society. By allowing all economic classes to seek their self-interest in a competitive system, capitalism would produce the most productive outcome possible; therefore, government intervention in the economy could only be harmful. Smith allowed for a few government functions, such as education, police protection, and national defense. But, he thought an economy that was largely unregulated by government would be both superior and self-regulating.

In the central tradition of economics,[1] then, between 1776 and 1936 business cycles were ignored as a legitimate subject of study and, further, public policy to try to lessen their damaging effects was ruled out of the question. In the United States during these years, the classical school's domination of economic thinking on the part of both academics and capitalists claimed countless victims. President Herbert Hoover, responding to the ravages of the Great Depression of the 1930s, could only bleat to a disbelieving public the classical article of faith that "Prosperity is just around the corner." Irving Fisher, among the most respected U.S. economists

---

[1] There are many ways to classify the different schools of economics, and we will use the following one: the "classical school" refers to the mainstream of economics from Adam Smith to John Maynard Keynes; the "neoclassical school" refers to the mainstream of economics since the 1930s, with its two broad branches of "microeconomics and macroeconomics." The "central tradition" refers to both the classical and neoclassical schools, thus the mainstream from the time of Adam Smith to our time. "Political economy" refers to schools of thought outside the mainstream, particularly those that emerged in the thinking of Karl Marx and Thorstein Veblen, about whom there are other essays in this book. There is also a critique of mainstream economics from a political economy point of view in the last chapter of this book.

of the time, no doubt helped to confuse Hoover by declaring, just prior to the 1929 stock market crash that began the Depression, that the economy was on a "permanently high plateau." It was into this theoretical morass that Keynes stepped in 1936 with the *General Theory* to change forever the way we all think about the capitalist business cycle.

So, who was this Keynes fellow?

JOHN MAYNARD KEYNES, THE PERSON

Keynes was an Englishman who lived from 1883 to 1946 and after 1913 produced a torrent of books and articles about the economic world. He was a compelling person. In the course of his 63 years he was: a brilliant student at England's most famous prep school; an equally brilliant student and then professor at Kings College in Cambridge; a financier who made a fortune for himself and, later, for Kings College by overseeing its endowment fund; president of a life-insurance company; patron of the arts; husband of a famous Russian ballerina; member of the influential "Bloomsbury set" of intellectuals; esteemed official of the British Treasury; board member of the Bank of England; and the principal designer of the international financial system after World War II. Most important to his lasting fame, Keynes' writing held the rapt attention of the political and intellectual world during his adult life, and continues to have wide influence now half a century after his death. He was, we should add, also an extremely confident man, so much so that in a 1935 letter to another famous British writer, George Bernard Shaw, Keynes wrote, "I believe myself to be writing a book on economic theory which will largely revolutionize—not, I suppose at once, but in the course of the next ten years—the way the world thinks about economic problems." It turns out he did exactly that.

The *General Theory* is only the most famous of his widely influential economic writings. One of Keynes' earliest works was an acclaimed book on probability theory. Another early book, *The Economic Consequences of the Peace* (1919), catapulted him into an international spotlight that never dimmed while he was alive. In this book, Keynes argued with impressive foresight that the victorious allies in World War I had exacted such heavy reparation payments from the Germans that the German economy would sink into ruin, then into dangerous political chaos. From the early 1920s on, Keynes concentrated most of his writing on capitalist economies, particularly their aggregate domestic and international dimensions. Though most

of Keynes' voluminous economic analysis merits the attention of economists, here we necessarily confine ourselves to two aspects of it. The first is Keynes' critique of two central conclusions of the classical explanation of business cycles, and the second is his critique of the classical view of the proper role of government in capitalism. It is Keynes, the political economist, that most concerns us in this book.

DEFINING OUR TERMS

The enormous effect of business cycles on life in capitalist societies has focused attention on their nature and causes, and provoked an array of different designations for them. In the early nineteenth century some economists referred to economic declines "gluts" or "overproduction." Later in the nineteenth century these gave way to the more ominous "economic crises," popularized mostly by Marx.

During the 1930s, the collapse of U.S. capitalism was so deep and prolonged it came to be known permanently as the "Great Depression." When, however, the economy took another dip in 1937-38, after four years of slow growth, economists came up with "recession" as a way to distinguish that dip from the Depression. A few mainstream economists, their thoughts clearly under the mesmerizing spell of the classical school, tried in the 1950s to popularize a particularly hopeful term, "rolling readjustments." Fortunately, this term didn't stick but it's useful to note that profoundly different political ideologies are embedded in the concepts "economic crisis," and "rolling readjustment."

We will use the term "business cycle" in a general sense, and we will use other terms—gluts, recessions, depressions, or crises—as they fit what we are then discussing. Like all descriptive language, which of these descriptions one uses often reveals personal biases. For example, an oft-quoted description of downturns is rooted completely in subjective circumstances: if you lose *your* job, we're in a recession; if I lose *mine*, we're in a depression.

No matter what they were called, capitalist business cycles produced a long-standing debate throughout the nineteenth century, and the two sides can be expressed in a compressed form:

The Classical School: Economic recessions and depressions are natural, self-limiting and localized consequences of capitalism that are essentially harmless.

The Alternative Schools: Economic crises are complex, inevitable, potentially deeply damaging, and unpredictable consequences of the capitalist order.

THE CLASSICAL SCHOOL OF BUSINESS CYCLES

Adam Smith expressed the most fundamental aspect of the classical view about aggregate spending in a capitalist economy in the following cumbersome way:

> What is annually saved is as regularly consumed…and nearly in the same time too; but it is consumed by a different set of people. (This, and the next quotation, are from: Guy Routh, *Unemployment: Economic Perspectives*, Macmillan, 1986, p. 56-57.)

About a century later, Alfred Marshall, another luminary in the classical school and Keynes' own mentor at Cambridge, made the same argument in a somewhat more complicated way that reflected nineteenth century development of Smith's theory. He wrote that:

> All sellers are inevitably, and by the meaning of the word, buyers. Could we suddenly double the productive powers of the country…we should, by the same stroke, double the purchasing power…Everybody would be able to buy twice as much, because everyone would have twice as much to offer in exchange.

What these two quotations have in common is that both make the similar claim that overproduction cannot occur in capitalism. How and why do they say that?

To answer our question, we will construct a hypothetical model of an early nineteenth century capitalist economy with three classes of economic actors: wage earners, capitalists, and landlords. Let's suppose that during a given year the owners of capitalist firms produced $10 billion of goods and services and were successful in selling it all during the same time. To produce that level of output, the

capitalists would have had to buy materials and labor time, and rent space from landlords. Thus they would have paid out most of the receipts from their sales in material costs, wages, and rents. Whatever was left after making all the payments to these "factors" of production could be kept as profits.

The process we are describing here is a key one to understand, and it means this: at the aggregate level of the economy, the process by which the capitalists produce goods is the same as the one by which participants in the economy receive income to buy back the output from the capitalist. If we break into this flow of income and spending at the beginning of production, and look at just one part of the stream during a particular month, we can see that, in exchange for their labor time, households received wage payments. And, during the same month that they receive this income, they will send most of it back to the capitalists in exchange for consumption goods and services. This interdependence between producers and consumers and workers is now called the "circular flow of income and output," and you were part of it the last time you cashed your paycheck and headed off to buy something. The circular flow is so crucial to an understanding of aggregate economics there is always a circular flow early on in principles textbooks. And, because it is the conceptual center of macroeconomics, it will help the beginner to study such a diagram long enough to understand its basic meaning (and perhaps before you go on here).

Now, let's go back to the circular flow of our own model and assume that as the $10 billion in sales revenue flowed into the capitalist coffers during the year, they paid it out as follows:

$7 billion went to laborers as wages
$1 billion went to the landlords as rents
$2 billion was kept by capitalists as profits

We are going to suppose that the laborers spent *all* their $7 billion of wages on goods and services, and the landlords spent *all* their $1 billion on consumer goods, too. This money, as you now know, will have gone back to the capitalist producers during the same year, and it will be the biggest part of what they have in order to start up the next year's cycle of production.

Concerning the $2 billion going to the capitalists this year, let's suppose they spent $1 billion on consumer goods for themselves, and "saved" $1 billion. We'll also make the quite reasonable assumption that the $1 billion they saved was soon put back into the spending stream when they purchased—"invested in"—new capital goods, such as machinery and factories. Machines wear out, and new technologies emerge that could lower costs for the capitalist, so that each year capitalists use up part, or all, of that year's savings to buy these new capital goods in a process that is sometimes called "capital accumulation." In our model, the upshot is that the capitalists will have put all their profits back into the spending stream by purchasing $1 billion on consumer goods, and using all their $1 billion of savings to purchase capital goods. We can sum up this key element of our hypothetical model in this way: during the year, capitalists produced $10 billion because they thought they could sell it. They actually did sell it all because every dollar they paid out in the form of wages and rents, as well as the profits they paid themselves, came right back to them in the form of someone's consumer spending, plus their own spending for capital goods.

Let's connect this idea to Alfred Marshall's statement that if we *doubled* the output—in our example, to $20 billion—"everybody would be able to buy twice as much, because everyone would have twice as much to offer in exchange." This means simply that the *level* of the economy is not the point: no matter how high or low the level of capitalist production, the savings/accumulation process will always keep the economy from overproduction. With twice as much output, there will be twice as much income, and the need for roughly twice as many new capital goods, so all that is saved will be invested in capital goods. This theory—that all output will find a buyer—became known as "Say's Law" after a French economist, Jean Baptiste Say, and it remained the core of the classical business cycle theory that held sway until Keynes' *General Theory*.

What's the basic problem with this theory? Not all savings are automatically converted into spending *during the same* year or month, or six months, or whatever time period we might be analyzing. Going back to our example, let's take a closer look at the $1 billion saved by our capitalists. What might the capitalists in our economy have done with that $1 billion if, during the year, threatening events—such as epidemics, or catastrophic weather or a financial crisis—had produced a sweeping wave of pessimism

among them? Such events might also have frightened the other potential savers in the economy, the landlords, and what would be the effect of their fears on their own spending? Both of these classes might reasonably have responded to fears about the future by saving for the coming bad times, rather than using all the income we gave them in our model to buy consumer goods or capital goods. If they had done this, that is, not put back all the $3 billion we gave them in our model, there could only have been one result: the capitalists would have produced goods that were not then sold, causing them to accumulate unwanted, unsold goods—inventories—and very likely to produce less output during the next time period. An economic downturn would have begun because all of the supply would *not* have created its own demand.

Despite the reign of a modified version of Say's Law in the central tradition up to the 1930s,[2] some economists saw through the classical error. Thomas Malthus in the early part of the nineteenth century, Karl Marx in the middle, and John Hobson at the turn of the twentieth century, are only the most famous who argued that savings not returned to the income stream quickly enough could cause a downturn. Marx probably spoke for many of these ignored and heretical economists by referring to Say's analyses of the aggregate economy, as "trivial," "tedious," and "insipid nonsense." Whatever they might have thought about Say and his Law, these critics could not break its transfixing hold on classical economists. That break would have to wait for Keynes in 1936. We now turn to a second foundation stone of classical thinking: the idea that sustained involuntary unemployment in capitalism is not possible.

---

[2] In our brief discussion of Say's Law we must leave out two important additions by later economists that made the macroeconomics of the classical more sophisticated than his simple law. These additions are an explanation of how interest rates equilibrate the market for loans, and a theory of the role of money in capitalist societies. Omitting these two, we are thus presenting an oversimplified version of classical macroeconomic theory, yet the parts that we are discussing—Say's Law and its theory of unemployment—were its central tenants and can reasonably be discussed on their own.

THE CLASSICAL THEORY OF UNEMPLOYMENT

All schools of economic thought give a central role to labor markets, where the price for labor—the wage—rises and falls in relation to the supply of and demand for the labor time of the wage earners. In economic models, on one side of a labor market sits the profit-seeking capitalist ready to hire an individual worker as long as the market value of that worker's output is greater than the wage the worker is paid. This theory will hardly be news for any of us, because it is the central economic relationship of capitalism: workers get jobs if they can make profits for capitalists! On the other side of the labor market, facing the profit seekers, are the workers themselves. The classical economists believed, with good reason, that work for capitalist wages was essentially irksome. This meant that below a certain level of wages nobody would work and that as wages rose more people would offer their labor power to the highest capitalist bidder. Given the two sides of this labor market, if the supply of labor were to remain constant, for instance, but capitalists decided to increase their output, they would need more workers and this would drive up wages. And, alternatively, if the supply of labor remained constant, but the demand for labor time fell, wages would fall. Our readers probably already know this part of the theory, because it is based on simple supply and demand analysis that you may have studied.

To connect this theory of a single labor market to the classical theory of unemployment, we will develop the following example: take a hypothetical large city with an active labor market for skilled carpenters, where the going wage is $15 an hour, and as we begin our analysis there are 10,000 carpenters on the job. Suppose that, for whatever reasons, there is a substantial decline in the demand for construction throughout the whole region. This event will likely reduce the selling prices of construction projects and thus the value of the output of the carpenters who work on them. As the value of what carpenters produce declines, their services will also be less in demand, and given that, we would expect their wages to fall. However, suppose that these wage rates don't fall because the carpenters make it clear they will fight wage cuts individually, or collectively through labor unions, or in other ways. This kind of resistance is known as "wage rigidity," and in response to it, if the decline in construction demand is steep enough, some employers will lay off some of the carpenters.

Suppose the capitalists lay off 2,000 carpenters, and the remaining 8,000 of them continue working for the old wage. Now, in terms of the classical theory, here is a crucial question: are these 2,000 laid-off carpenters "unemployed"? According to the classical economists they are unemployed, but *voluntarily* so. That is, they are *choosing* to be unemployed, and if they lower their wage demands enough construction firms will once again find it profitable to hire more carpenters. Perhaps, if all the carpenters were willing to take, say, $10 an hour, and if that wage fit the new market conditions, it would again be profitable for the capitalists to hire all 10,000 of them. In other words, as long as carpenters are willing to accept lower wages in the face of falling demand for their services, there can be no *in*voluntary unemployment. The implicit and connecting idea here is that hiring the carpenters at a lower wage will allow the builders to sell their output at a lower price. This lower price will produce a greater demand for the projects, and that will lead to an increase in the demand for carpenters. Our unemployed carpenters are out of work because of their resistance to wage cuts.

The classical school generalized this theory—that without wage rigidity all individual markets were always at, or tending towards, full employment—to the entire economy. So strong was the hold of this model on the minds of economists in the central tradition that it was, as Guy Routh reports, "maintained right into the depths of the depression of the 1930s," when unemployment in both Britain and the U.S. was about 25%. He gives two examples, the first of them are comments made in 1932 by the president of the Royal Economic Society, the principal organization of the British classical school:

> General unemployment appears when asking too much is a general phenomenon… [The world] should learn to submit to declines of money-income without squealing.

And, in 1933, Professor Pigou, the successor to Alfred Marshall at Cambridge, stated the classical mantra about labor markets and unemployment succinctly:

> There will always be at work a strong tendency for wage-rates to be so related to demand that everybody is employed. (Both quotations are from Routh, p. 57.)

To sum up this quick review of the classical school's explanation for economic downturns and the consequent unemployment, we have the following: (1) aggregate supply will always equal aggregate demand, except temporarily, because capitalists will automatically use any savings out of the income stream to purchase capital goods; and (2) deviations from full employment in *all* individual labor markets result from worker resistance to falling wages in contracting industries. How, then, did Keynes go about putting these models, more or less, into the dustbin of history?

THE BROAD OUTLINES OF THE "KEYNESIAN REVOLUTION"

To begin with, we want to be quite clear about our purposes in this section. The central structure of the Keynesian macroeconomic framework is formed by interrelated theories of consumption, investment, government spending, and net exports and the way in which behavior in these various sectors causes a capitalist economy to go up and down. Such a framework is central to any introduction to modern macroeconomics, and all economics students will thus be made to learn its structural outlines and most important details. We will leave to economics courses the proper development of macroeconomics and take up only what helps us to explain the broad impact of Keynes' ideas on economics and on public policy, and of course, the relationship of these to political economy.

In 1936 when Keynes published the *General Theory,* many economists eagerly seized upon the details and implications of this theory, especially as it related to explaining the causes of the Great Depression all were living through. Most of them were young and from the United States, and Harvard's economics department had more than its share of them. At the same time, this book produced a great debate among economists throughout the capitalist world, and many were not then, nor are they now, convinced of the usefulness of the Keynesian structure. However, enough economists in the United States and Britain were converted to his way of thinking to begin to sink the classical ship. One such young economist, Paul Samuelson at Harvard, legitimized Keynesian economics by putting it on a par with classical microeconomics in a 1948 principles textbook that remains, even now, the model for most such books.

Another reason that Keynes' critique took hold was that others outside the central tradition, who understood and accepted his principal conclusions,

had already developed much of his critique in books, lectures, and in other ways. As early as the 1700s, arguments about savings, involuntary unemployment, and the policy measures that might solve the problem of depressions, had been advanced, respectively, by a Frenchman, Pierre de Boisguillebert, and an Englishman, William Petty. And in the 1860s, Marx had developed a number of ideas about business cycles, including that in part they resulted from an imbalance of spending in the investment and consumption sectors of the economy. Toward the end of the nineteenth century, in 1899, an Englishman we have already mentioned, John A. Hobson, had argued in a book he coauthored that unemployment was caused by "over-savings." Hobson, however, was soon to realize that he had made a heretical argument and would be punished for it. According to him, there were several negative responses to the book, and:

> The first shock came in a refusal of the London Extension Board to allow me to offer courses of Political Economy. This was due, I learned, to the intervention of an Economics Professor who had read my book and considered it in rationality as equivalent to an attempt to prove the flatness of the earth…[The second came] when suddenly, without explanation, the invitation [to offer a course to a charitable organization] was withdrawn. Even then I hardly realized that in appearing to question the virtue of unlimited thrift [savings] I had committed the unpardonable sin. (Quoted in Keynes, *The General Theory,* 1936, pp. 365-66.)

By the late nineteenth century it had become, at least according to Hobson and Keynes, an unpardonable sin not to agree with the classical explanation of the business cycle! And, we have seen, right up to the point when Keynes was writing the *General Theory,* that in 1932 and 1933 Britain's most widely respected economists were still telling the world that the only way out of the Great Depression was to lower wages, all around.

More substantive than these largely ignored critiques of the classical theory were the actual practices of two European countries, Sweden and Germany, which had implemented their own "Keynesian" policies before the *General Theory* was published. John K. Galbraith has described (in *Economics in Perspective*, Houghton Mifflin, 1987) how, since the early part of the century, Swedish economists and government planners had instituted policies that made sure that "over-saving" in the Swedish economy was offset by government expenditures. Swedish fiscal policy, in practice before Keynes argued for it, was part of the Swedish "middle way" we discuss in another chapter. In Germany, the Nazis, after achieving power in 1933, instituted a wide array of government interventions in the economy, including such public works as the famous Autobahn highway system. This, and other such measures, helped to bring the country out of its own Great Depression brought on by the "consequences of the peace" Keynes had written about in 1919.

All this theory and practice was well known by Keynes, a fine student of history and of his own discipline, and he drew upon both to build his own system. He also chose as a specific strategy in the *General Theory* to write the theoretical parts in the language of the classical school and, many parts of his analysis begin from one or more of the conceptual foundations of that school. If you were to try to read the *General Theory,* almost certainly you quickly would be cornered by confusion. Yet, if you plowed on, perhaps with only bits of understanding here and there, you would find that the book opens up towards the end, as if coming upon a beautiful valley after driving for many miles through strip-mined hills. The reason is that, quite intentionally, Keynes wrote the closing chapters of the book for the general public. There he takes up a number of the most important implications of his theory for public policy in a discussion that draws upon his renowned eloquence as a writer.

The Keynesian Critique of Say's Law

Concerning Say's Law, Keynes argued conclusively, in terse theoretical parts of his book, that this "law" was the wishful thinking of those who dreamed of a self-regulating capitalist system. The assumption that savings would always be spent on capital goods during the same production period was not quite so far-fetched when made by Adam Smith. In his time the merchant and landlord classes did virtually all the savings, and it appears that usually— but certainly not all the time—quickly converted their savings into capital goods in order to profit from the rapidly expanding capitalist markets. However, by the nineteenth century, and certainly by the early twentieth

century, industrial capitalist systems had become vastly more complex, and governments had, even in a world in which their economic role was supposed to be minimal, become ever more involved in these economies. Increasingly, the saving "leakage" from the economy was joined by the "tax" leakage, because whatever governments took in taxes reduced the circular flow of income and thus could lead to underconsumption if the tax leakages were not spent. In fact, from the point of view of Say's Law, we can think of taxes as identical to savings: They are a drain from the system that must be returned or overproduction will occur.

We can express Keynes' idea with more clarity if we consider the magnitudes of these leakages from the spending flow in our own economy. In 1997, for example, U.S. business firms gave employment to over 120 million people and these people produced output that was sold for over $8 trillion. As this $8 trillion flowed through the U.S. economy, much of it was drained out of the expenditure stream as savings and tax leakages, as follows:

- More than 10 million businesses firms saved—"accumulated"—about $1 trillion to help finance their expenditures for capital goods. [3]
- More than 90 million household units saved about $267 billion and put most of that in banks or other financial institutions to be lent out to others.
- All the levels of government took a total of about $1.5 trillion out of the expenditure stream through taxation.
- Households and firms spent about $.5 trillion on imports, another leakage from the domestic expenditure stream.

This means that during 1997 the tax and savings "leakages" out of the flow of income were almost $3.3 trillion, or about 38% of all the expenditures! Of course, at the same time that these leakages were occurring, governments were putting money

---

[3] These savings come from two sources: *retained earnings*, which is the part of total profits the capitalists keep for the firm rather than paying them as dividends to the stockholders; and *depreciation allowances*, funds they also retain out of sales revenue that are used for replacing used-up capital goods and for buying new capital goods.

back into the expenditure stream by buying such things as military hardware and education; business firms were adding to the stream by buying machinery and equipment; banks were lending the savings out to all kinds of spenders; and there were exports sold to foreigners.

These figures lead us to the relevant theoretical point: while U.S. capitalists were deciding to produce the $8 trillion of output during 1997, they had no idea, of course, how much of the income they generated would be lost to leakages, and how much would be gained back by injections. The reason is that these leakages and injections result from an impossibly large number of decisions by people who, at the time they save, tax, or spend, do not typically know anything about how others are putting money into, or taking it out of, the income stream. The capitalists in this process are not operating in total darkness, because they have past sales experiences to draw upon. However, the volume of output that the capitalists produce for sale, say, next month, depends upon hunches, or other best guesses, about something they *cannot know*: the level of leakages and injections that will occur as the income their production generates flows through the economy. If their estimates of sales are not realized—which, in theoretical language, will occur if there are too many leakages that are not offset by injections—they will likely accumulate inventories, and during the subsequent time period they will likely produce less total output. Thus, when the *typical* business firm is not selling all the output it is producing there will be general overproduction, and this will ultimately lead to a decline in output, less employment offered, less income generated; that is, the economy will move into recession.

The Multiplier and the Liquidity Trap

Two other parts of Keynes' critique of Say's Law merit a brief description here. The first of these, called the "multiplier," Keynes developed with other Cambridge economists, and it was a powerful addition to his model of the macroeconomy. We will explain the multiplier with a simple example. Imagine a rosy scenario in which the local billionaire decides to pay back the community by giving the first person he or she sees a $100 bill. Suppose you are the lucky recipient, and you spend it on that tattoo of your favorite professor you've been aching to put on your arm. Your purchase alone increases spending in the economy by $100; and it also increases the income of the tattoo parlor by $100, as we can see. Suppose the owner of the parlor spends $80 of it for a new hairdo.

This then will add $80 of new spending and income to the $100 spent for the tattoo, both of them additions to spending brought about by that initial $100 the billionaire gave to you. The beautician now has some more money to spend, and on down the line each new level of spending would create multiples of its own. The successive transactions would thus "multiply" the first round of spending, the $100 on the tattoo, and make the total change in spending some multiple of that first round. The multiplier adds a certain speed and energy to upward and downward movements of the economy, and it added to the new macro-theory that Keynes used to undermine the classical theory. It is also carries with it depressingly bad news for those committed to laissez-faire, for, as you can see, our $100 bill would have produced a similar multiplier effect had it been new government spending for goods and services, or simply handouts to needy citizens. More about that later.

The theory of the "liquidity trap," another of Keynes' principal ideas in the *General Theory*, has recently resurfaced in public discussion in relation to the current long-term depression of the Japanese economy. In trying to explain the depth of the Great Depression, Keynes argued that societies could wallow in a slump for long periods of time even if interest rates—which at low levels are supposed to induce capitalists and consumers to spend more and end the downturn—fall to zero. He called this problem a "liquidity trap," and it would occur if there were a collapse in confidence among consumers and capitalists that encouraged them to seek "liquidity," meaning they would choose to hold on to money, rather than buy things, until they perceive an improving economy. We will briefly return to this idea in another context below.

KEYNES AND THE CLASSICAL THEORY OF UNEMPLOYMENT

Concerning the classical claim that there could be no long-lasting *involuntary* unemployment, Keynes developed several levels of critique, and we will concern ourselves with the two most prominent ones. Remember that, for classical economists, lasting unemployment resulted when workers were not willing to take lower wages in declining product markets. Thus, their suggestions for unemployment policy—even in the middle of the Great Depression, when the unemployment rate was 25% in both the United States and Britain—was for the working class to take lower wages. Keynes saw at least two fatal errors in this thinking. The first had partly to do with the relative power between workers and their bosses, for it was apparent to Keynes, and almost everyone else, that unless there was a sustained and deepening downturn workers mightily resisted wage cuts. However, because the classical economists ruled out government intervention as a way to lower wages, nothing was left to do except to wait for workers to see the light and accept the necessary wage cuts. When they didn't—which was almost always—this meant that wages never fell quickly in recessions, preventing the economy from self-adjusting as the classical theorists believed it would. To the classical school, this resistance from workers to falling wages also meant that the recessions should be blamed on them, rather than on the system itself. Thus, the first big mistake of the classical school was to substitute wishful thinking for observable facts about how promptly wage rates would fall in declining labor markets.

The second error of the classical school about unemployment can be explained like this: Suppose that an economic contraction becomes deep enough, and sustained enough, to lower the demand for labor in all the principal labor markets. There would be a point in such a contraction that wages would begin to fall, when and by how much depending on countless conditions. We have already pointed out that, according to the classical economists, falling wages would lower costs and prices and would invite a greater demand for goods and services. And, it was thought that this greater demand would *automatically* turn around the economic decline. Keynes pointed out, however, a *general* fall in wages—the largest single part of national income—would likely cause an eventual *decline* in the demand for goods and services that workers buy, rather than an increase encouraged by the lower prices.

Keynes offered several other possible consequences of a fall in wages, some of which might be expected to raise expenditures by business firms, but he did not see them as having the capacity to offset the decline in total spending that would come from falling wages. Falling wages, if they did have the effect of reducing total consumer demand, could also greatly reduce the optimism of the capitalists and lead them to reduce their spending on new equipment. This latter possibility was important to Keynes because he knew that the sustained and deep

depression of the 1930s had, by 1936, done exactly that in the leading capitalist countries. Such a progression would mean that the decline in consumption spending, along with the decline in capitalist spending on capital goods, would send the economy spiraling downward even further.

To Keynes, then, the levels of employment and unemployment depended on the collective decisions of people to spend as consumers and capitalists and to fund government spending programs, the decisions of foreigners to buy U.S. products, the multiplier, and all the remaining parts of his theoretical framework. That is, in his model the unemployed are victimized by crises in capitalism, and the classical solution of lower wages would only make the crisis worse. In his argument, Keynes came closer than he probably would have liked to Marx's idea of an "industrial reserve army" of unemployed that we discussed in the essay on Marx. What these two theories share is the conclusion that unemployment is an inevitable feature of capitalism over which workers have no control. Unemployment goes up when aggregate spending declines, and thus if we are looking for culprits to blame, it would have to be the millions and millions of individuals in households and business firms deciding to cut back on their spending. Unemployment in capitalism, therefore, *is systemic and inevitable*, rather than the result of individual decisions to work or not to work at market wages. It is hard to imagine a more resounding rejection of classical economics than this Keynesian conclusion about unemployment.

THE CURRENT STATUS OF KEYNESIAN ECONOMICS

Aside from pushing from the limelight central parts of classical economics, the principal long-term influence of the *General Theory* has been to broaden the focus of macroeconomics to include aggregate sectors of spending, and their dynamic interrelationships, as central to the study of the capitalist business cycle. Keynes had no particular qualms about the microeconomic models that his own mentor, Alfred Marshall, had been so important in bringing to the mainstream; and, as we have said, his principal work in 1936 built on many of the theoretical foundations of the classical school. For this reason, in one sense, Keynes never really left the central tradition of economics. In fact, the macro-theory he produced gradually became part of the mainstream, a process that led Paul Samuelson to write in the 1964 version of his textbook that:

> [Today] the broad fundamentals [of Keynes' theory] are increasingly accepted by economists of all schools of thought, including, it is important to notice, many who do not share Keynes' particular policy views and who differ on technical details of analysis (*Economics: An Introductory Analysis*).

Samuelson's point here does not mean, by any stretch of the imagination, that there have not been challenges, before and after 1964, to Keynesian ideas. These have come particularly from economists unhappy with his conclusions about the need for government intervention in the economy. Two of these challenges, called "monetarism" and "rational expectations," have come from the economics department at the University of Chicago, where key economists responded negatively to Keynes' ideas in the 1930s and which remains one of the strongest bastions of anti-Keynesian sentiment in the United States academy. Economists in the monetarist and rational expectations schools have had considerable influence in the academy over the past three decades and have helped to focus attention on aspects of the microeconomic foundations of the economy that they see as crucially shaping the aggregate economy. There are also several schools of Keynesian economics, and they compete with the others for the attention of other macroeconomists in the academy and the policy makers in government.

It is far beyond the scope of this essay to go into the current academic debate about macroeconomic theory. We will merely present fresh evidence of the fact that, even after 60 years of challenges from many mainstream economics, Keynesian ideas continue to play a role in the current debate among academics about the macroeconomy. Keynes' theory of the "liquidity trap" has surfaced recently in the arguments of such prominent mainstream academic economists as Robert Gordon and Paul Krugman to explain current economic depression in Japan. Louis Uchitelle, economic correspondent of the *New York Times*, writes that:

> Mr. Gordon, who is 58, is already giving fresh emphasis in class to a concept that has received little attention since the 1970s. And so are other professors, although the idea of an utter consumer shutdown runs so counter to the standard, modern day beliefs of their profession...The professors are, in effect, dusting off a phenomenon first described by the British economist John Maynard Keynes in the 1930s and soon termed, in economic jargon, a liquidity trap. It means that the demand for goods and services consistently falls short of a nation's capacity to produce them despite short-term interest rates as low as zero. The central bank loses its power to steer the economy. That may be hard to imagine in the United States today, where the Federal Reserve, with its constant attention to interest rates, has helped to keep consumer spending robust for the better part of a decade (*New York Times*, June 2, 1999, p. C-1).

Professor Krugman also suggests that the long recession in Japan is the kind that could also happen in the United States, even though the current economic boom makes that seem unlikely. Krugman, according to Uchitelle:

> ...traveled to Japan to see conditions for himself. He constructed a mathematical model, a standard tool of modern economics, to demonstrate that printing more money and lowering interest rates, even down to zero, would succeed in stimulating demand and expanding an economy. "Instead, I succeeded in proving to myself that this was not necessarily true," he said. He concluded that a liquidity trap was possible after all. It was no longer just a historical curiosity —a fading memory of the Depression and the teachings of Keynes. It had happened in Japan....Among professional economists, Mr. Krugman was not the first to conclude that Japan had fallen into a liquidity trap. A small group of Keynesian economists already had this in mind. And as early as 1996, some conservatives, among them John Makin of the American Enterprise Institute, who does not consider himself a Keynesian, wrote that Japan was caught in a liquidity trap ...

In our view, a particularly interesting aspect of this article is that it takes us back to the 1930s, when Keynes launched his major attack on the classical school's theory of economic crises and ushered forward a debate about his ideas that won't go away. We have mainstream economists, like Professor Gordon, coming back to Keynes after relegating one of his major theories to the lowly status of a footnote. And, we have a few Keynesians saying, as they always say when capitalism begins to slip and everyone scurries back to Keynes, "We told you so!" His run, in this regard, has been a long one.

KEYNES, THE POLITICAL ECONOMIST, I: ECONOMIC METHODOLOGY

We now want to expand our argument for having included Keynes in a book on political economy. The Keynes you will encounter in your regular textbook will seem to conform to the "scientific method" used by mainstream economists. But there was another important, political economy side to Keynes' thinking—a side that demonstrates the broad sweep of Keynes' ideas. We will let Keynes demonstrate this by speaking for himself at some length here and below. Writing in 1931, he said:

> The study of economics does not seem to require any specialized gifts of an unusually high order. Is it not, intellectually regarded, a very easy subject compared with the higher branches of philosophy or pure science? An easy subject, at which very few excel! The paradox finds its explanation, perhaps, in that the master economist must possess a rare *combination* of gifts. He must be mathematician, historian, statesman, philosopher—in some degree. He must understand symbols and speak in words. He must contemplate the particular in terms of the general, and touch abstract and concrete in the same flight of thought. He must study the present in the light of the past for the purposes of the future. No part of man's nature or his intuitions must lie entirely outside his regard. He must be purposeful and disinterested in a simultaneous mood; as aloof and incorruptible as an artist, yet sometimes as near the earth as a politician (*Essays in Biography*, W.W. Norton and Company, 1963 edition, pp. 140-41).

More precisely about the quantitative techniques of the mainstream economists, Keynes wrote in the *General Theory* that:

> Too large a proportion of recent 'mathematical' economics are mere concoctions, as imprecise as the initial assumptions they rest on, which allow the author to lose sight of the complexities and interdependencies of the real world in a maze of pretentious and unhelpful symbols (p. 98).

As an example of the kind of ideas that Keynes was willing to entertain, we will quote from him concerning what motivates economic actors in capitalism. In the following passage from the *General Theory*, where his specific focus is what motivates capitalists to invest in capital goods, you should note that Keynes implicitly dismisses as badly misleading the constricted creature called economic man in mainstream quantitative models.

> [A] large proportion of our positive activities depend on spontaneous optimism rather than on a mathematical expectation, whether moral or hedonistic or economic. Most, probably, of our decisions to do something positive, the full consequences of which will be drawn out over many days to come, can only be taken as a result of *animal spirits*—of a spontaneous urge to action rather than inaction, and not as the outcome of a weighted average of quantitative benefits multiplied by quantitative probabilities... Thus if the animal spirits are dimmed and the spontaneous optimism falters, leaving us to depend on nothing but a mathematical expectation, enterprise will fade and die— though fears of loss may have a basis no more reasonable than hopes of profit had before...In estimating the prospects for investments [in capital goods], we must have regard, therefore, to the nerves and hysteria and even the digestions and reactions to the weather of those upon whose spontaneous activity it largely depends (*The General Theory*, pp. 162-63, emphasis supplied).

If we combine the argument in these three passages, we can see in Keynes' methodology a far-flung net—or a particularly big vacuum cleaner if we use the metaphor of U.S. economist, Robert Solow—in which to catch things that might help his analysis. For Keynes, apparently, the entire universe of ideas and knowledge had potential for helping theorists to understand the world outside the swirl of prejudices and confusions inside their heads. It seems hardly to have mattered to him whether economics was a science, though he insisted often that economic *theory* was a matter of simple logic. Economists generate ideas and plans of action to avoid economic crises and the political chaos that always accompanied them. In other words, though Keynes's ideas about the economic world were in some ways deeply embedded in classical thinking, they were outside it in critical ways. As we have just seen, his methodology for studying economic activity broke all the self-imposed bonds of the central tradition. Perhaps now, after reading about Veblen and Marx, readers can see how much closer are his research impulses to theirs than to those of the economic mainstream. His method of work was that of a political economist, despite the fact that so much of what he wrote was in the terms of the classical system of ideas about the economy.

KEYNES, THE POLITICAL ECONOMIST, II: THE POLITICAL KEYNES

By the early 1920s Keynes had come to believe in the need for government intervention in certain areas of economic life, and thus the policy prescriptions he offered in the General Theory merely extended ideas he had held for some time. The specifics of his antirecession policies will not come as a surprise to readers at this point. When an economy is mired in an economic contraction, Keynes argued, it is a consequence of inadequate spending in all the key sectors. Economic downturns were most likely to originate from a decline in capitalists' purchases of capital goods, because these expenditures were ruled by volatile and unpredictable "animal spirits." When the spirits led the capitalists to reduce their spending on buildings and equipment, all those who had been supplying such products before would now be out of jobs and income, and the effects of their declining spending would spill over into the consumption sector, causing a decline there as well. Further dragging the economy down would be a negative multiplier effect, and soon enough an economic crisis would be underway. Given this theory of how the aggregate economy could quickly slide into a recession, the solution seemed obvious to Keynes: as investment and consumption spending fell, the government should take up the slack in demand by borrowing money for its own expenditures, and it didn't matter for what those expenditures were made. As this spending worked its way through the economy, it would ultimately produce a better outlook for businesses, which meant more investment on capital goods. This would then start the whole process moving back upward, with the help of the multiplier, to recovery and economic growth.

Aside from the Swedes and German Nazis, whom we described earlier as having tried this kind of "fiscal" policy before Keynes argued for it, other capitalist governments did not readily jump on the Keynesian bandwagon. The "New Deal" in the United States generated a spate of new government programs, such as unemployment compensation, federal welfare, and public works projects that gave jobs to the unemployed, but the government was not ready to risk the huge deficits that Keynesians were urging on it as the way to end the Depression. However, starting in

about 1940, Keynesian policies were "tested in the field" by most capitalist governments during World War II. In the United States, government leaders tossed aside the classical school's admonition about government intervention in the economy, including its rule against deficit spending, to fight the war against Japan and Germany. Running massive deficits to finance the construction of bombs, planes, and ships, federal government spending led to a massive recovery. By 1943-44, the unemployment rate fell to its lowest recorded level, about 1 percent of the work force.

With the war as a gigantic lab experiment that seemed to prove the Keynesian theory, most in the scholarly and political world gradually came to adopt it. After World War II, most capitalist nations passed laws, such as the Employment Act of 1946 in the United States, making the maintenance of stable prices and full employment a job for the federal government. These were laws in part written by, and certainly reflecting the views of, Keynesian economists. A symbolic highpoint of the influence of Keynes occurred in 1963, when in a speech at Yale University John Kennedy used the idea of the Keynesian multiplier to justify the cut in personal income taxes he was urging on the Congress as a way to cause a sluggish economy to grow faster. The essentially Keynesian basis of domestic U.S. economic policy remained in place for about 25 years, and, in 1971, an economic conservative, Richard Nixon, argued that "we are all Keynesians now."

Even as Nixon spoke, the U.S. economy had already begun to develop a number of structural problems, particularly pockets of hard-core unemployment and rising inflation, that could not be readily resolved by Keynesian policies. These problems in the United States and in Britain in the 1970s deepened through the decade and they propelled into power Margaret Thatcher in Britain in 1979 and Ronald Reagan in the United States in 1980. These two were elected by espousing the old laissez-faire slogans of free enterprise, individual initiative, and most especially, the sentiment that government in principle was a bad thing for the economy. Indeed, by the middle of the 1980s, the U.S. Republicans and British Conservatives held sway with an increasingly antigovernment rhetoric that gradually took hold and is now the stated economic philosophy of the major political parties in both countries. By the end of the 1980s, it was virtually impossible in the United States to be elected to public office at any level if one championed higher taxes. According to many political analysts, George Bush was pushed from the presidency by Bill Clinton in 1992 because he went back on his famous "read my lips" pledge not to support tax increases.

For his part, Bill Clinton jumped on the bandwagon when he came into power as a "new Democrat," claiming that "the era of big government is over." His economic policies—including "ending welfare as we know it"—are now indistinguishable from those of the Republicans. Catering to business and financial interests is economic policy, under the assumption that their good fortunes will trickle down onto the rest of us. Partly, Clinton has moved toward the Republicans in order to get elected and re-elected; partly he has done so because, more than any Democratic president before him, he has aggressively and successfully financed his campaigns with money from rich individuals and especially from powerful corporations.

Yet, this antigovernment posturing is mainly the rhetoric of politics, and it is utterly at odds with the extensive role government plays in the U.S. economy. Federal spending was 21.7% of Gross Domestic Product in 1980 when Reagan started his rhetorical war against government. By 1992, when George Bush's defeat ended twelve years of Republican control of the White House, this proportion had actually risen to 22.5%. Looked at another way, between 1980 and 1992, federal spending per capita—the average amount the federal government spend on each of us each year—actually increased from $4,232 to $5,610, after taking account of inflation. Thus, while Republicans were claiming to be delivering a laissez-faire utopia, in fact, the governments they largely dominated at every level responded to our demands to spend more on each of us each year.

A principal reason the U.S. economy is currently performing relatively well is that most people are confident that the national government will not hesitate to intervene, and massively if necessary, should the economy turn downward. Before Keynes, and certainly in the middle of the Great Depression, no one could reasonably have had that confidence. If people believed the economy was slipping into recession, they would not tolerate Bill Clinton, or other economic policy makers like the Federal Reserve Board, pronouncing week after week that government would only make things worse if it intervened in the economy, and prosperity was "just around the corner."

This widespread involvement of government in capitalism is the political reality in all modern capitalist countries, no matter what their politicians say in speeches or at press conferences about "keeping government off of peoples' backs." These same people expect their governments to manage the macroeconomy, and presidents who have failed to do so in the public perception—Jimmy Carter and George Bush are two recent examples—don't get a second term.

To sum up this section, we again return to an assessment by John Kenneth Galbraith, who recently lectured on these matters at the London School of Economics. The *Vancouver Sun* reported on that lecture and, in addition to pointing out that Galbraith "worked with Keynes in the late 1930s," the story included the following:

> Let us not assume that the age of slump, recession, depression is past. Let us have both the needed warnings against speculative excess and awareness that the ensuing slump can be painful,' said Galbraith, who has written more than 40 books including the classic *The Affluent Society*. He said the writings of the economist John Maynard Keynes will come back into fashion with the inevitable slowdown, as governments seek ways to alleviate its effects (June 29, 1999).

KEYNES AND INTERNATIONAL CAPITALISM

There is a counterpart to all of this regarding the international economy. An important element of Keynes' fame derived from his having been the principal designer of the post-World War II system of international finance. In 1944, representatives from the allied nations met in Bretton Woods, New Hampshire to plan a framework for developing world capitalism once the war was over. The system that Keynes and others designed was in place from 1945 until the early 1970s. It formed a matrix of regulations analogous to Keynesian domestic policy in the sense that government bodies at the international level would be directly involved in regulating the post-war international economy. This, too, was an assault on the classical system because "free trade" was, in that system, the analog to an unregulated domestic economy. One observer, looking back on the effects of the system the delegates produced, has written:

As an experiment in economic policy, the Bretton Woods agreement, proved equally impressive. Between 1945 and 1973, when the regime of [international] financial controls remained in effect, the war-ravaged economies of Europe and Asia were rebuilt, and the developed world as a whole enjoyed annual economic growth rates exceeding four per cent, which translated into the virtual tripling of total output (John Cassidy, "The New World Disorder," *The New Yorker*, October 22/November 6, 1998, p. 200).

The ideology of "free trade" was quite naturally a part of the Reagan/Thatcher adoption of laissez-faire, and picking up where they left off, Democrat Bill Clinton has campaigned more vigorously for unregulated international capitalism than any president since before the Great Depression. In their championing of "free trade," presidents Reagan, Bush, and Clinton have used the considerable authority and power of the U.S. government to dismantle the system of international controls established at Bretton Woods. Some of these, such as regulating the values of currencies, were dropped in the 1970s. Other controls, such as the regulation of capital flows across borders, are now being eliminated as countries come under pressure from the United States to adopt their own "free trade" policies. It is not possible to know if these trends will continue, particularly after many experts blamed the recent collapse of the financial system in several Asian countries on the lack of international controls over capital flows.

Though we cannot know now the long-term effects of this age of laissez-faire rhetoric, there is one measure that might help us to put into a sensible context the real, rather than the rhetorical, effects of government intervention in U.S. capitalism. That measure is the comparable rates of growth in the size of the U.S. economy during two periods. During the first of them, 1945-1970, when Keynesian ideas shaped domestic fiscal policy in the U.S., and the international system established in Bretton Woods was still in effect, the average real growth rate in our economy was about 3.5%. During the second period, 1970 to the present, by which time both domestic and international controls have been rolled back in significant ways, the annual real growth rate has been between 2-3%. Because so many elements determine growth rates, in addition to government's role in the economy, we can safely extract but one conclusion from this comparison: the most sustained period of economic growth in U.S. history occurred during the period in which U.S. economic policies were most thoroughly "Keynesian."

CONCLUSION

Keynes and his ideas are included in this book because he shared two important ways of thinking with political economists. For his study of economic life, no information was outside his purview. He was a thoroughly erudite man, a voracious reader and constant conversationalist, and he believed that dependence on all the senses—what one had read, heard about, seen, could intuit, and even what one felt—was central to the work of any good economist. This is a far, far cry from the methodological stance that dominates mainstream economics and restricts its scope. Unlike those who dominate mainstream economics, and who claim to be "making correct scientific judgments," Keynes never stopped giving his opinions to the day he died.

Keynes also shared with political economists the view that laissez-faire ideology, still at the underbelly of so much mainstream thinking, is an invitation to economic mayhem. The lessons of the Golden—Keynesian—Years of the U.S. economy, 1945 to 1970, confirm what political economists have been teaching all along: unregulated capitalism is an unsustainable system, and for it to last over the long, long run it will have to be held in check by ongoing and reasonable public policies.

Chapter V

SOCIAL CLASSES IN CAPITALISM

INTRODUCTION

The Class System at Bucknell University

The *Catalog* for Bucknell University, as is typical of such catalogs, contains a lofty "Mission Statement" telling the world that the university is dedicated to noble goals. Of these goals, the following are representative:

> *To develop new experiences that will enable students to grow in moral sensitivity and in respect for other persons. To engage in institutional programs and practices that exemplify compassion, civility, and a sense of justice.*

Only the most churlish person could fault such goals for a university. And wonderful, indeed, it would be for professors if our students leave their classrooms morally sensitive, respectful of others, compassionate, civil and having a sense of justice. Wonderful, too, if professors were that way as well!

These goals, alas, are up against a jarring social reality carefully ignored at most universities: *social class.* The existence of an undeniable array of social classes at universities, among the students and among those who work as faculty, staff, and administrators, is the constant reminder that some of us are accorded more respect than others. And, it is especially hard to know what "sense of justice" a student might infer from an institution whose "practices" generate benefits and status so unequally.

Students will learn from dorm life the first week of classes that some are from very privileged backgrounds, some from merely privileged backgrounds, and some from considerably lower stations. The expensive cars and clothes, or the lack of them, and all the talk about one's family make the case. And, soon forgotten will be the more than 50% of the eighteen and nineteen year olds off campus, almost all of them from the lower half of the class system, who are not at universities but heading for low wage jobs or the military service.

Concerning those who work for a living at Bucknell University, this year the president is being paid about $170,000, an income supplemented by over $30,000 of benefits and an elegant, sprawling home to live in. Between him and the faculty are a number of other top administrators whose salaries range from about $90,000 to $130,000. Beneath them, in this hierarchy of money and power, are the faculty members whose average income is between $55,000 to $60,000, and below them are those called, in a perfect word for a class system, "support staff." They make annually somewhere between the minimum wage, about $14,000, up to $50,000 for the heads of nonfaculty departments, and most of the support staff are in the lower ranges of this spread. Secretaries with decades of experience can make less than $30,000, or less than the value of the benefits paid to the president. For all the apparent reasons, the inequality of this income is matched, and quite closely, by the varying amounts of power and status attached to each of the income strata, thus obeying a simple rule of life in any hierarchy.

All this relative privilege and power utterly contradicts the goal to cultivate a sense of justice among our students. As a principal such contradiction, but only one of many possible examples, consider the effect on the children of this university community of the greatly higher incomes of the president and other top officials and higher incomes of the faculty, relative to those of most of the support staff. The higher salaries of the leading administrators and faculty members unquestionably allow them to pass on to their own children a number of advantages, such as: better odds to attend the best schools; better access to superior food, clothing, doctors and dentists; and a better environment in which to learn the linguistic styles and the cultural prejudices of other elites who will then eventually hire them for the better jobs. In most dictionaries, the term "just" is synonymous with "fair." Thus, it is hard to imagine how either term could be used to describe a community that systematically allows a minority to pass on to its children significantly greater opportunities for "the good life" than those passed to the children of the majority. Particularly this is true where, as at our university, there are no processes in place, nor planned for in the future, that would lessen this great inequality.

No university community, or any other kind, which truly is committed to "exemplifying a sense of justice," would construct a system of compensation that trickles down so unequally to the children in it. As the children might put it, and they tend to begin to understand these things at an early age, "That's not fair!"[1] Why then, this lofty but unattainable language about justice in our *Catalog*? Is it simply a guise to attract unwary students, to pry lucre from their parents' pockets?

The answer to our question above is "no," our university *Catalog* is not lying to the world (at least not beyond generating the half-truths that, like all vendors, it publicizes to attract its customers). We are merely lying to ourselves, and doing so is as All-American as apple pie. Americans have worked mightily to explain away the system of social classes that shapes their lives and whose ugly consequences are taken for granted in every other industrial society in the world. Most prominent of these efforts is the belief in myths such as "melting pot" and the "American Dream." The first of these suggests that once on our shores, all meld into a similar kind of being: American! And, the second, that anyone can make it to the top with a little guts and gumption, contests the very idea of barriers between the classes. Meanwhile, as history has unfolded, the structure of social classes brought here by Europeans has remained more or less intact. The highest social classes remain inhabited mostly by rich white men and their families, who are at the top because they dominate the economic order, and the political order along with it. And, at the bottom of our social order are disproportionate numbers of the kind of people who were down there in 1800: people of color, women, and white men who are unskilled and uneducated.

Social Class in More General Terms

This system of social classes—whether we recognize it or not—is both interesting and consequential for what happens to any of us. It is interesting because of its complications, its

layerings, and its changes over time. In the United States the subject of social class is more compelling yet because our need to deny its existence gives a hint of the illicit to discussions about it. Despite our desire to avoid the subject, this compelling interest and the great consequences of social classes in capitalist societies have produced sometimes competing, sometimes complementary, theories about how classes originate and how they change over time.

The first part of this essay briefly reviews central ideas in the broad literature about social class. In the second part, we will discuss the consequences of social classes, particularly the differential effects of social class on the physical and emotional health of people in modern capitalist societies. We will find in this section good evidence that the lower your social class the more likely you will suffer from psychological stress, heart disease and related illnesses, and the more likely your life will be shortened by all of these conditions. What could be more consequential? In the last part we look briefly at the issue of "upward mobility" in capitalist societies, and we will construct a direct challenge to the popular myth that the road upward is available to most, if not all, and always fulfilling to those who make it.

Finally, before we turn to the theorists, we want to emphasize what this essay is *not* about. In isolating social class as a determinant of our behavior, we do not mean to ignore the other things that also mold and make us. We all know that race and sex are two other powerful shaping forces in our lives, and both of these act interdependently with social class. Black people in the United States, for example, make about 60% of the income of whites because an ingrained and unrelenting racism has for all our modern history denied most blacks access to the schools, neighborhoods and jobs that one needs to reach the higher social classes. Further, this example of the interdependence of race and class in creating limited options for black people is but the tip of an iceberg of profound structural complexity. As one writer, John Boylan, put it in a response to an early draft of this essay:

> While economics and class structure play a significant role in the creation of culture, they must be factored in with a whole pattern of other

---

[1] Dennis Gilbert reports that studies on children's attitudes about social class show that 3rd graders have begun to recognize different social classes, that 70% of 6th graders see about the same class alignments as their parents, and that most 12th graders will see such alignments the same as do their parents (pp. 116-117).

elements...Individuals also develop their individual personalities from countless influences, forces, and circumstances, including, of course, class background, many of which they are only dimly aware... [We] live in [and are shaped by] a culture that is a tremendous ever-shifting web of words, images, rules, lies, taboos, prejudices, fears, hopes, and dreams. It pervades laws, norms, rules both stated and unspoken...[Once] you start examining it, it shifts, changes, camouflages itself, and envelopes the observer. I think of it is as a huge tinker toy in which the pieces are constantly being reassembled...We tend to understand it the same way that the blind men know the elephant by describing only the part of the animal that each is actually touching.

Thus, in this essay we proceed seeking only to bring into a sharper focus one part of an elephant we can never know completely but which unendingly shapes us into the persons we are becoming.

Theories of Social Class

The two predominant ways that people today think about social class come from Karl Marx, writing in the middle of the nineteenth century, and from Max Weber, who wrote at the turn of that century. We will introduce their ideas on social class, along with those of Pierre Bourdieu, a recent interpreter of Weber. Our focus on these three writers means, or course, that we are not providing the broad survey that one might find in textbooks on social class. However, in what we do take up we will introduce all the important categories and dimensions of the current scholarly discussion of social class. And, along the way, we will mention a few other authors our readers might want to look at for greater depth and details.

Marx and Social Class

The term "class" originates in the Latin word, "classis," used by fifth century Romans to describe the various income levels of their day. As a way to describe the different roles people play in the social hierarchy of capitalist societies, the specific

usage of the word "class" emerged in the early eighteenth century in the work of Daniel Defoe, an English political pamphleteer best known for writing *Robinson Crusoe*. Soon, theories of class found their way into French analyses of society, and thus became part of the nexus of ideas that fueled the French Revolution and the overthrow of the French aristocracy in the late eighteenth century. The most influential writers in the British classical school of economics, Adam Smith and David Ricardo, both recognized that the different streams of income in capitalism—wages, profits, and rents—flowed into the households of separate groups, or classes of people, the laborers, capitalists, and landowners.

Ricardo was especially important for modern conceptions of social class, because he argued that conflict between the social classes was inevitable. His reasons need not deter us, except to note he saw capitalists and the workers ever engaged in a struggle over the distribution of what was left to them after rents were paid to the landlords. Marx was aware of these earlier French and English theories of social classes and, typical of all his work, he built on such theories to develop his own. At least two things distinguished his ideas about social class from earlier ones, the first that they were central to a larger, more complex analysis of capitalism that continues to attract significant attention. And, second, Marx and his frequent coauthor, Frederick Engels, argued that class conflict would ultimately generate a revolution that would bring an end to capitalism.

In a brief section on social class in our earlier essay on Marx, we quoted economist Teresa Amott's comment that "Marx's original conceptions continue to define and shape the argument" about social class in capitalism. To refresh memories about that essay, in Marx's analysis the capitalist class (or bourgeoisie) rules over capitalism because it owns the major firms that dominate the economic order, and this preeminence provides capitalists the money and power to rule the political order as well. We also described Marx's argument that the income and wealth of the capitalist class derive from "surplus value," that part of the workers' output that goes to the capitalists in profits rather than to the workers in wages or salaries. These wage workers, by far the majority, comprise the other major class in capitalism and the continual struggle between capitalists and laborers over their wages and working conditions is the dynamic center of the system.

Marxists say that class position is defined by one's "relationship to the means of production" (the factories, equipment, and other productive assets used to produce goods and services). If you own these, or manage them in the very top positions in corporations, you are in the capitalist class. If you don't, you are in the proletariat. Marxists are aware that people such as doctors, postal carriers, high-school teachers, librarians, and countless others, are not so easily crammed into one of the two social classes that Marx believed would ultimately come to be in developed capitalist systems. His two-part class system was a broad, abstract construct used as a way to see the most essential structural features of capitalism. However, when he wrote about contemporary events, he would always introduce a host of highly specialized class groupings, including the dominant capitalists and their allies in struggle with an unruly amalgamation of working class groups. As it turned out, most theorists of social class after Marx abandoned his two-class model, but retained the idea that one's place in the economy is crucial in determining one's social class.

Max Weber and Social Status

Max Weber was a German social theorist who lived from 1864 to 1920 and whose writings were central to the development of modern sociology. He constructed a carefully reasoned and complex theory of social classes, in which he introduced several key terms in this field of study such as "social class," "status hierarchies," and "lifestyle." Weber was successful enough in countering the Marxian two-class theory to produce a way of thinking about social class that is now much more influential among U.S. academics. Most essentially, Weber replaced the idea of two classes endlessly struggling against each other with the image of their "stratification." This metaphor implied that such classes are more like layers of rocks at a geologic site than the two warring classes of owners and workers in Marx's model. Weber's social geology is responsible for the current popular image, where the "upper class" rides atop a hierarchy of classes that descends to the "middle classes" and on down to the "underclass."

Yet, Weber did not abandon Marx's position that employment, one's relationship to the economic order, mattered greatly in determining class position. Weber argued that a person's participation in the economic order, especially whether he or she was a capitalist owner, determined *social class,* and that played the dominant role in determining *life chances*. However, a person's overall class standing also depends on what Weber called social *status*, how one's economic position, activities, and possessions are perceived by others in the community. Dennis Gilbert, author of an excellent survey of theories of social class, has summarized Weber's ideas about how one's status is interdependent with one's economic class. He writes that:

> [Weber] specified many of the interrelations between class and status, between economy and society. Because of class position, a person earns a certain income. That income permits a certain lifestyle, and people soon make friends with others who live the same way. As they interact with one another, they begin to conceive of themselves as a special type of people. They restrict interaction with outsiders who seem too different (that may be too poor, too uneducated, and too clumsy to live graciously enough for acceptance as worthy companions). Marriage partners are chosen from similar groups because once people follow a certain style of life, they find it difficult to be comfortable with people who live differently. Thus, the status group becomes an ingrown circle. It earns a position in the local community that entitles its members to social honor or prestige from inferiors (*American Class Structure in An Age of Inequality*, fifth edition, Wadsworth, 1998, p. 9).

In this Weberian system, therefore, one's economic class is *objectively* determined, meaning that it is what you do in the economy, along with the power and benefits you get from it, rather than how others might value it. On the other hand, social status is a *subjective* determination, meaning that our views about where in the status hierarchy we abide, and the place where others might be, is a complex, shifting mosaic of attitudes. As Gilbert notes above, Weber knew of the interdependence between economic class and social status, and that the former always shaped the latter. Elite groups, such as the socially prominent families in a city, typically get their income and wealth from an economic and political order they dominate by owning factories, banks, and service companies. They translate this advantage into a life style not affordable by most others, and they understandably consider themselves "better" than others because the evidence seems so obviously that way to them. As important, they thrust their privilege into the future by making sure, through schooling and networking, that their children will be more likely to dominate the economic and political order, and thus the world of status, in the future. A critical feature of status groups, Weber argued, is that they bond together to construct boundaries between themselves and others, and the higher the status of a group the thicker are the walls that separate it from all the others.

Over the years, Weber's distinction between the economic base of social class, and the life style basis of social status, has gradually been replaced by wide acceptance of the idea that the term "social class" includes both elements. This means, for example, you can improve your "social standing" (another phrase for class position), either by getting a more highly paid job, or keeping the same job and moving into a more prestigious neighborhood. In most such cases, of course, the higher pay will be the reason one moves to a more prestigious neighborhood, because as we have said, one's status is mostly shaped by one's income.

Recently, a few writers have advanced the idea that barriers between U.S. social classes are thinning because status determinations now change so quickly that those on top know that any moment they might be hurled into the hated oblivion of being like everyone else. Recently, the *New York Times* published a lengthy survey of relative status *within* particular groups in the United States, including the following ones:

- Among long distance truck drivers, there is A Million-Mile Club of those who have driven that many miles without an accident. One of those with the highest status is the legendary Kenneth Caudle who has driven more than five million accident free miles.

- Among some of the richest families, buying whatever you want no longer distinguishes you because so many others can do the same thing. However, you can achieve extra status in this group by getting what you want *more quickly* than they do. An example is the "young investor" from Long Island who wanted his driveway widened ten feet, *in one day*, to accommodate his four luxury cars. He found a local contractor to do the job and thus became the local hero (at least until someone could find a contractor to do such a job in half a day).

- Among those who live in mobile homes, a new status symbol, which can be bought for $5,000 to $6,000 dollars, is a pitched roof. And, for more money, you can get more status by installing a vaulted ceiling in your trailer park home.

- U.S. Navy fighter pilots gain status by bombing targets accurately and for landing gracefully on an aircraft carrier. But, they get the most by engaging an enemy plane in the air and shooting it down. Mongo Mogillo did exactly that during the Persian Gulf War, and now refers to himself as "a proven commodity. I've got 25 missions in combat; I've shot down a plane. Been there, done that." Thus to get the highest status among such pilots, as one of them put it, "A fighter pilot needs an air-to-air kill."

In this *New York Times* list, there are several other examples, such as the status stay-at-home moms get in certain quarters, and that given to immigrants based on how much they can help the people back home. There is extra status given among vegetarians to those who eat only *raw* vegetables.

There are two aspects of these examples of status that are worth emphasis. The first of them is how often status in one group will not travel well to another one. Stay-at-home moms might tend to see that ace fighter pilot's "something special" as merely a quick trigger and an ability to see the enemy pilot as a thing, rather than as a human being. Truckers who drive safely might laud each other while being seen by upper class drivers as a menacing feature of highway life who possess few, if any of the symbols of status rich people ordinarily admire. And, what kind of respect do you think truck drivers have for the drivers of expensive sport cars that dash around and between their sixteen wheelers?

The second, and more important, aspect of these examples is that they point to how fleeting and unpredictable these kinds of status symbols can be. Unlike money, the nature of one's job, and level of education—those attributes that most scholars, and we, believe confer much more permanent elements of social standing—one can still get status by possessing other qualities, or other things. And, in the information age, with its 24 hour media and Internet supermarket advertising the rapidly increasing kinds of things available, and the rapidly expanding ways one might behave as a human being, the production of status symbols has quickened dramatically. That is why some writers believe that the old Weber-Warner strata, with its array of classes from the rich elite down to the underclass, is considerably less rigid than it used to be.

There is surely merit in this criticism, for it points most directly to the extreme fluidity and unpredictability of the world in advanced countries where people are regularly bombarded with *thousands* of advertising messages every day. Nonetheless, the old status symbols—a high status job, money and power, and the graduate education and tastes that usually come with such jobs and income—continue to create genuine boundaries between people in capitalist culture that have discernible and important effects on people's lives. These boundaries might be more difficult to ascertain and shifting all the time, but most people who study social class continue to see them as still able to absorb the fleeting nature of the new fads that come and go with increasing speed.

Pierre Bourdieu: Class Position and Cultural Capital

The French sociologist, Pierre Bourdieu, for his work *Distinction: A Social Critique of the Judgment of Taste* (1979), gathered interview data in the 1960s about the living and spending habits of 1200 French men and women. He analyzed this data in the terms of a conceptual framework about

social class that derives directly from those before him, especially Max Weber. However, Bourdieu added as part of this framework an extended discussion of what he called "personal capital" which is quite useful in discussing the barriers between social classes. According to Bourdieu's framework, one's class position is ultimately determined by one's "personal capital." Such capital can take several forms, including economic capital (the income and/or wealth to which you have access), educational capital (roughly how many years and where), and social capital (your network of family, and other associations). All these "capitals" are implicit in the work of Weber and his followers, but Bourdieu enriched the old mix by focusing on what he called *cultural* capital. Douglas Holt, an interpreter of Bourdieu, describes cultural capital as being "fostered in…the social milieu of cultural elites" and as including the following crucial elements.

> Upbringing in families with well-educated parents whose occupations require cultural skills, interaction with peers from similar families, high levels of formal education at institutions that attract other cultural élites studying areas that emphasize critical abstract thinking and communication over the accumulation of particularized trade skills and knowledges, and refinement and reinforcement in occupations that emphasize symbolic production ("Does Cultural Capital Structure American Consumption?" *Journal of Consumer Research*, June, 1998).

Bourdieu's focus on styles of consumption as manifestations of cultural capital has drawn much attention to his arguments about how cultural elites draw "distinctions" between themselves and others. To give an example of this process, we will follow Bourdieu's own, in *Distinction* (pp. 27ff.), about the different ways that social classes "consume" commercial films. Although we will use a film as our example, it is easy enough to see how the consumption pattern of other cultural items, such as newspapers, literature, magazines, and theatre, are all shaped by social class. Further, such cultural products purchased by elites are the subjects of considerable discussion among them in a language mostly inaccessible to nonelites, as our example seeks to demonstrate.

Try to imagine yourself the daughter of parents with a high school education, your father a brick layer, your mom a homemaker, and yourself a college freshman. The mother of your assigned roommate is a professor and her father is an ambassador to a foreign country. Now, imagine spending a weekend with your friend at her country home when at dinner the subject of the film "Titanic" comes up and someone at the table asks you what you think about it. You say that the film was a great experience, with fantastic special effects, a wonderful love story, and an interesting dose of history that you didn't really know. Then, mom and dad weigh in with a few ideas about films that are new to you, such as comments about the director's choices, the twisted version of history the film portrays, and its odd casting. Then, finally dad sighs with a dismissive gesture that the film was "overwhelmed by typical Hollywood sentimentality." And, a bit peeved by it all, mom dismisses all Hollywood films as being that way, and, additionally, always inferior to French films. After such an exchange, in addition to feeling inferior because of already having compared your family house and contents, cars, and lawns to those at the country home, and after not being able to identify one of the foods you were served and two of the implements you were supposed to eat with, you also realize you're in a world of *ideas* you didn't know existed.

To understand the importance Bourdieu places on cultural capital as defining social classes, and their role in maintaining barriers between the classes, one only has to consider all the other kinds of situations where such capital serves us well, or badly. Any of us who has felt out-of-place, whether with people we look up to or down to, it is often because we find ourselves running with a crowd with very different accumulations of cultural capital. Bourdieu's idea of cultural capital also focuses attention on how the social classes differ in both what they buy and the way they think and talk about, and ultimately value, such items. A conversation about *Titanic* which never goes beyond simple platitudes—such as "Wow! What a flick. The special effects were awesome!" —is not exclusive. Anyone can engage in it, though highly educated people would probably choose not to if they could do so gracefully. The conversation we have imagined, however, is highly exclusive because the parents' comments about the film are bold signs that they have ample

amounts of cultural capital that, of course, they will have all along been passing on to their daughter.

Concerning how cultural capital fuses with other kinds of personal capital, we can already guess which of our two first-year women will most likely be a cultural elite in the next generation. Clearly, the daughter of the professor and ambassador will have been accumulating more educational and social capital to have a great early advantage over her roommate. In addition, by not living in a house with these kinds of consumption items, and not expressing the way in which such items are used and talked about, our working class student will have already fallen far behind in the accumulation of this, and of other kinds of, cultural capital.

It is quite apparent that all these kinds of capital—economic, educational, social, and cultural—are more readily accessible to the children of the privileged than those of the middle class, and in turn more accessible to the middle classes than to the working classes below them. And, the decreasing access to social capital as one descends the class ladder substantially lessens the quantity and quality of choices one has in life. None of this is to say, of course, that we can know which of the two young women in our example will work her way highest up the social ladder and how life will be there. Our privileged student might, indeed, fall into the grip of a destructive eating disorder while our bright and persevering working class student works her way to the top of a corporate ladder. Our argument is only that the richer your family the greater your odds to accumulate crucial kinds of personal capital. We shall see some stunning consequences of these odds in the discussion below on social class and health.

Regenerating Social Class Privilege

The Children's Defense Fund (CDF), an advocacy research group, has published data that explain more directly how the children of the privileged acquire more of all kinds of personal capital than other children. In 1998, the CDF published a report based on information from a U.S. Department of Agriculture document, *Expenditures on Children by Families* (www.usda.gov/fcscnpp/using2.htm). The CDF report includes the following information on expenditures by "husband-wife" families, in terms of differing family incomes:

Annual Family Income	Average Expenditures on each child to Age 18
Under $34,700	$110,040
$34,700-58,300	$149,820
Over $58,300	$218,400

These numbers mean that the upper third (roughly) of the income distribution will spend about twice as much money on each of its children to age eighteen than the lower third. Thus, we can presume that—on average—the richer kids will get more and better food, clothing, health care, schooling, travel, and all the rest. And, these will, of course, directly or indirectly allow them to develop more economic and social capital along with other advantages that result from living in a relatively high income family. Actually, there were slightly over 10 million U.S. families in 1996 whose average incomes were *over $100,000*, and we can only imagine how much more cultural capital will be accumulated at that level, where all the food, clothing, schooling are better yet.

Our argument, we want to emphasize, is that larger family incomes lead to greater accumulation of personal capital, including cultural capital, for children and thus greater opportunities to become elites as adults. It is *not* our argument that a larger family income necessarily leads to a happier or more productive life. In fact, economist Juliet Schor, in her engaging book, *The Overspent American*, reports that 39% of people in U.S. families with incomes between $75,000-$100,000, and 27% of those with incomes over $100,000, told interviewers they did not have enough money to buy all they needed. We all know unhappy rich people, and people who gain contentment with modest means. Indeed, aside from extreme wealth compared to extreme deprivation, there is probably no way to know whether more money usually makes for more happiness. Nevertheless, most people in our society would prefer more income than less, and few parents would turn away the opportunity to give their children better health care, education services, and richer cultural experiences.

Without question, cultural capital is one way—along with the other advantages of being richer—that social classes tend to "reproduce"

themselves from one generation to the next. The best way to get into the most prestigious and powerful positions in the economy is still to have prestigious and privileged parents. Data we will introduce later show that sons whose fathers work in the highest paid sectors of the economy are more than twice as likely as those from the lower classes to end up in such sectors themselves. Yet, despite the great power of social classes to regenerate themselves over time, people from the lower stations do, in fact, make it to the top. Later in this essay, we will discuss this American Dream of upward social mobility to see if, in fact, getting happier in our society is simply a matter of more education, connections, money, and status.

Summing Up the Theorizing

In general, contemporary theories of social class, almost all having their origin in either Marx or Weber, conclude that the more wealth, money, authority, autonomy, power over others, education, connections, and high-status jobs you have, and the more you buy things that others cannot afford nor discuss as complexly as you can, the higher is your social class. As you move down from this class to the one just below it, no matter whether you call it "the second highest class" or "the upper-middle class," you will typically find less of all these possessions, and on down to the bottom where you find very few of any of them. Further, people at each level will use their money and education to construct lifestyles that are barriers between themselves and those beneath them. And, last, because the upper classes dominate the political order, the government's economic policies will be shaped to help them maintain their advantaged place in the economy. Such elites will also make sure that no laws can prevent them from passing on the essential ingredients of their advantages to their children.

But, there is more to these advantages of being in the upper classes than readily meets the eye, particularly in a society where most are blind to the issue of social class. Therefore, now we turn to other, related, consequences of the fact of social classes in U.S. capitalism.

THE LIVING CONSEQUENCES OF SOCIAL CLASS

Mainstream economists ignore social class principally because its existence conflicts directly with the benign view of capitalism they typically hold. This basic prejudice leads such economists to perceive themselves as "dispassionate experts" with the professional obligation to offer policy solutions for problems that arise in capitalism, rather than to consider the relative merits of the system itself. In the language of the modern "scientific" economist: "Our job is study *what is*, rather than *what ought to be*," without ever considering whether there *ought to be capitalism* as opposed to some other system. In this way of thinking, and especially in the United States, nasty aspects of capitalism—such as its inevitable ruin of the environment, gross inequality, its urging us to be as greedy as we know how to be, and its rigid and damaging hierarchy of classes—are necessarily kept out of sight like a lovable old dog with mange. Thus, in the mainstream there is the assiduous avoiding of the study of social class, for within that world of analysis are powerful challenges, indeed, to the notion that capitalism is an essentially benign system that needs to be tinkered with rather than overhauled or replaced. What, then, are these powerful challenges?

Life, Itself

In a nutshell, social classes in U.S. capitalism divide people into a hierarchy of place and privilege where one's social class might reasonably be considered one of the crucial indicators of whether one will live a relatively long and reasonably successful life. What evidence do we have to make so broad a claim? To begin with, consider the following statement about income and health in a recent The *New York Times* article:

> Scientists have known for decades that poverty translates into higher rates of illness and mortality. But an explosion of research is demonstrating that social class—as measured not just by income but also by education and other markers of relative status—is one of the most powerful predictors of health, more powerful than genetics, exposure to carcinogens, even smoking. What matters is not simply whether a person is rich or poor, college educated or not. Rather, risk for a wide variety of illnesses, including cardiovascular disease, diabetes, arthritis, infant mortality, many infectious diseases, and some types of cancer varies

with relative wealth or poverty: the higher the rung on the socioeconomic ladder, the lower the risk. And this relationship holds even at the upper reaches of society, where it might seem that an abundance of resources would even things out (Erica Goode, "For Good Health, It Helps to be Rich and Important," *New York Times*, June 1, 1999, p. 1).

This is the overall conclusion of an article that refers to the finding of some 193 papers about socioeconomic status and health that have appeared in scientific journals during the past five years. A principal cause of this burst of interest by medical professionals was the findings of a study, begun in the 1960s, of 18,000 male civil servants in Britain, in which "astonished" researchers found that:

> Mortality rates varied continuously and precisely with the men's civil service grade: the higher the classification, the lower the rates of death, regardless of cause…A 25-year follow up of the subjects [of this study in 1996]…found that the social class gradient persisted well past retirement, even among men into their late 80s (Goode, p. 9).

Intrigued by these findings, the British researchers began a second study in 1985, in which they included both men and women, from whom they collected more details, including information about the "amount of control people had" on the job. The researchers found that:

> Job control…varied inversely with employment grade: the higher the grade, the more control. And, the less control employees had, as defined either by their own or managers' ratings, the higher the employees' risk of developing coronary disease. Job control, in fact, accounted for about half the gradient in deaths from pay grade to pay grade (Goode, p. 9).

This article also reported that, while blacks in the United States have lower life expectancies (for instance a black man age 45 can expect to live five years less than his white 45-year-old counterpart), studies accounting for social class difference showed that black and white men had about the same life expectancies. Some of these studies used such evidence as the fact that the richer your neighborhood the more likely "you can trust your neighbors" and the less likely you believe they are trying "to take advantage of you." These aspects of neighborhood life are analogous to loss of control on the job, in that people who cannot trust the safety of their own neighborhood have a good deal less control over their ability to protect themselves and their loved ones.

These kinds of findings are not surprising, to say the least. As early as the mid-nineteenth century, Marx and Engels, and novelists such as Charles Dickens wrote extensively about the awful circumstances that limited the lives of the working classes. In *Capital* (1867), Marx presented considerable data from British Parliamentary studies showing that the health and the life span of British workers depended importantly on what they did for a living and where they did it. In the United States, many scholars have long studied this connection between social class and health and life. One of them, Vincente Navarro at Johns Hopkins has been writing about the subject for three decades.[2] In 1991, Professor Navarro explained why U.S. health researchers were just then discovering a relationship between health and social classes in capitalism that had been apparent all along:

> The way in which the U.S. government collects health and vital statistics reflects [the fact that class is rarely discussed in the scientific and mainstream media]. The government collects statistics about mortality rates and causes of death by race, gender, and region, but not by class. The overwhelming majority of other developed capitalist countries do collect mortality statistics by class....Most Western European countries, with the active encouragement of the European

office of the World Health Organization, have chosen the reduction of class mortality differentials as a major objective of government policies. The United States is absent from this international debate. There is a deafening silence in our country regarding class and class mortality differentials. Instead of class, the U.S. government uses race, and consequently lists the reduction of mortality differentials by race as one of the nation's top five objectives ("Class and Race: Life and Death Situations," *Monthly Review,* September 1991).

As an example of Navarro's point, recently the *New York Times* (October 11, 1999) reported that black men are more likely than white men to die from heart attacks because of two factors: lack of health information and access, and occasionally inferior treatment at health facilities. In this case, there is an admixture of both socioeconomic class background and racism.[3] If we look only at income, this higher inclination of the poor to die from heart attacks than the rich is also true of poor white people, and for the same reasons. However, as Navarro points out, because we don't look at these matters according to social class, we must explain them all in terms of race. Navarro summarizes a 1986 report on the relationship between social class and health care as "one of the few occasions" that the U.S. government reported on this relationship. The report broke people down into several categories, with their mortality rates for heart disease, per 10,000, as follows:

Heart Disease Mortality Rates, per 10,000	
Management/Professional	37
White Collar Workers	43
Service Workers	59
Craft Workers	69
Blue Collar Workers	86

[2] In addition to Vincente Navarro, mentioned in the text, two other scholars have been making these arguments for a long time. One, Leonard Sagan, covered much the same territory as Navarro in *The Health of Nations* (1987), particularly in chapter 8 on "Mortality Gradients Among Social Classes." Another, Harvey Brenner, has for twenty years produced a long series of books and articles about the relationship between socioeconomic variables and health, particularly its relationship to unemployment.

[3] By isolating social class in this essay, we do not mean to imply gender and race are unimportant, or less important. For us, the idea of social class enriches the discussion of how things and privileges are distributed in a society, rather than to obscure it. We hope that the example from Vincente Navarro provides a good idea of the complexities of determining how much the relatively low class position of (for example) Hispanics in the U.S. is determined by racial factors and how much by social class.

As we travel down the hierarchy of these innocent numbers we also descend into a world in which people have less and less control over their work. This relationship between control over one's job and health is so central to research on the matter, we will return to it in a later section.

Personal Capital and Access to Health Care

One explanation for this data on health and social class can be explained in terms of Pierre Bourdieu's idea of personal capital, and all that it implies. Having more rather than less educational and cultural capital, for instance, makes it easier to negotiate for one's self in public life. Knowing about how to get health care when you need it is importantly a matter of reading skills, access to information and understanding what to do with it, and regular contact with others who themselves have the same skills and have sought the same health care you seek. Then, of course, having more rather than less economic capital allows you more readily to pay for the care. Added to these limitations for wage earners relative to professionals, for instance, is that their work schedules are typically less flexible. In a nutshell, it is easier for lawyers and dentists to arrange their schedules to include health care visits than for wage earners who work from nine to five. Further, most professionals have health care insurance, more and more wage earners don't; professionals typically have longer vacations; and professionals seek health care from other professionals, thus people like themselves who have the same linguistic habits and are on the same wave length in other respects. And, because they have more education, income, and access, professionals are much more likely to participate in stress-reducing leisure at such places as sports clubs, golf courses, and similar places where one can simultaneously work off the fat and have fun.

Social Class and Emotional Health

The evidence gathered by scholars over many years concerning mental health and social class is quite persuasive, if not indisputable. Yet, before we present the overall dimensions of this evidence we need to make certain readers do not confuse our point. All of us know people from different social classes, and we can all cite instances where someone from the working class seems happier, and more emotionally sound, than someone who is rich and privileged. Here, our argument is comprised of generalizations with no power of prediction whatsoever about a single individual, or even a small group of individuals. We will be discussing qualitative aspects of the behavior of large groups of people, and these are always relatively imprecise and given to many and conflicting interpretations. Nevertheless, we believe the data at this general level comprise a persuasive and powerful argument.

An especially influential study about the relationship between social class and mental health was done in Illinois in 1985, and the results of this study are consistent with all comparable ones we know about.[4] In the Illinois study, 809 people were interviewed in depth about their lives, their feelings, and the extent to which these could be identified as symptoms of depression. The results were divided into several categories, income and education the two of them most directly related to social class. For both education and income, the 809 respondents were broken down into "deciles," ascending from the bottom 10% to the top 10% (meaning that those in the bottom 10% had the least income and education, respectively). The results of this survey are analyzed by John Mirowski and Catherine Ross, in *Social Causes of Distress* (1989), and they are straightforward enough: the less income you have, the more likely you are to be depressed; and, the less education you have the more likely you are to be depressed.

On the matter of "severe psychological distress," Mirowski and Ross wrote the following:

> Social factors account for a great deal of distress, but do they account for severe psychological distress? To address this second question, we defined extreme distress as a level of symptoms greater than that evidenced by 95% of the population. Approximately 61% of these

---

[4] One of the first well-organized, and continually influential, studies on this issue is August Hollingshead and Fredrick Redlich, *Social Class and Mental Illness: A Community Study* (1958). This book contains a clear and comprehensive discussion of the methodological problems of this kind of research, and is the basic "textbook" for research being done in the field. Hollingshead and Redlich concluded that the lesser (neurotic) disorders tend to be clustered in particular classes and that the more debilitating disorders (psychoses, such as schizophrenia) were inversely related to social class: the lower your social class, the higher the probability you will be seriously mentally ill.

people would qualify for a psychiatric diagnosis. If we split society into two halves, socioeconomically, better and worse, the worse half of society has 83.2% of all the severe distress. The advantaged half has only 16.2%. Stated another way, the odds of being severely distressed are 5.9 times greater in the worse half than in the better half.

Mirowski and Ross give as major reasons for these outcomes that rich people are more likely to detect mental illness in its earlier stages, more likely to know how to seek treatment, and better able to afford better treatment than their lesser counterparts in the class system. All these factors would produce statistical evidence of mental illness being less a burden for the rich than for all others and particularly less a burden compared to that of poor people.

In this kind of research, we must be wary of the enormous practical difficulties, such as defining mental illness, the limitations of interview data, and record keeping by hospitals and mental health workers. Nevertheless, we have reported the data from Mirowski and Ross because, like that of Hollingshead and Redlich, it is consistent with other studies in its general conclusion that the best way to avoid mental illness is to be born into the upper classes. We say, "born into" because getting there by upward mobility can itself create mental distress, as we shall see.

The Central Role of "Control" in Health and Longevity

There are a host of factors, other than one's social class, that determines how healthy you are and how long you live. Diet, habits, and especially genetic makeup all have a great deal to do with our well being and longevity. And, within particular social groups, researchers have found that it matters greatly whether your family and community is nurturing when you are young, understanding and tolerant when you're older. It also matters greatly whether you have stable and loving intimate relationships. Yet, when we take all those into account, statistically, certain other aspects of our lives remain central determinants of how well we fare.[5] We are going to focus on one

of these, the amount of control over one's work, because it is closely related to all definitions of social class, and because there have been quite a few recent studies about it. The issue of job control gathers attention in our society because the workplaces in the United States have been designed such that in most of them (as Marx once put it), "the hand is separated from the brain."

This separation is importantly a consequence of the work of Frederick J. Taylor, the father of "scientific management" in the early part of this century. He convinced the owners of many of the largest firms to use time and motion studies, and other techniques, to divide production processes into their simplest components as a way to reduce costs. Thus, increasingly U.S. firms developed ways to produce goods and services where specific tasks were imagined and designed by a relatively small number of professionals, such as engineers and management specialists, and overseen by top officers, including financial specialists. The work of producing the goods or services, though, was mostly done by wage earners who were gradually "deskilled" by the process. The goal was to establish work places where workers were told what to do, when to do it, and how to do it, and these production processes gradually spread their way through the economy. Indeed, they became known as the "American Way" of production, or what we now call a "bottom line mentality."

What, then, are the consequences of this lack of control over work, which is the basic fact of the life of most employed adults in our society? Consider first this very general statement about "control" and well being:

> Of all the things that might explain the social patterns of distress, one stands as central: the sense of control over one's own life. Many studies in many sciences find the sense of control associated with lower distress. This sense reflects the reality of the individual's experiences,

---

[5] The following is an example of "controlling statistically" for these kinds of characteristics. Assume we were to select

randomly two groups, one from poor families and one from rich families, and all members of both groups had similar diets and exercise habits, smoked about the same number of cigarettes and drank similar amounts of alcohol, and all were in reasonably happy marriages. Even though these were all the same, we would expect statistically to find the rich people living longer than the poor ones on average. That would then lead us to look for other variables to explain this difference in longevity between the two groups, such as the nature of their work, where they lived, or a host of other things.

opportunities, and resources. It implies an attentive, active, and proactive approach to problems...Psychologically beneficial control comes from the power to get things done, not the power to win conflicts; and from power over your own life, not from power over the lives of others. Because the different forms of power are associated, they are easily confused, causing some people to go beyond the beneficial limits of control...[For]the large majority, though, a greater sense of control would be psychologically beneficial (Mirowski and Ross, p. 167).

It is certainly not hard to translate this assessment of control and well being into a system of social classes, particularly as they are related to the hierarchy of work in capitalist societies. For instance, Robert Karasek, an engineer at University of Southern California, and Tores Theorell, a physician and professor at Sweden's National Institute for Psychosocial Factors and Health, have produced one study that has gathered considerable attention to the matter, *Healthy Work: Stress, Productivity, and the Reconstruction of Working Life* (1990). In this book, Karasek and Theorell pay particular attention to what they call "decision latitude," a measure of the degree to which workers control the dimensions of their work. This concept implies that it is not the demands of your job that make it stressful, but the extent to which you determine what good or service you make, how you make it, and at what pace. Concerning, for example, the effect on blood pressure of having a lack of control at the job site, Karasek and Theorell wrote:

If an employer increases the demands on employees while concomitantly decreasing their decision latitude, the employees will experience rising blood pressures levels. Only some of them will react, and they will probably be the best workers--highly motivated and cooperative. Certainly the toll of badly designed jobs is high: our evidence builds a strong case that the work environment can become a biological prison that the average human being cannot endure

without adverse physiological effects in the long run (p. 157).

Karasek and Theorell divided jobs on a grid in terms of two dimensions, "low/high psychological demand" and "low/high decision control." They found the following breakdown consistent with their data on heart disease:

Examples of jobs under the most stress (high psychological demand/low control):	
sales clerk (female)	freight handler
waiter and waitress	garment stitcher
fireman	mall worker
telephone operator	cashier
cook	

Examples of jobs under the least stress (low psychological demand/high control):	
sales clerk (male)	peddler
architect	auto repair man
natural scientist	forester
dentist	skilled machinist

These categories do not bode well for the health of workers in the next century, since the federal government predicts that some of the fastest growing job sectors in the U.S. economy into the next century will be cashiers, sales clerks, waitresses and waiters, and mall workers. Karasek and Theorell argued in their book that the United States was woefully behind other countries in studying the relationship between stress on the job and health. More recently, Professor Karasek, just back from a year advising the government of Norway on the issue, told a Boston Globe writer that; "The government used to fund large-scale occupational health studies but stopped about 20 years ago."[6] Can our readers guess why this happened about 20 years ago?

A recent study done by Peter Schall, director of the Center of Social Epidemiology at the University of California at Irvine, confirms the data from Karasek and Theorell on hypertension (high blood pressure) and job strain. According to the same Boston Globe writer, Dr. Schall:

---

[6] Delores Kong, "Jobs Don't Kill People, But Stress in the Workplace Can," *Boston Globe*, August 30, 1999, S. 7, p. 19.

For instance…cites an automobile plant in California, where the assembly line is sped up so much that employees were timed spending 58 seconds out of every 60 seconds working. 'Every second of every minute of every working hour is accounted for in plants like this,' Schall said.

Schall and his colleagues:

[M]onitored the blood pressure of nearly 200 men for 24-hour periods. Those who had the highest job strain had on average a systolic blood pressure (the upper number) nearly 12 points higher and diastolic blood pressure nearly 10 points higher than those with the least strain…. Dr. Schall said, after looking at all possible causes of high blood pressure, job strain was found to be more important than smoking or salt in the diet.

This kind of data, like that on relative degrees of mental health, is qualitative, tentative, and subject to differing conclusions depending on the nature of the studies made, basic definitions, and research methodologies, to name the most obvious limitations. However, the experts increasingly agree that people who work at jobs over which they have little control, and at which they can use few of their skills, are affected in the same way as by a lack of control over their personal lives. Such work can depress them, make them sick, and take years off their lives. These findings are particularly important in focusing on one's economic position in the world, one's "relationship to the means of production," as Marx put it, as crucial to one's well being. The findings also support Marx's broad two-class structure, in that we have two such classes: the minority who controls work and the majority who labors at their beck and call.

It is also the case that, precisely because the jobs at the top always pay much better and they are the healthiest places to be, that most everyone in the lower classes tries to get there. When those from the bottom half get to the upper half, it is an example of significant "upward mobility," and this event in someone's life is better known as realizing "The American Dream." This Dream,

implying that anyone can pull himself or herself up "by the bootstraps" is therefore presented as a powerful antidote to the damages wrought by the class system. If anyone can "make it" by trying hard enough, no matter how deprived life had been down below, the awful effects of work in the different social classes is, somehow, justified. Those at the bottom remain there because…well, because they deserve to be. We need to look at this claim carefully.

SOCIAL CLASS AND THE AMERICAN DREAM

The claim that upward mobility allays the damages of the class system is actually composed of two related arguments. The first of these is that anyone can make it to the top with enough effort; and the second argument is that those who do make it are, in fact, delivered into the Promised Land. We will look at these separately.

How Much Mobility is There?

Though data on this important question is surprisingly sparse, Dennis Gilbert, in *Class Structure in an Age of Growing Inequality* (1998), has produced a look at the trends between 1962 and 1990. Gilbert compared data from several studies over the years and their different classifications made it necessary for him to force them all to one set of categories. After doing that, he ended up with the following five class system, in the terms of the nature of work, in which to look at mobility:

- *Upper white collar* (professionals, managers, officials, non-retail sales)
- *Lower white collar* (proprietors, clerical workers, retail sales workers)
- *Upper manual* (craftsmen and foreman)
- *Lower manual* (unskilled, service workers, operatives, non-farm laborers)
- *Farm* (farm workers and farmers)[7]

---

[7] Two things about this information need pointing out. In our analysis we have dropped the last category of farm workers because they represent less than 3% of all workers, and because they are such a mix—ranging from migrant workers to more highly paid workers in corporate farms—that their *average* circumstances do not give us useful information. Second, as Gilbert points out, almost all U.S. studies on mobility have focused on men. He shows, however, that available data on women, as a group, show a

The figures below, as we explain in the footnote, are about males only, and they describe the percentage of each group that ended up either above, the same, or below the economic position held by their fathers. (This data relates to the period between 1982-1990, and the percentages are roughly similar to those in other studies done since the 1960s.)

Up:	44%
Stable:	36%
Down:	20%

As simple figures, these are interesting and informative, confirming the idea that there is a great deal of mobility in the U.S. economy, with almost half of the sons achieving a higher standing in the economy than their fathers. Most of this mobility, however, was the movement across one class barrier, such as the movement from lower to higher manual labor, or lower to higher white collar labor. Crossing a single class boundary is hardly the stuff of the American Dream, with its symbolic "rags to riches." Such success stories imply movement across several class barriers. What can we say about these bigger leaps?

We will define significant upward mobility as moving from the bottom of Gilbert's classification to the top, or the sons of lower manual laborers who ended up in upper white-collar work. An example would be the son of an unskilled laborer who became a doctor, or the son of a cashier who becomes a top corporate executive. The following numbers express in percentage terms what kind of jobs were attained by the sons of men who were lower manual workers:

Upper white collar:	27%
Lower white collar:	11%
Upper manual:	25%
Lower manual:	37%

We can see that 27% actually made it to "the top," ending up with jobs as professionals, managers, officials, or non-retail sales workers. Though

---

similar mobility pattern to that of men, but its sparseness leaves the mobility of women a subject badly in need of study. Blacks, as we might expect, have greater numbers in the lower class categories and less upward mobility than whites, but the rate of their upward mobility has steadily increased since 1960.

Gilbert's data doesn't show us how many of these sons became, say, high status doctors and how many became lower status "officials" in small firms, we will assume that all these stories embody the dream of going from nowhere to the top. We can also see from this data that 62% of the lower manual workers remained manual workers. This means that, along with the mobility, there is for the sons of most manual labors a consignment to wage earning, manual labor. It is also true, according to Gilbert, that about 60% of all those who are in upper white-collar jobs had fathers who were there as well. Nevertheless, one might reasonably conclude from the data that our system is remarkably and successfully "open," given that over a quarter of those who start so low can get to the top. Before we draw that conclusion, however, we must ask ourselves this question: once they get to the top, what actually happens to the sons—and daughters—of factory operatives, or service workers, who became doctors, and lawyers and professors?

Strangers in this Fine Place So Far From Home

What does happen, say, to a person from a working class family who ends up at an elite university, then accumulates enough educational capital to land a job with a Wall Street firm dominated by fancy Ivy League types? That's an important question for two principal reasons. The first of these is that upward social mobility actually lessens the genuinely unfair constraints of social classes. Since the distribution of opportunities closely mirrors the distribution of income, and is thus greatly unequal, mobility allows at least some people to make their up way up and out of the their lower class standing. Second, upward mobility allows for more political stability than would be possible without it: if everyone in the bottom half was consigned there for life, particularly in a society claiming itself as "free," rebellions would always be only slightly beneath the surface of social life. Much depends, then, on whether upward mobility "works" as it is supposed to for those who achieve it (and, we should remember that we are talking only about substantial upward mobility, whereby someone crosses from "manual labor" to "upper white collar" as described above).

This question of whether upward mobility works for those who experience it is considerably complicated and the results of studies trying to answer it are mixed.[8] However, there are some important conclusions that scholars have reached who have done the most influential studies. Consider, as a general statement, this dramatic claim from Hollingshead and Redlich, *Social Class and Mental Illness* (1957), about "social climbers," those upwardly mobile people who appear to have made their move "successfully":

> The climber may impress an observer as pleasant, successful, and very able if he is successful and appears well integrated. Only on longer acquaintance and after a deeper search does one become aware of the climber's conflicts and defenses. His deeper anxieties become manifested when his mobility drive becomes blocked; then his defenses do not function properly…When these social climbers were rejected by those who "are there" socially, their reactions were characterized by severe anxiety, depression, sometimes by antisocial acting out, and in …extreme cases by suicidal attempts…(p. 368).

The tone and overall conclusion of this quote are more important to us than its specific claims, because it signals that the literature on upward mobility is always in part about the stressfulness—called "status dissonance" in the literature—that comes with it for so many who make the trip. One body of research that encompasses all the relevant issues about upward mobility focuses on essays by college professors who have working class backgrounds.[9] By going from the lower or upper manual classes to becoming a college professor, such people have clearly made a substantial upward movement from their family backgrounds. In the books (mentioned in the footnote) from which we will draw examples, there are dozens of different voices and they all tell different stories. Some of these professors, for instance, expressed relief at having been lifted up from the drudgery of the wage work; others found pleasure at having a foot in two worlds; while still others found having their feet in two worlds often wrenching and painful. Yet, while all these voices were unique, there were unmistakable dominant themes overall, of which one can find examples in virtually all the essays.

One such theme was a genuine feeling of alienation from professional (often in these essays called "middle-class") life. The first voice here expresses this alienation in the context of a considerable anger about colleagues, most of whom in the academic world—probably about three-fourths in the top tier of colleges and universities—originate in the middle or upper classes:

> My friends have been a handful of fellow outsiders who share my contempt for the rest of "them." I feel quite unapologetic about these prejudices. I feel "they" are all deeply worthy of contempt. They parade a sense of inflated self-importance; take pleasure in feeling smarter than students; pretend they contribute meaningfully to GNP; dance for favors; create parochial empires; cower before symbols of authority; wallow in bogus professionalism; and submerge themselves in their narrow expertise, which, for many, is their ticket to a legitimate place in the academy. The tone and the anger in what I've written above give some indication of the depth of my alienation (*Strangers in Paradise*, pp.261-2).

[8] One such study, still in progress, concerns over 100 working and lower middle class students who attended Bucknell University between 1963-1997, and who were raised in a coal mining town about 40 miles from the campus. John Anderson, an economist, contacted all these alumni and got essays or did extended interviews with about half of them about their experiences at Bucknell. Anderson and historian Mary Hill (who joined him in the middle of this project) included the following conclusions to the current draft of their study: "[While] some found their four years at Bucknell a positive, even exciting experience, for many these years brought much pain and hardship. The most common—but not unanimous—feeling of these students during their first year was that they were economically and socially inadequate. [However, most] were genuinely pleased with their Bucknell education and felt it had a positive impact upon their lives."
[9] Four studies that make up part of this research, each with a different focus from the others, are: Jake Ryan and Charles Sackrey, *Strangers in Paradise: Academics from the Working Class*

(1984; rev. ed., 1996); Michelle Tokarczyk and Elizabeth Fay, eds., *Working Class Women in the Academy* (1993); and C.L.B. Dews and Carolyn Law, *This Fine Place so Far From Home: Voices of Academics from the Working Class* (1995); and a more quantitative look at the issue, Michael Grimes and Joan Morris, *Caught in the Middle: Contradictions in the Lives of Sociologists from Working-Class Backgrounds* (1997).

Another voice from these collections carried a second theme, mixing a recognition of the "stick-ability' of one's class origin with a hopefulness that suggests a way to mitigate the conflicting circumstances:

> How can these feelings of marginality and estrangement be reduced? How can working-class academics begin to integrate the divided or split sense of self that arises from belonging (yet in some fundamental ways, not belonging) to two distinct class cultures? As members of a transition class, it is likely that working-class academics will always feel marginal to some degree. However, if this outsider status is to become a source of empowerment rather than a source of internal conflict, it is imperative that such faculty begin to validate the working— and middle—class parts of themselves. To do so requires that they recognize and confront the ways in which they have internalized the classism of the larger society and, thus, their own oppression. This process is essential if working-class academics are to reclaim their power and develop an authentic or integrated sense of self (*Working Class Women in the Academy*, p. 54).

Another of these professors sounded a third theme that resonated in all the essays, about how long the path from home had become. She reflects on these matters by recalling the time when her parents were about to drive her back to her studies at Dartmouth, but her father was called back to duty at a paper mill.

> My father left [for the mill] a bit earlier…and as my mother began the drive out of town with me in the passenger seat, I remember being struck with the feeling that my father was out there somewhere, driving too, but on a very different road. With the greatest clarity I have ever experienced about the question of mobility, I saw myself on the road to my life of bright and interesting friends, a glut of culture and ideas, comfort and privilege. My father was on the road he took every day to the paper mill. Huge and noisy and noxious, the mill was where my father spent lonely, dirty days among men who shared none of his interest in reading about ideas (*This Fine Place so Far From Home*, pp. 157-58).

Alienation, anger, the unending reminder that your parents went down a different road, the unmistakable power of social class to "stick with you" all the way down your own path, mixed in with a hopefulness and willingness to struggle for legitimacy—these are the themes common to the literature on upward mobility. You might get to another place, but once there, you need to figure out how to deal with the fact that, unlike most people, you have a dual-class experience. Therefore, whatever else might happen, whether you are happy for most of your days or miserably angry at the pretensions of life at the higher reaches, you must construct a way to negotiate a new terrain. Going from the working classes to the more prestigious professions is literally to move from one neighborhood to another one. At first, people in that new world might not even notice you; or, worse, they might despise you and all your trappings. Upward mobility puts you in a world in which those already there have likely accumulated more of all of Bourdieu's personal capital than you have. They will have a greater ease with the neighborhood, and, especially a built-in savvy about how to negotiate the terrain. If, for instance, you were raised in rural Texas, and find yourself in a room full of New England elites, you must keep it to yourself that you prefer George Jones to Mozart, and corn bread to croissants. Such a revelation of the dearth of your cultural capital could well permanently signal your marginality.

The upward traveler must, therefore, develop a strategy to survive. The literature on upward mobility is in agreement on this point, without exception. These strategies range from assimilation (trying to be like them), separation (trying to keep your job while staying to the side), war (fighting them tooth and nail until they fire you), and so on. The absolute necessity of such strategies makes our essential point that social class is, however ambiguous and hard to tie down, a powerful shaping mechanism in our lives. These social classes exist because of invisible, but nonetheless real, barriers that separate us from each other in terms of our income, education, habits, and all the rest. Thus, to cross them one must learn to navigate in enemy territory and, perhaps as a precaution, wear a helmet.[10]

This brief discussion of upward mobility has meant to invite our readers to the growing literature on the subject and to suggest what one will find there. We have ended our essay with it because the alleged "freedom" of the U.S. capitalist order presumes some semblance of equality of opportunity for the good life. Every Jack and Jill must have an equal chance to hit the big time. However, that kind of equality can only occur in a society in which most people have the opportunity to move upward, and that most of them who get there find their experience a joyful relief from the lesser life below. None of these two conditions exist in the U.S., as we have tried to show. Most people stay where they started, bossed around by the same people who bossed around their parents. And, if they do move up, they go to a new neighborhood in which they are at the bottom, often despised, isolated, misunderstood, and more. These, then are the two principal reasons that the fact of social classes makes the American Dream a particularly deceitful myth.

CONCLUSION

Our hope is for readers come away from this chapter considering the likelihood: that social classes exist and play a crucial role in determining who we are; that most people inherit the class position of their parents and stay there; and that numerical representations of social class, such as by income levels, badly understate the overall effects of the class system. On this last point, if we say, for instance, that the top 10% of the income classes has about four to five times as much income as the bottom 10%, the numbers understate our point. Access to four or five times as much income as the next person gives you

multiple advantages beyond the income, including especially the kinds of personal capital we have described. Being at the top of the income system means more of life itself, more of that thing that living creatures seem most dearly to cherish. Most critically, such higher income is usually translated into such advantages as healthier lungs, a stronger heart, straighter and whiter teeth, and more things about which to smile.

Given the complexity of the issue, particularly that critical dimensions of social class cannot be measured precisely, if at all, it is no surprise that in mainstream economics it is simply ignored, left for the sociologists, or other "soft" scientists to consider. And, it is no surprise that in the work of political economists, such as Marx and Veblen, and in social policies aimed at civilizing capitalism such as those developed in Sweden, the idea of social class is central. All societies generate what Shakespeare was the first to call "pecking orders," and capitalism does so in particular and predictable ways. Thus, we have brought this issue to the forefront, where it belongs.

---

[10]We should emphasize a point we mentioned briefly before, that all these barriers to upward mobility are greater for most women than for men with similar circumstances and in particular if they have children along the way. Michelle Tokarczyk and Elizabeth Fay, eds., *Working Class Women in the Academy* (1993), a book we mentioned above, has a number of essays making this point, particularly the one by Donna Langston. Another book that focuses on the relatively greater barriers to upward mobility for black women, is Lois Benjamin, ed., *Black Women in the Academy* (1997).

Chapter VI

The Middle Way: Swedish Social Democracy[1]

[In Sweden] the state, the consumer, and the producer have intervened to make capitalism "work" in a reasonable way for the greatest good of the whole nation . . . . That this constitutes a . . . middle course seems to me obvious; it is a course between the absolute socialization of Russia [the USSR] and the end development of capitalism in America. In Russia . . . the rulers of the state attempted to make all of life conform to an idea, an ideal. In the United States the profit motive was put above every other consideration and it worked to the end of blind self-destruction.
Marquis Childs, *The Middle Way*, 1936

INTRODUCTION

What Childs describes in the quotation above are two forms of economic extremism. The Soviet Union developed an economic system based on command-style communism, where the state controlled almost all aspects of the economy, while the United States over the course of its history has always had a market system, where capitalists and individuals made most economic decisions. What we will discuss below is an example of what Marquis Childs refers to as the *middle way* between command communism and unregulated capitalism: *social democracy*. Sweden developed an economic system that successfully incorporated many of the ideas of Marx, Keynes and Veblen into the economy. As a result, we can see in Sweden's system the practical application of many of the ideas of these influential thinkers. The Swedes created a society that demonstrates impressive levels of equality, stability, and productivity.

The Social Democratic Labor Party (Socialdemokratiska Arbetarparti, or SAP) that governed Sweden for most of the twentieth century took its cue from Marx, and actively worked to make Sweden an egalitarian society where there was little poverty and where all persons had the opportunity to build a good life for themselves. The SAP believed that all Swedish citizens should have the right to a decent job, to security in their old-age, to health care, to day care, to a decent standard of living. These rights evolved over the years through the ongoing implementation of innovative policies, which we will show in our brief sketch of Sweden's economic history.

In Sweden's system we also see the application of the ideas of John Maynard Keynes. Sweden was the first industrialized nation to employ Keynesian policies. Moreover Swedish economists took Keynes' ideas much further than most. During the 1920s, the Swedish government made some small efforts at stabilizing the economy, such as creating of low-wage private sector jobs for the unemployed. But during the Great Depression of the 1930s, under the direction of the "Stockholm school" of economists, the Swedish government began a large-scale implementation of Keynesian stabilization policies.[2] By 1936, the year Keynes' *General Theory* was published, when other developed countries had only begun to consider Keynes' ideas viable, Sweden had already successfully used these stabilization policies to create jobs and raise wages to their pre-Depression level. Beginning in the 1950s, Sweden took even bolder steps, carefully managing the economy so that *even in recessions*, the unemployment rate remained exceptionally low.

Sweden also incorporated the ideas of Thorstein Veblen into its system. Sweden sought to limit the predatory and wasteful aspects of capitalism, such as advertising; and instead emphasized the productive side of the economy. For instance, the media in Sweden is publicly owned and operated and high quality programming is aired without commercials. Likewise, companies in Sweden are allowed to keep their profits as long as they are reinvested in productive activities, but wasteful or destructive practices, such as polluting and downsizing, are penalized.

---

[1] Our thanks to Ellen Campbell, who helped with the research and writing of this chapter.

[2] Although Swedish economists were writing about and implementing stabilization policies at the same time Keynes was advocating them, these ideas came to be known as "Keynesian" policies because of the widespread influence of Keynes' masterwork, *The General Theory*.

In short, Sweden has a remarkable economic system that is worthy of careful study, as it provides an interesting counterpart both to the command economies of the former Soviet block and the unregulated market economies of the United States and Japan. In what follows below, we will outline what it means to have an economic system described as "social democracy." We then take you through a sketch of Sweden's economic history, which describes the evolution of what came to be called the "Swedish model" or the "Middle Way." Finally, we make the argument that Swedish socialism is a humane, productive, and civilized economic system that improves upon many aspects of the U.S. economy. We begin by exploring the curious resistance to forms of socialism seen in America.

WHAT IS A SOCIAL DEMOCRACY?

The terms used to describe the Swedish economic system, as a rule, do not carry positive connotations for Americans. For example, the term "socialism" often draws a suspicious reaction, as does the idea of a "big government" interfering with the "free" market. Consider your own reaction when you see or hear the word "socialism." Does it conjure images of Communist Russia? Anti-Americanism? A vast and inefficient bureaucracy that limits personal freedom and rights?

But what is the *real* meaning of "socialism"? In a 1967 Webster's dictionary, socialism is defined as "any of various economic and political theories advocating collective or governmental ownership and administration of the means of production and distribution of private property." Yet in a 1923 Webster's dictionary, the definition of socialism is "political and economic theory of social reorganization, the essential feature of which is governmental control of economic activities, to the end that competition shall give way to cooperation and that the opportunities of life and the rewards of labor shall be equitably apportioned…" Consider the difference between these two definitions. What happened to the meaning of this word over a period of 44 years? In the early 1900s, the philosophy of socialism was a response to the philosophy of individualism, a *cultural* philosophy and movement that encouraged self-awareness and personal gain (greed). Therefore, this earlier "socialism" was not strictly political, but social, cultural, and essentially philosophical. However, over time its meaning became more and more politically extreme as the opponents of socialism sought to demonize it. As one can see, we have so politicized the term over the years that our more contemporary dictionaries, our supposedly non-biased sources for meaning, have lost sight of its roots and define it only in political terms.

The word "democratic" has also been politicized over the years. In the United States, we promote democracy as government by and for the people. Yet there are other possible applications of democracy. Democracy in the workplace can mean workers having input into how things are produced and how the workplace is run. Democracy in a community can mean people deciding how to allocate health care and jobs. The U.S. focus on *political* democracy, especially electoral activity, over and above other arenas for democratic action, demonstrates the extent to which we narrowly define social philosophies in purely political terms. Similarly, the word "freedom" is heavily politicized in the United States. We are used to referring to "free markets," where the word "free" applies to freedom from a meddling government. But freedom comes in many forms, and historically Sweden's Social Democrats have been more concerned with a broader range of freedoms: freedom from the domination of an employer, from poverty, from the ravages of a recession.

In this essay we will challenge the traditional definitions of "socialism," "democracy" and "freedom" by moving beyond the simplistic, *politicized* uses of these terms. Forget the Republican-Democrat, right-left, conservative-liberal labels we have been trained to apply. Instead, keep in mind the philosophies that originated the meanings of these words. Unlike the caricature of socialism as a massive bureaucracy controlling every aspect of our lives, socialism is an economic system designed to promote cooperation, equality, and a high standard of living, but not necessarily at the expense of individualism. Social Democracy means the freedom for people to control collectively many aspects of their lives, not simply to choose political leaders. As we trace the evolution of the Swedish model below, we will see an example of real, democratic, socialism in practice.

THE ORIGINS OF THE SWEDISH "MODEL": 1847-1932

Many books and articles written about Sweden's economic system refer to it as the "Swedish Model." Implied in the word "model" is the idea that this was an experiment, something planned by a centralized group of intellectuals, and then implemented for the world to observe and critique. This was not the case. Sweden's system developed slowly but persistently throughout the twentieth century as a result of many decisions made by many groups striving toward the same goals of equality and quality of life. These groups included the business community, unions, politicians as well as scholars. In other words, the majority of Swedish citizens built this socioeconomic structure democratically over time.

Sweden's democratically created socioeconomic system is also referred to as a "welfare" state. "Welfare" is another term that has been politically demonized. But the fact that Sweden has a welfare state does not mean that its populace doesn't have to work because the government supports it, or that poverty is so pervasive that widespread welfare benefits are required just to keep its citizens in shoes. It means exactly what it says: "welfare" is to "fare" "well." In other words, the welfare state is designed for the benefit of the whole society.

Historically, Sweden's welfare state evolved from a society that was admirably enlightened long before its Western counterparts, and even before the Social Democrats first came to power in 1920. In 1847 and 1853 Sweden passed "poor relief laws," taking the first step toward the implementation of its social philosophy of helping those whose impoverished circumstances were beyond their control. In contrast, most of Europe still had debtors' prisons and indentured servitude at this time, when people who were too poor to pay their debts were imprisoned, enslaved, or forced into "workhouses" to work for a pittance. As examples, Paris had the Bastille, most of the first colonists in America were indentured servants from Europe, and Australia was a penal colony for Britain's criminals, many of them debtors. Whether it was a mother of three whose husband died, or a worker who was injured and disabled, the cause of the indebtedness was irrelevant. The inability to pay one's debts in these

countries was treated as a willful, punishable act. But Sweden recognized that poverty was usually neither willful nor deserving of punishment. The Swedes saw poverty as a product of economic factors, and began taking responsibility for helping their people out of poverty.

The Social Democratic Labor Party (SAP) was founded in 1889. Around this time the philosophy that produced the "poor relief laws" began to mature and expand. Instead of assessing the health of their economic system through stock prices and GDP, the Swedes began to develop a system wherein the health and value of the economy was gauged by the quality of life of its entire population. As early as 1913, Sweden's Liberal Party government (non-socialist), with the support of the populace, began broadening the range of social benefits. It took most other developed countries until the Great Depression of the 1930s to take similar steps.

In contrast, at the turn of the century Mark Twain coined the phrase, the "Gilded Age," to describe the excesses and decadence of wealthy American society. This was when the most powerful people in the American economy, appropriately termed the "Robber Barons," controlled the direction of our country. It was the economic climax of the Industrial Revolution in the U.S., and the U.S. was an exceedingly wealthy nation—or at least a few people were wealthy. The Gettys, Rockefellers, Vanderbilts, Goulds, *et al*, held virtual monopolies on our natural resources, banks and railroads, and did business without any significant government intervention. There were few corporate taxes or regulations and no laws to protect labor.

Today we take our labor laws for granted, but we can try to imagine life for the worker who didn't have the protection of the forty-hour work week, or health benefits, or safety in the work environment, or the minimum wage. In the late nienteenth century, workers had few rights in the workplace; those who weren't in unions—the great majority—were completely at the mercy of the employer who understood that the most efficient way to increase profits was to cut the costs of labor, to lengthen the workday, and even to employ children. One out of six American children under the age of 16 worked to support the family, spending twelve-hour days in unventilated, poorly lit mills, operating dangerous machinery without breaks.

This was also a time in American history when the difference in quality of life between those who owned the means of production and those who did not, was strikingly evident. Those who owned property along with the few who could afford an education had the means to consume lavishly; the lines of class division were never clearer. But for the poor of the Gilded Age, a lack of income could have devastating consequences. Being poor meant not being able to pay a doctor when sick (there was no medical insurance) or to put food on the table (there were no programs in the United States to keep people from starving).

To view the poles of this class division, begin with Newport, Rhode Island, the lovely ocean resort where the Robber Barons built their summer homes. Their architectural beauty is breathtaking -- imported Italian marble, elaborate frescoes, exotic woods, rare works of art, crystal and gilt. They installed in these palaces every known amenity and luxury, staffed them with dozens of servants, and hosted only the world's most wealthy elite for their soirees. America's laborers, who paid for these displays of decadence with their sweat and sometimes their lives, lived in a very different world. They lived in city slums that a state board of health described as "choked up with garbage, filth and mud." Workers daring to strike against low pay and poor working conditions were sometimes killed, or driven from their homes. In 1886, after sugar laborers went on strike asking for a wage of one dollar a day, thirty were killed and hundreds wounded by local authorities. In the Homestead strike of 1892 at the Carnegie Steel plant, laborers were killed, the state brought in the militia, and the strikers were arrested. Time and again, employers and the government suppressed any efforts by laborers to improve their lot.

The schools, churches and popular literature of the time taught that "to be rich was a sign of superiority, to be poor a sign of personal failure…." This attitude is reflected in the words of James Mellon's father, who declared, after his son paid a substitute only $300 to take his place in the Civil War, that "a man may be a patriot without risking his own life or sacrificing his health. There are plenty of lives less valuable." John Rockefeller, Andrew Carnegie, Philip Armour, and Jay Gould also hired substitute soldiers to go to war for them. These cowardly men were our "industrial giants."

This was laissez-faire capitalism at its *worst*. U.S. governments of this era believed that the economy should be left alone, relying on the arguments of Adam Smith, despite the fact that the economy in the late 1800s little resembled the early industrial economy of Smith's era. Competition was no longer atomistic due to the massive size of corporations, and the "invisible hand" discriminated according to wealth and privilege.

At the same time as the United States became increasingly mired in inequality at every level of society, Sweden took steps toward the development of a more humane, egalitarian system. The Liberal Party government passed the National Pension Act in 1913 to provide security for the aged, more than twenty years before the United States implemented its own social security system. In 1918 a Liberal-SAP coalition government passed a new poor law, turning the responsibility of assisting anyone in need over to local governments, while the central government contributed administrative support. This law was to remain the cornerstone of Sweden's assistance programs for the next 40 years.

By 1918, America had made only a few changes in an effort to dampen the ravages of uncontrolled capitalism, and these small efforts targeted the corporations, not the people. One was corporate taxation, and another was the Sherman Anti-Trust Act, used to inhibit only the worst abuses of the most obvious monopolies. As is typical of the United States, the government did not take actions directly to improve the quality of life for the majority, but acted indirectly, hoping to improve their lot by forcing business to mend its ways. The power and responsibility for the welfare of the worker was still solely in the hands of industry, whose main concern was, of course, profit. In the 1930s, after America's unregulated capitalism burned itself out in the form of the Great Depression, the United States finally implemented some modest social policies. But America spent ten years trying to repair the devastation caused by the Depression, and endured massive suffering in the process. Sweden largely avoided these problems because of their welfare state and their implementation of Keynesian policies.

THE SAP'S FUNCTIONAL SOCIALISM: 1932-1968

Social and Political Philosophy

The SAP began to influence economic policy immediately after its formation in 1889. At that point, it stated its guiding principles as follows:

1. Legislation to guarantee to every Swedish citizen a simple and decent standard of living…[Social Democrats] hold that it is the duty of society to provide for the needs of the aged, invalids, widows, and those who have lost their income through no fault of their own.
2. Housing and child benefits for needy families so that they should not be forced to lower their standard of living because they have children to raise. [The] idea is to distribute the expense over the entire population as a collective responsibility.
3. Social welfare to be…the inherent right of every citizen irrespective of his financial status.

In order to implement its philosophy, the SAP was forced to compromise with employers and political opponents. Compromise was possible because although the philosophy behind the SAP's ideas was socialist in nature, the SAP was not dogmatic or rigid. The Social Democrats pursued the goal of a better life for all Swedes, and it allowed the economy to operate within a capitalist system as long as they could achieve this goal.

The Social Democrats saw the problems associated with free-market as well as with state-controlled systems. From 1920 to 1932 recessions plagued Sweden's free-market economy as a succession of governments, some including the SAP, failed to stabilize the economy adequately. There was also an unequal distribution of income and wealth, and a significant percentage of the population lived in poverty. But the SAP did not adhere to the idea of state-controlled production in response to these problems, fearing the inefficiency that could come from a command-style economy. Instead, once the SAP was firmly entrenched as Sweden's ruling party in 1932, they allowed the capitalist norm of private ownership to continue, intervening in the economy whenever the needs of labor were not met. As in the U.S.

capitalist system, there were wealthy entrepreneurs who owned and controlled much of Swedish industry, but the SAP limited their power and influence. The SAP devised taxes on income and profits so that it was profitable for business owners to reinvest in productive activities and to create jobs. Entrepreneurs were allowed to make a fortune in Sweden, but only if they expanded employment, produced socially useful products, and limited the destruction of the environment. Thus the SAP permitted the private sector to pursue profits as long as firms achieved social goals. In some sectors, the SAP organized consumer and producer cooperatives, and in other sectors, such as health care, dental care and child care, the SAP socialized the provision of services, but overall the SAP preserved private ownership.

The Social Democrats established early on that equality and economic growth were not necessarily incompatible. Conservative Swedish economists who followed the ideas of Adam Smith insisted that some measure of inequality was necessary to stimulate growth: if investors, business owners and the wealthy in general, were not allowed to keep what they earned, they would have no incentive to continue investing and growth would stagnate. Thus they argued that measures to improve equality through high taxation of corporations and wealthy individuals would slow growth. Swedish Social Democrats rejected this argument, and demonstrated that public investment, stability and careful macroeconomic management could stimulate growth, which would ultimately be very profitable for industry and private individuals, providing incentives for continued investment. The Social Democrats prevailed and were able to win over industry leaders to this approach.

By no means did the Social Democrats have free rein when they came into power. The democratic electoral process remained in place, with political parties (socialist and non-socialist) and special interest groups wielding influence and power, keeping partisan measures from dominating the political arena. Powerful interest groups included both labor unions and employers' associations, and all actors within the economic system were included in the decision-making process for negotiating mutually beneficial policy and legislation. The leaders of the SAP could not have achieved their egalitarian goals without the cooperation of employers, and the fact that employers cooperated indicates the benefits all parties realized in a democratic socialist economy. Thus through pragmatism and compromise, the SAP gradually implemented socialist policies and ideals *without* a revolution or large-scale nationalization, the first socialist party in the world to do so.

De-Commodification

One of the primary (socialist) goals of the SAP was the de-commodification of the Swedish people. "De-commodification" meant taking people, and what they needed to live decent lives, out of the marketplace as mere commodities to be bought and sold. To Marx, treating people as a commodity—buying and selling labor—is exploitative, because the market value of people is measured simply by how much economic profit (surplus value) they produce. De-commodifying people meant ensuring that all people had decent lives, irrespective of market outcomes.

People need certain basic goods and services in order to live full lives. In the SAP principles mentioned above, for example, child-care is treated as a fundamental need because, as is stated, "[Swedish citizens] should not be forced to lower their standard of living because they have children to raise." In many market systems, families that have children must lower their standard of living because, in paying for the costs associated with caring for and raising children, they have less money to spend on other goods. In the United States, child-care is sold as a commodity only to families that can afford the service. When examined objectively, privatizing childcare is an exploitative practice that impacts the lower wage earners most dramatically.

The same can be said for housing, medical care, dental care, and services for the disabled. In an unregulated market system, these fundamental needs are at the mercy of for-profit industries where the bottom line, and not quality of life, is the only concern, and not everyone can purchase these necessary items. In the United States, those who cannot pay for these basic, life-sustaining services are often forced to go without, and suffer the consequences. But Sweden does not choose to value its people by such standards, and will not deny these necessities to those without money. All Swedish citizens have the *right* to essential goods and services under the Swedish welfare state.

After the Social Democrats were voted into power in 1932, they introduced legislation that began to fulfill the principles of de-commodification embedded in their social philosophy. Augmenting the Pension Act of 1913 and the Poor Law of 1918, the SAP instituted housing subsidies and a national pension scheme in 1935, and in 1938 added socialized dental care. By the 1950s, the SAP had installed a national health plan and laid the foundation for a comprehensive network of de-commodified rights for all Swedish citizens.

To this point, the provisions mentioned are those needed to survive physically. But the SAP wanted to guarantee a full *quality* of life as well. Their two main goals when they came into power were *equalization* and *integration*. Equalization refers to a better distribution of wealth and income, and integration refers, not to racial or ethnic issues, but to issues of social class. The primary objective in this realm was full employment. Putting everyone to work would diminish the exploitation of labor, reduce income inequality, and thereby further reduce class divisions. This would also eliminate what Marx refers to as the "reserve army of the unemployed." As we will describe in more detail below, policies designed to achieve full employment were put into action after World War II, policies that went far beyond simple stabilization of the economy and provision of basic services.

Equalization and integration were also accomplished through investment in *human capital*. This was, and is, primarily accomplished through education. Although the primary reforms in the Swedish educational systems took place between the 1950s and 1970s, education had for a long time been considered vital to the well being of the nation. Schooling is free at all levels in Sweden; as a result, the inequality seen in the U.S., for instance, of personal wealth buying the best education, is non-existent. All citizens are entitled to the best education, regardless of financial status, giving every person a start from a level playing field. Sweden's population is one of the most widely and best educated in the world.

As we can see, the "Swedish model" was not a planned experiment, but in fact an evolutionary process that resulted from a series of actions over long periods of time. And although the pace of structural change picked up in the 1950s, the groundwork had been in place since 1889.

Economic Stabilization and Full Employment

Most countries instituted Keynesian stabilization policies, designed to boost spending and create jobs during recessions, following the advent of the Great Depression. As noted above, Sweden's stabilization efforts preceded the Depression. The national pension system of 1913 and the comprehensive poor law of 1918 both served to boost spending when times were tough, and the Swedes instituted policies to stabilize employment as early as the 1920s. Stabilization policies in the 1930s were even more aggressive and successful. But because capital was privately owned, there was still a natural dependency on industry to stimulate the economy. The state recognized this, and a pattern of compromise between capital, labor, and the government became the method for ensuring stability, equality and growth within a highly regulated, but still capitalist system.

The Swedish government engaged in an extensive stabilization policy beginning in the 1930s, spending money counter-cyclically. When an economy enters a recession, tax revenues decrease as businesses downsize and workers lose jobs. In such circumstances, many governments decrease spending to counter the reduction in tax revenues, thereby keeping the budget balanced. But cuts in government spending during a recession put even more people out of work, making the recession even worse. Instead, Sweden *increased* spending in recessions by borrowing money to invest in public works projects, to train workers and to create jobs. This way the flow of production and income was stabilized, spending didn't decrease dramatically in recessions, industry was encouraged to invest, and the economy was bolstered until industry's investments brought employment back to normal levels.

In addition to using government spending to stave off recessions, the Swedish government instituted a counter-cyclical investment tax credit system called the Investment Reserve in 1938. Firms were allowed to deposit funds with the government which could be invested tax free if invested *in Sweden at specified times*—during a recession. If invested at another time, the firm would have to pay taxes on the funds. Thus the government encouraged the private sector to invest counter-cyclically, stabilizing the economy even further.

In the 1950s, the Rehn-Meidner plan, named after its two economist authors, was implemented to manage the economy more carefully. Included in the plan were two main areas: the solidaristic wage policy, and active labor policies. The primary goal of this plan was to ensure *full employment*.

In the U.S., full employment (or "the natural rate of unemployment") is considered to be an unemployment rate of about 5.5%. Many mainstream economists believe that an unemployment rate of less than 5.5% guarantees inflation. Labor becomes more powerful when unemployment is low because there are fewer workers available to fill jobs, and at the same time firms need labor to increase production because more goods are sold when more people are employed. Workers are able to demand wage increases, therefore driving up costs. In theory, a wage-price spiral would result from dramatically low unemployment: labor's demand for higher wages forces business to raise prices to cover the higher cost of labor; the higher prices of goods force workers to demand even higher wages, and so on. But this theory, that low unemployment always causes inflation, does not necessarily hold true.

With cooperation between the unions, employers' associations, and the government, unemployment in Sweden exceeded 3% only *three times* from 1951 to 1991, without causing significant inflation. The agreement was that real wages were increased annually at the rate of ½% below the national average rate of labor productivity growth. This meant that if workers increased their productivity by 3%, they would receive a raise of 2.5%, and employers would keep the rest. This formula insured that workers benefited from increases in productivity but also guaranteed that wages did not increase too quickly, thus keeping inflation in check.[3] In other words, wages were voluntarily limited by labor unions so that they wouldn't increase faster than

---

[3] The key point here is that if workers increase their productivity by 3%, this lowers firms' costs by 3%, since the same work force is now producing 3% more than before. Because firms' costs have decreased by 3%, firms can increase wages by as much as 3% without having to increase prices at all. Ultimately, wage increases only cause inflation if wages increase *faster* than productivity increases.

productivity, keeping inflationary pressures down, despite full employment and the accompanying power that a tight labor market gives to unions. As a result, workers did not need to strike to force pay increases, and workers and employers were cooperative rather than antagonistic—both labor and capital had a direct incentive to increase productivity since both groups benefited. Following this pattern of compromise, Sweden had full-employment without spiraling inflation for 40 years (1951-1991) and laborers received a substantial share of the benefits from economic growth, equalizing incomes to a significant degree. Sweden's experiences call into question both the theory that equality and growth aren't compatible, as well as the assumption that full employment and low inflation aren't possible. Sweden offers a striking contrast to the U.S. system where productivity increases by laborers often do *not* result in higher wages. From 1973 to 1997, the average productivity of a U.S. worker increased by 34%, but average wages for workers actually *declined* by 14%. U.S. workers actually lost ground when they increased productivity!

Solidaristic Wage Policy

Another key economic policy was Sweden's *solidaristic wage policy*. This meant equal pay for equal work: all workers at all firms doing the same type of work would be paid the wages that workers in the most efficient, internationally competitive firms were paid. Wages were set nationally in a centralized bargaining process that included employers, labor unions and the government. The equalization of wages reduced competition between workers, creating a more cooperative environment for labor and removing the inequality of less pay for comparable work. An important byproduct of this policy was that women began receiving pay equal to men. All workers then received the same annual wage increases, based on productivity growth. A provision was later added to the solidaristic wage policy to increase the wages of low-wage workers faster than the rest, to make Sweden even more equal.

Another consequence of the solidaristic wage policy was that firms experiencing rapid growth did not have to raise wages faster than other firms did. Typically, firms in growing industries (such as the internet in the United States today) have to pay laborers a premium in order to keep them.

But because of the solidarity wage policy in Sweden, the best, most competitive firms did not have to grant additional wage increases when they were doing well, allowing them to make large profits. Meanwhile, firms experiencing hard times were not able to reduce wages. As an example, in a year with 3% average productivity growth, a firm that increased productivity by 10% would only have to raise wages by the national rate of 2.5% (½% below the average rate of productivity growth). A firm with only 1% productivity growth would still have to increase wages at the same rate of 2.5%. The former firm earns excess profits, while the latter firm loses money. Thus the solidaristic wage policy caused expanding industries to do better, and contracting industries to struggle even more. The result was a reallocation of capital to profitable, expanding industries from contracting industries. The systematic elimination of the least efficient, least profitable firms, and the promotion of the most productive firms, was an explicit goal of the SAP -- an attempt to encourage the best businesses with the greatest comparative advantage. And it succeeded: from 1950-1970, the golden age of U.S. Keynesian capitalism, Sweden's per capita GDP increased by an average of 4% per year, higher even than the U.S. growth rate of 3.5%. Sweden found that the economy's overall productivity improved as the firms that increased productivity gained excess profits, which were then pumped back into the firm, generating economic growth. The unions, employers associations and government, working to energize the economy, supported this reallocation of capital.

An interesting point here is that declining industries were not "bailed out" by the government, but if they failed, they were reabsorbed by successful industries. This harsh but realistic approach kept the economy growing and competitive. Instead of pouring funds into dying industries, investing resources in growth industries stimulated productivity and improved competitiveness. This is one of the reasons why Sweden's economy performed successfully even with all of the restrictions on corporate behavior imposed by the SAP.

Active Labor Market Policies

Another way of maintaining full employment was via *active labor market policies*. For those who became unemployed, there were generous unemployment benefits with a time limit, training and education with a stipend, and money for relocation costs if needed. If a worker was still unemployed when the benefits ended, there was employment available in short term public works projects (the Swedish government established itself as the "employer of last resort" for those workers who could not find work after a certain period of time). Unemployed Swedish workers were given money, time, training, and moving assistance to make sure they could find a good job to replace the one they lost. And if they could not find a job, they were put to work in community projects that needed attention.

Active labor market policies, along with stabilization policies, produced full employment without accelerating inflation in Sweden from 1951 to 1991, as noted above. Full employment is beneficial to any economic system: all workers remain productive, the stream of income and spending supports the economy, industry profits and invests, tax revenues support the government, which in turn supports the full employment system, resulting in a self-sustaining economy in which everyone benefits. The cooperation between labor, capital and the government in the institution of the "middle way," and the benefits that each group received as a result of it, helps to explain the widespread support in Sweden for a socialist model of development that is almost inconceivable in the United States. By 1968, Sweden's system was the envy of much of the world. Swedish firms were internationally competitive, Swedish workers were among the best paid in the world, and poverty and homelessness were eliminated. But labor leaders still thought Sweden could be improved.

SWEDEN BECOMES MORE SOCIALIST: THE LABOR OFFENSIVE, 1968-1976

Despite the relative generosity of the Swedish welfare state, labor leaders during this period decided that is was time for Sweden to become even more socialist in nature. They were dismayed at the vast profits being earned by Sweden's huge transnational corporations that in part resulted from the solidarity wage policy that controlled wage increases at the most profitable firms. The SAP believed that the vast wealth being generated for a few wealthy individuals was unfair and threatened the integrity of the system. Labor wanted to negotiate a fairer distribution of the excess profits that firms were receiving because of union wage restraint.

Furthermore, labor leaders became increasingly concerned with the boring, stressful jobs, typical in Swedish industries, that Marx would describe as alienating in nature. In keeping with the idea that all Swedes have the right to *meaningful* work, labor leaders began to push for greater labor control over the workplace. A series of strikes and work slowdowns led to concessions from employers and workers did gain more control over the workplace. Factories were redesigned to be more flexible, to increase efficiency, and to give workers more control over the work process. Jobs were rotated so that no one laborer was stuck with a particularly dull task for too long a period; the most repetitive jobs were mechanized and workers were retrained for more highly skilled work. Workers also gained more control over job security and promotion. Thus Swedish workers were able to avoid many of the negative consequences of deskilling that Marx saw as an inevitable part of capitalism.

During this period, the SAP also increased the benefits provided to Swedish citizens. Employees were given the right to take educational leaves to upgrade their skills or change professions, health benefits and industrial safety measures were expanded, and the government instituted new programs to promote gender equality. The SAP also began to move more explicitly towards traditional socialism during this period through the institution of *wage earner funds*: employee investment funds that were to be funded by taxes on corporate profits. The SAP intended the funds to be used to buy up shares of companies, so workers could gradually gain a voice in all business decisions. Once labor leaders became owners, they would sit on corporate boards and directly influence corporate decision making. Laborers could then keep firms from moving overseas, or downsizing workers unnecessarily. The funds would also inject Swedish firms with new capital for investment, and gradually generate a more equitable distribution of ownership and wealth as workers became part owners, and eventually majority owners, in all large Swedish firms. Note that although the principle of worker ownership of the means of production is certainly a Marxist concept, the Swedish vision differed from that of the Soviet Union. The Swedish vision was for workers at each firm to control how it was run. This differs from the Soviet approach in which a centralized government bureaucracy controlled the direction of all firms.

Swedish economist, G. Adler-Karlsson, eloquently stated the ideals behind the push for wage earner funds in 1970:

> Let us look upon our capitalists in the same way as we have looked upon our kings in Scandinavia. A hundred years ago a Scandinavian king carried a lot of power. Fifty years ago he still had considerable power. According to our constitutions the king still has equally as much formal power as a hundred years ago, but today he is in fact powerless. We have done this without dangerous and disruptive internal fights. Let us in the same manner avoid the even more dangerous contests which are unavoidable if we enter the road of formal socialization. Let us instead strip and divest our present capitalists of one after another of their ownership functions. Let us give them a new dress, but one similar to that of the famous emperor in Hans Christian Andersen's tale. After a few decades they will then remain, perhaps formally as kings but in reality as naked symbols of a passed and inferior development stage.

Thus the SAP pushed for the gradual transition from highly regulated private ownership to a socialization of the means of production in the hands of the working class—a peaceful transition to socialism. As one can tell from Adler-Karlsson's statement, the SAP believed that socializing the means of production would lead to a superior society. But it was not to be. Wage earner funds were controversial even within the SAP, and they were never fully instituted. Nevertheless, the SAP was able to extend the welfare state during this period, as noted above.

Unfortunately, these demands by labor and concessions by employers came at a time when the world was facing a global recession. The oil crisis of 1973 began a period of world-wide economic instability that would change the economic landscape of many industrialized nations. Sweden in particular suffered, because it was totally dependent on imported oil as its energy source. Inflation reached 10% in 1974, unemployment increased, and capital experienced rapidly rising costs in a highly regulated system that limited the ability of a firm to escape these high costs. This is when profound economic, political and welfare changes began to take place, resulting in what some have termed "the decline of the Swedish model."

CAPITAL'S OFFENSIVE, 1976-1999.

The economic difficulties of the early 1970s caused Swedish voters to oust the SAP and elect a center-right government that was more conservative, and more sympathetic to industry. This ushered in an era in which big corporations successfully fought to roll back taxes and the welfare state. The erosion of the Swedish system began when employers abandoned the practice of centralized bargaining with labor that had been in existence since 1938. Instead, they turned to bargaining individually with their labor unions, undermining the solidaristic wage policy that had been a cornerstone of Swedish democratic socialism. The "divide and conquer" strategy was somewhat successful. With such a vital element of the system disempowered, corporations excluded workers more and more from the decision-making process, and increasingly moved operations overseas.

Along with the center-right government, employers worked to cut taxes and decrease government spending and government control over the economy. For example, the investment tax credit system, which gave businesses incentives to invest during recessions, was abolished. Corporations were now free to invest whenever they wished without tax penalties. But an even more significant change was the deregulation of capital markets in the 1980s, as Swedish firms were allowed to invest abroad instead of just at home, and funds could be moved freely internationally for the first time in many years. The result of the newfound ability of capital to invest wherever it wanted, and tax cuts that increased the amount of money at capital's disposal, was a boom in asset markets. Money flowed rapidly into real estate, art, and other speculative, non-productive assets, resulting in huge price increases for these assets—a speculative boom. Unfortunately, as spending increased but productivity did not, an overheated economy resulted, generating inflation as high as 10.5% in 1990. Gregg Olsen, in his article entitled "Re-Modeling Sweden," (*Social Problems*, February 1996, p. 8) describes the debacle that followed:

> The Swedish credit market . . . was rapidly deregulated throughout the 1980s. By the end of the decade, Sweden's long standing system of controls over foreign investment and exchange and the financial sector were effectively eliminated. Finance houses proliferated during this period, and money flooded into office buildings and real estate, both in Sweden and abroad. However, the speculative boom ended in short order. The Swedish credit system foundered by the end of 1991, forcing the government to divert tax revenues to bail out several of its major banks at a cost of 3% of GDP. The near collapse of the key banks and insurance companies that comprise the financial industry helped to bring the international recession to Sweden.

As a result of the collapse of the speculative boom, many assets became worthless, leading to large financial losses for many banks and businesses. Sweden's central bank responded to the overheated economy of the late 1980s with tight money policies, generating huge increases in interest rates to rein in inflation. Real interest rates reached an incredible 14% in 1992, leading to significantly higher unemployment, as consumer spending dropped and business investment collapsed. The combination of high interest rates, the bursting of the speculative bubble of the 1980s, and an international recession all during the same period proved devastating. In 1991, the Swedish economy entered its deepest recession since the Great Depression, with unemployment reaching 8%. The economy has since rebounded, although unemployment remains much higher than it was previously (unemployment was still 8% in 1996, vs. the post-World War II average of 2.4%).

The rise of Sweden's business interests and the subsequent decline of the power of labor unions parallels the experiences of the U.S. as well as other developed nations with the advent of globalization. In essence, globalization erodes the power of labor, because instead of paying organized laborers higher wages at home, businesses will now move to a country where wages are low and where labor unions are suppressed. As a result, we see employers worldwide pursuing a race to the bottom, seeking out the lowest wages and the least organized labor.

The Swedish Welfare State Since 1976

A major goal of the conservatives who ruled Sweden from 1976-1982 and 1991-1994 was to reduce the size of the Swedish welfare state, by reducing taxes and cutting government spending on social programs. They reduced the top tax rate from 85% to 50%, extended sales taxes to make up revenue, and reduced but did not eliminate benefits for parental leave, health and dental care, housing, unemployment, retirement and sick leave. These policy changes helped to produce a doubling of the poverty rate in Sweden from 1978 to 1992, although as we will see below, the Swedish poverty rate nonetheless remains the lowest in the world. Sweden also experienced the inevitable decrease in equality in all areas—the rich grew richer while the poor grew poorer, wage inequality between men and women increased, and opportunities were no longer as equal. The "fare well" state was under attack.

Even more drastic changes in the welfare state were enacted during the 1991-1993 recession. A new center-right government, elected in 1991, instituted corporate welfare programs (subsidies and tax breaks for corporations), and privatized education, child-care, and health care in some cases. Prior to this time, Swedes had widely accepted the idea that benefits should be universal, and not subject to the inequities of the market (i.e., de-commodified), so these changes marked a significant departure in philosophy. Nevertheless, much of the Swedish welfare state remained in place, and the return to power of the SAP in 1994, as voters rejected the conservative government because of its failure to improve Sweden's economic performance, meant a renewed commitment to democratic socialism. The partial erosion of the welfare state in Sweden led some conservative commentators to talk about the "end of the Swedish model." However, as we will see below, Sweden retains a vast government sector that still safeguards the social and economic rights of its citizens. And overall, Sweden's recent experiences are not unique: the Swedes faced the same hardships that all developed countries faced beginning in the early 1970s.

Sweden's Economic Performance Since 1970

In general, the economic performance of Sweden deteriorated after 1970 due to a number of factors, including globalization, industrial decline, and the aging of the population. With the advent of increased global competition, traditional manufacturing industries that Sweden specialized in, such as cars and household durable goods, faced more competitive markets. Furthermore, Sweden's huge industrial giants were unable to adjust and move out of declining sectors and into rising sectors of the global economy, much as the rust belt industries in the United States had trouble adjusting. Some industries even gave up producing in Sweden and moved operations to less costly locations in the Third World.

Sweden also faces an aging population, which means fewer working people supporting more and more elderly. Gregg Olsen ("Half empty or half full?" *Canadian Review of Sociology and Anthropology*, May 1999) notes that Sweden has the largest proportion of seniors in the world today. A natural byproduct of these demographic changes is a less productive economy. The United States will be facing a similar problem in the years ahead as the baby boomers retire in larger and larger numbers.

These forces—global competition in traditional manufacturing, the flight of transnational corporations to the developing world, the aging of the population—have presented problems throughout the developed world. For instance, both Sweden and the United States experienced slower economic growth and a more unequal distribution of income since 1970. Although Sweden faced higher levels of unemployment and stagnation in the 1990s, while the U.S. economy experienced relatively more economic growth, Sweden's average real economic growth rate from 1967-1996 was 2.1%, while the real growth rate in the U.S. was 2.5%.

Conservative commentators argue that the generous benefits of the Swedish welfare state also may have contributed to the difficulties in staying competitive in the global marketplace of today, although the evidence on this issue is mixed. Sweden's welfare state expanded dramatically after World War II, yet as noted above, Sweden's

average real economic growth rate from 1950 to 1970 was 4%, ½% higher than the U.S. average real rate of growth over the same period. Given this fact, there is clearly no reason to think that the welfare state is inherently inefficient or that it constrains economic growth. In actuality, it was when the welfare state was eroded and markets deregulated that Sweden's economic performance began to decline, a trend we also see in the experiences of the United States.

The problem with the Swedish approach may actually have been that their government was not active enough in guiding industrial development. Unlike the government of Germany that focused government resources on key growth industries such as computers, the Swedish government allowed its industries to determine where to invest their funds. While Sweden's active labor market policies successfully solved their unemployment problem, the lack of an active industrial policy to help Sweden's industries evolve created problems. The efforts the government did make in the last 20 years, to prop up declining heavy industries, were very costly and did not succeed in making these industries competitive.

The Results of Capital's Offensive

Since capital's offensive began in the 1970s, all Swedish governments have pursued a less regulated form of capitalism. Even when the SAP has been in power recently (the SAP governed from 1982 to 1991 and from 1994 to 1999), it, too, largely pursued a market-based agenda. The pursuit of these policies on the part of all political parties in Sweden is strikingly similar to political developments in England and the United States, where conservative groups pushed the economy in a free-market direction, formerly liberal groups (Democrats in the U.S., the Labor Party in England, the SAP in Sweden) turned to a moderate market-based approach, and organized labor ceased to be as powerful a voice in national politics.

As in the United States, Sweden is now dominated by huge Transnational Corporations (TNCs). Industrial concentration in Sweden is extremely high (a small number of large firms dominate the economy), in part because of the solidaristic wage policy which made it more profitable for large, efficient, export-oriented companies. As these companies increased in size and power, they pushed for a deregulated market approach to the economy, along with membership in the European Union so that they would have even more mobility and more markets in which to operate. Swedish TNCs now attack any form of government regulation in the popular press, criticizing the "public sector," the "welfare state," and "collectivism," while supporting the market economy, which supposedly generates a "free and good society." Sweden's CEOs now regularly threaten to relocate outside of Sweden unless the government creates a more business-friendly environment for them. And many businesses are carrying out these threats. Despite being profitable, Volvo closed its taxpayer-financed plants that experimented with worker autonomy and a more humane work place, moved some operations overseas, and sold out to Ford.

Meanwhile, as TNCs offer a united front in favor of unregulated markets, Swedish labor unions fight amongst themselves, and the SAP is no longer directly associated with the labor movement. The welfare state is largely intact, shored up by the return of the SAP to power in 1994, but industrial relations between employers and unions have been dramatically altered, and the new government's ability to pursue equality and stability is, in the words of Gregg Olsen (1996, p. 16), "severely circumscribed in a neo-liberal [laissez-faire] environment dominated by TNCs and global financial markets." In order to qualify for the Euro and to appease the huge conglomerates that dominate Sweden, the SAP-led government recently agreed to deeper cuts in the welfare state and new efforts to fight inflation. [4] The cuts in government spending and the high interest rates necessary to fight inflation resulted in chronically high levels of unemployment in the 1990s. But it is important to remember that being unemployed in Sweden does not have the

devastating consequences that it can have in the United States, because of the generous welfare system and the potential for retraining for a new job. And Sweden remains committed to equality and to collective decision-making, with the participation of labor, capital and the government. With the SAP continuing to enjoy broad-based support and with labor unions still relatively powerful, the "Swedish model" will be in place for the foreseeable future, albeit in a somewhat less progressive form than its 1970s incarnation.

CONCLUSION: THE CASE FOR SWEDISH DEMOCRATIC SOCIALISM

Despite the recent erosion in some areas of the welfare state, Swedish social democracy remains intact, and there is no denying the effectiveness of the Swedish model over the last 60 years. The SAP returned to power in 1994, as voters tired of conservative policies that failed, to solve Sweden's social and economic problems. Over the last few years, the SAP has resumed its egalitarian approach to running the economy and restored most of the welfare state. Ultimately, Sweden's system for most of this century has been, and still is based on the following general goals and principles:

1. **Economic development and efficiency**. In order to have a prosperous society, the economy must function efficiently, and in a worker-friendly manner. This means cooperative management of the economy to serve the needs of society, but not necessarily government control of the entire economy. Cooperation between labor and capital can increase efficiency and productivity, resulting in fewer strikes, less litigation, more rapid technological change, and innovative forms of work organization.
2. **Economic well-being for all**. The benefits of prosperity should be shared with all citizens. This can only be accomplished with the de-commodification of all basic necessities.
3. **Solidarity**. Individuals are members of a community, not only with rights but with obligations to that community as well. A society based on mutual cooperation is preferable to one based on unmitigated competition.

---

[4] Sweden signed the Maastricht treaty to link their currency with other European currencies, with the ultimate goal being the establishment of one currency in Europe -- the Euro. Hence, the Euro is the currency that all European countries that sign the Maastricht treaty will use in the future. But in order to qualify for the EURO, Sweden must obey the following strict macroeconomic rules: 1) budget deficits cannot exceed 3% of GDP; 2) the national debt cannot be greater than 60% of GDP; 3) inflation cannot be more than 1.5% above the average of the inflation rates of the three EU members with the lowest level of inflation; 4) long-term interest rates cannot be more than 2% higher than that achieved by the three nations with the lowest inflation rates; and 5) exchange rates must fall within the Exchange Rate Mechanism.

4. **Universality and equality**. All Swedes rely on the same network of services and participate in deciding how the local government operates these services. This network gives everyone a stake in the system as well as a voice. The provision of a wide range of services is a buffer against the predatory nature of an unregulated market system, while local control over services is a buffer against an overly controlling or inefficient national bureaucracy. This builds both equality and community.

5. **Democracy and cooperation**. Every society needs rules, which should be determined by the people themselves, and not unduly influenced by money. True democracy means that workers should have input into management decisions as well as political decisions, otherwise society degenerates into a barbaric system in which only the wealthiest and most aggressive prosper, and where workers are exploited. Firms influence the direction of the economy, as do labor unions and community groups. These groups must work together and compromise for the economy to work effectively.

6. **Education and access to information**. In order for a democratic society to work, all citizens need to be well-educated and informed. One measure taken by the Swedes is public control of the media in order to insure an unbiased flow of information. Swedish radio and television is run by the Swedish Broadcasting Corporation and contains no commercials. Programming emphasizes education and information in addition to entertainment.

7. **Pragmatism**. The SAP is remarkably free of dogmatism, and has shown itself to be quite flexible. The goal is to establish a society that benefits all people, and if this can be achieved without worker control of the means of production then the SAP accepts that. On the other hand, the SAP refuses to accept the social costs associated with unregulated capitalism.

In Sweden, democratic socialism resulted in an economy that is remarkably prosperous, and one that has the least poverty, the most equitable income distribution, and the highest levels of spending on health and education in the developed world.

Further, Sweden has succeeded in Keynesian stabilization policy and the pursuit of full employment far better than any other developed country. From 1950 to 1991, a period of 42 years, Sweden's unemployment rate only exceeded 3% a total of three times, whereas U.S. unemployment exceeded that level 38 times. Sweden's average rate of unemployment, even including the deep recession of 1991-1993, is amazingly low when compared with other European and developed (OECD) countries, as table 1 below indicates.

Table 1. Average Unemployment Rates for Sweden, the U.S. and Other Developed Countries, 1960-1994

Country or Group of Countries	Average Rate of Unemployment
Sweden	**2.4%**
All OECD countries	5.2%
15 European Union Members	5.6%
United States	**6.0%**
Canada	7.3%

Source: Olsen 1999.

Sweden was able to maintain full employment because of the following factors: 1) wage restraint on the part of labor, as part of the nationwide collective bargaining agreement; 2) an unemployment benefit system with a fixed duration of benefits, a wide range of labor-market programs to promote the acquisition of skills, and strict work requirements; 3) an active labor-market policy in which the government created jobs (through public works and employment subsidies), provided training, assisted people in finding jobs and moved them to areas where there were jobs (there is a nationwide labor-market exchange which matches job seekers with jobs).

Sweden demonstrated conclusively that there is no reason for a country to live with a high "natural" rate of unemployment in order to have price stability. As Swedish economist Rudolf Meidner stated, "There is no such thing as a natural rate of unemployment. The level of employment and unemployment is significantly influenced by what the government does. It is a result of economic policies. . . . Price stability and full employment are not incompatible goals." Sweden's inflation rate averaged 6.4% from 1961-

1996, 33% higher than the U.S. average inflation rate of 4.8% over the same period, but the average unemployment rate in the United States was *150%* higher than Sweden's unemployment rate.

Despite the existence of extensive benefits for those who do not work, Sweden has the highest labor participation rate in the world. Whereas mainstream economists predict that generous welfare benefits provide a disincentive to work, the Swedish experience demonstrates that people *want* to be productive (Veblen's instinct of workmanship), and that if work is not drudgery people will work willingly and enthusiastically.

Sweden's experiences with economic growth are similar to those of the United States, with relatively high rates of growth for much of the 1870-1970 period, and slower growth since 1970. The build-up of the welfare state in Sweden was quite compatible with their economic growth.

The benefits of social peace and stability along with public investment in infrastructure and human capital more than offset the high taxes and the restraints on businesses. The cooperative nature of economic decision making, with businesses, labor unions and the government all participating, insured that economic growth could occur in a socially responsible context.

Meanwhile, Sweden also succeeded in creating one of the most peaceful, crime-free, egalitarian societies in the world. They de-commodified many aspects of the market system, thereby insuring that all citizens have the right to a good education, housing, health care, and a job. As table 2 below indicates, the rights of a Swedish citizen are much more extensive than the rights of an American citizen. If you came from an average family, which society do you think would be most

Table 2. Rights of a Swedish Citizen vs. Rights of a U.S. Citizen.

	SWEDEN	U.S.
PARENTAL LEAVE	All parents have the right to stay home and care for an infant for up to one full year per child at 90% of normal salary. All parents also receive a child allowance to cover the costs of raising children.	All parents have the right to six weeks of unpaid leave to care for a newborn child. Some parents receive monetary assistance for a limited period of time if they are very poor.
VACATIONS	*All* workers get at least five weeks of paid vacation per year plus extensive sick leave benefits.	U.S. workers *may* get at least two weeks of unpaid vacation per year *if* they are permanent employees; there are no mandatory vacations for temporary employees, and no one is guaranteed sick leave.
HEALTH CARE	All citizens receive high quality health and dental care, with modest co-payments up to a maximum yearly payment. Care is generally so good that even the wealthy use public health care.	Medicare and Medicaid provide health insurance to the elderly and very poor. Many workers receive health insurance through their employer, but over 43 million Americans, including 10.7 million children and many of the working poor, have no health insurance.
EDUCATION	Free education is provided for all citizens at all levels, including college, vocational and adult education (for those people who want to explore new careers). Adult students receive time off from work and a stipend. The quality of education is so universally high, that even the children of the Swedish King attend public schools.	Free primary and secondary education is available to all citizens, with the quality varying widely depending on where one lives. People living in a poorer school district generally receive an inferior education. Some limited funding is available for college students, but college is often beyond the reach of the poor and the lower middle class. What funding is available is usually in the form of loans, creating a long-term debt for most.
JOB TRAINING	Free training is provided to all citizens who desire it. Those undergoing training receive a stipend from the government.	Some training programs exist, but they are limited in nature, and usually only to the poor. Trainees do not usually receive a stipend.
EMPLOY-MENT	The Swedish government believes that every citizen has the right to meaningful work. Unemployed persons receive unemployment benefits, retraining, or a job in a public works project.	*Some* of the unemployed receive up to 6 months of unemployment benefits and job search assistance. After six months, benefits are cut off.
SOCIAL SECURITY	All Swedish citizens receive a pension from the state, which pays people at least 75% of what they earned when they were working, or a guaranteed minimum amount if they did not work.	Most U.S. citizens receive social security benefits, but often the payments are not enough to live on.
HOUSING	If Swedish citizens cannot afford a house, they are given a housing subsidy. Sweden does not have a problem with homelessness due to the success of their housing and anti-poverty programs, and they have no slums.	Some U.S. citizens receive housing subsidies or a spot in public housing. But many citizens do not qualify for these benefits, and the U.S. has a significant number of homeless people. Every major U.S. city has slums.

Figure 1: The Size of Government in Advanced Industrial Countries

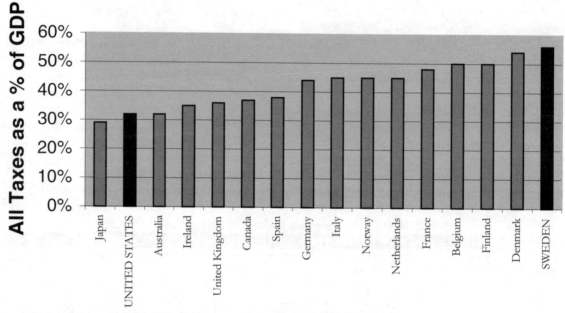

Source: *Statistical Abstract of the US*, 1998. Since government regulations and programs require tax revenues for funding, the tax rate is a good proxy for the size of government. All taxes (state, local & federal) are included.

pleasant place to live in?

Because of its extensive system of benefits and rights, proportionally Sweden has the largest government sector in the world. The Swedes believe this to be necessary to control aspects of life that should not be left to the market. As figure 1 below indicates, Sweden and the other social democracies of Europe have the largest proportional governments, while the United States, United Kingdom and Japan have among the smallest governments. This is a clear indication of the economic philosophies of the different countries. Sweden, Denmark, France and the Netherlands, to name a few, believe that all citizens have the right to a decent standard of living and real opportunities. They use government programs to insure that all citizens have these rights. The U.S., the U.K. and Japan do have substantial governments, but these countries leave much more up to the market than does Sweden.

As figure 2 shows, through extensive spending on education and social programs,

Sweden has virtually eliminated poverty. Sweden's large government is accompanied by the lowest poverty rate in the world, a byproduct of its highly regulated economy and generous allocation of rights. Meanwhile, the U.S. has one of the smallest governments in the world, but also the highest poverty rate of all developed countries. Many, if not most, poor people in the U.S. are not able to lift themselves out of poverty through their own efforts, and often they are characterized as lazy or incompetent by those who are more privileged. The reality is that most poor people want to work, but do not have the necessary resources (education, a car, work clothes, child care, or opportunities) available to them that would allow them to find self-sustaining employment. Together, figures 1 and 2 conclusively demonstrate that a country *can* eliminate poverty if it is willing to spend the money, but without such intervention, many people will remain poor.

Table 3. Inequality in Sweden and the United States, 1989.

GDP going to each group (%)	Poorest 20%	2nd Poorest 20%	Middle 20%	2nd Richest 20%	Richest 20%
United States	4.6	10.6	16.5	23.7	44.6
Sweden	8.1	12.1	16.7	25.3	37.8

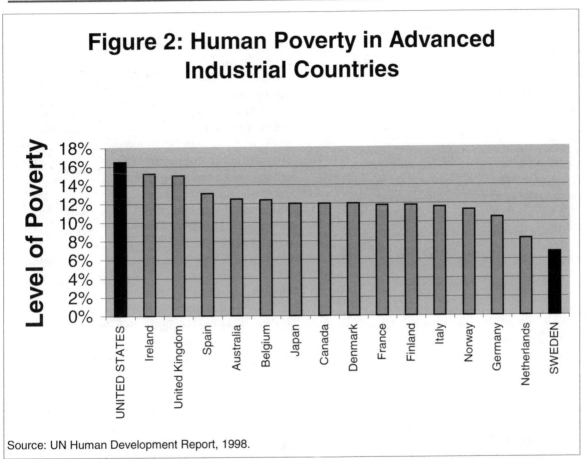

Figure 2: Human Poverty in Advanced Industrial Countries

Source: UN Human Development Report, 1998.

In addition to eliminating more poverty than any other country, Sweden has one of the most egalitarian societies in terms of income distribution. Its highly progressive tax and transfer system insures that those who have the most contribute the most, and those who have the least are guaranteed a decent income. Table 3 hows how much more equal Sweden is than the U.S. as a result of its different tax and transfer system. The bottom 80% of the population does much better in Sweden than in the United States. Sweden's highly progressive tax system contains within it a value judgment about different kinds of consumption based on the ideas of Thorstein Veblen. It is assumed that the consumption of basic necessities by all people is more important

than the consumption of additional conspicuous luxury goods by the wealthy. In contrast, most U.S. politicians argue that the wealthy have the right to spend all their money as they see fit. Many conservative politicians in the U.S. even want to create a flat tax, where the rich and the poor would pay the same marginal tax rate. In the United States, with the central position given to individual choice in consumption decisions, there is no stigma attached to a rich person spending $1 million for a yacht, but politicians who propose that society has a responsibility to spend an equivalent amount on health insurance for 250 uninsured children are criticized for advocating big government. Swedes find this U.S. method of allocating resources immoral and barbaric.

Explicit in Sweden's extremely high inheritance tax, which helps reduce incomes at the top, is the egalitarian idea that everyone should start life at a reasonably similar level. Most Swedes agree that people with money should not be able to live on the dividends coming from an inheritance simply because their ancestors made a fortune. True equality of opportunity means that all people have equal access to education and that even the children of the rich should have work. Furthermore, in order to avoid alienation, that work should be meaningful and workers must have some control over the workplace.

In another nod to Veblen, Sweden dramatically restricts advertising and instead channels funds into productive areas such as research and development. As noted above, the Swedish Broadcasting Corporation runs television and radio and airs all programming commercial free. Newspapers receive state subsidies so they are not entirely dependent on ads. Again, Swedes make a value judgment about economic activity: advertising is wasteful and commercial impulses distort the content of television and newspapers. While the U.S. media resists "restrictions" on programming, most Swedes believe the commercial nature of the media in the United States is much more restrictive, and not in society's best interests. Can we really depend on the huge corporations that own the media to present a balanced version of the news? If so, then why haven't we all heard more about the success of Sweden's economic system?

It is often said that the United States is the land of opportunity, yet most working people do not have an equal opportunity to succeed because they lack access to equal education and training. In Sweden, *all* citizens have access to a high quality education. The United States is spoken of as the land of the free because we have few government regulations over the marketplace. This gives us the freedom to succeed and to keep most of the money we make. We also have the freedom to work wherever we want—but often for next to nothing! This is, of course, a freedom much admired by some Swedes: the corporate bosses.

Swedish economists also question whether the United States is truly prosperous in any meaningful sense. Despite rapid GDP growth during the 1990s relative to the rest of the world, should the U.S. be boasting about a level of prosperity that is benefiting only a small percentage of the population and that was built on the low wages of workers with declining, or no benefits? Shouldn't U.S. citizens be concerned that despite this supposed prosperity, millions of people in the United States are condemned to poverty, including many children, and over a million poor people are in prison? The debtors' prisons of the 1800s are reviled in history books, but is imprisoning poor, desperate people who resort to crime really so different? Is the purpose of an economy to generate billions for Bill Gates or to generate the greatest standard of living for all that belong to that society? In all of these ways and more, the democratic socialism of Sweden serves most people better than the (largely) unregulated capitalism of the United States.

Thus the experiences of Sweden demonstrate the possibility of a "Middle Way" between unregulated capitalism and command communism: democratic socialism. Sweden may not be a paradise on Earth. Sweden has problems just like all other countries. People there complain about their high taxes and their sometimes inefficient government. But building on the ideas of Marx, Keynes and Veblen, Sweden proved that a country can maintain full employment, be efficient and productive, and give every citizen the right to decent levels of food, clothing, health care, to a job, and to some control over their lives. Ultimately, each country must decide what things to leave up to the market and what things should be determined by the collective decisions of all citizens. In the United States, most things are allocated based on how much money a person has, which gives unprecedented levels of freedom and choice to the very wealthy, but leaves much of the population without the basic necessities of life. Perhaps the United States is the land of the free— if you're rich. But for everyone else, democratic socialism seems to provide more freedom and better opportunities.

Chapter VII

A Political Economy Critique of Mainstream Economics

This essay is written in the spirit of a 1978 saying by the Chinese revolutionary, Mao Zedung: "Let a hundred flowers bloom." After three decades of dominating political discussion and practices in China, the communist revolutionaries were seeking the views of everyone else. The analogy to our essay is that the discussion about the economy in the capitalist world has long been dominated by one line of thinking, which we will define below as the "mainstream" of economics. Alternative ways of thinking about capitalism have emerged, but they have fallen from favor in mainstream economics and most students taking economics courses in the United States today will not hear about them.

WHAT IS THE MAINSTREAM OF ECONOMICS WE ARE TALKING ABOUT?

We are going to discuss different approaches to studying the economy, as well as their potential for producing useful information. Concerning mainstream economics, we must first of all emphasize that, like all social theory, the mainstream school constitutes a broad spectrum of often conflicting ideas. Practicing economists, like all real people, are never fixed on a particular point of any spectrum, but are closer to one part of it than to others. Economists from every school borrow, consciously or otherwise, from others because there is such a wide and open diffusion of economic ideas in the modern world. Thus, when we refer to "mainstream economists" we are necessarily lumping them into a single category that is an obvious distortion, and it is not altogether satisfactory to us.

Our critique in this essay refers mostly—but not exclusively—to economic models that (1) are narrowly conceived, (2) are quantitative and expressed in complicated mathematical terms, and (3) depend upon certain, restrictive assumptions about how people behave, always have behaved, and always will behave. Without question, there are mainstream economists who engage in lively debates on virtually all of the topics we take up in this essay. Many of them move beyond the strict confines of models and assumptions to examine institutional aspects of the economy. And many investigate empirically with statistics, and in other ways, the actual behavior of people, instead of assuming that they all behave in the same, predictable way.

Why, then, do we focus on those mainstream economists who most narrowly conceive the subject? There are two parts to our answer. The first is that this subset of economists dominates contemporary economics, and it exercises its dominance primarily through its almost exclusive control over graduate training in economics and the most prestigious economics journals. It is also the subset that has produced all but one or two of the Nobel Prize winners in economics. The second reason for our focus is that, of all schools of economic thought we know about, this one is least likely to produce results useful to the public. A genuinely interesting irony underlies what we write about in this essay: the very "best" economists, in the view of this dominating subset, produce the least useful kind of economics. Aside from the irony, given the difficulty of defining our terms, we can only hope that by the time our readers have finished this essay, our lumping distortion will have some justification and not preclude a consideration of what we argue.

Having made this disclaimer about our use of terms, there remains a critical distinction between *all* versions of mainstream economics and what we call political economy. This distinction is a matter of "methodology," or "method of analysis." Mainstream economists are trained to limit the scope of their analyses—that is to limit the breadth of knowledge they bring to bear on an issue-- compared to political economists. Moreover, in choosing a relatively narrow focus, almost all mainstream economists have gradually and systematically excluded from their studies the political economy point of view. As an example of the consequences of this kind of exclusion, it is difficult for political economists to accept gracefully the attention given in mainstream economics to, say, the theory of consumer demand when ordinarily none is given such ideas as Veblen's notion of "conspicuous consumption" or Marx's theory of "surplus value." In sum, the political economy critique presented here is both a general critique of the mainstream methodology, and a more specific critique of the subset of mainstream economics that is most narrow in its approach.

Now we will turn to a more concrete discussion of the terms we have introduced.

AN EXAMPLE OF THE DIFFERENCE BETWEEN THE MAINSTREAM AND ITS ALTERNATIVES

We will use the term "political economy" to refer to the major schools of economic thought that have developed alongside and in opposition to mainstream economics, and now have been purged from it. What do we mean by the "political economy" view? Consider an example that demonstrates the wide chasm between mainstream economics and Marxist economics, a principal kind of political economy, in terms of how each views the production of *business profits* in a capitalist system. A mainstream economist might put it like this:

> Profits are the payoff to private individuals for "entrepreneurship," for having saved, or borrowed, funds to invest in productive inputs, for having the foresight to know what goods or services to produce with these inputs and the talent to manage how the inputs are used and the goods marketed. Profit-making is the central vehicle by which capitalism is energized because: (1) by investing the funds, producing the goods, and making the profits, the enterprising capitalist gives jobs to people who are not capitalists themselves and who need those jobs in order to live; (2) the capitalist will make the highest profits only by producing goods and services most demanded by consumers; and (3) it is the competitive quest for profits that gives capitalism its extraordinary dynamism and proven ability to drive from the field all competing economic systems.

On the other hand, in the Marxist view, profit is looked upon in this different sort of way:

> Over the past 400 years, through its drive to accumulate profits, the capitalist class— by pillage (such as the enclosure movements), murder (wars against and systematic impoverishment of Third World Nations), and domination (of workers, consumers, and politicians) —has come to own the resources, factories, and other

capital equipment needed to produce goods and services needed by all. Prior to the emergence of capitalism, most people were peasants who owned enough capital goods to produce a livelihood. However, gradually they were stripped of these capital goods, and in order to live they necessarily became wage workers for capitalists. Further, at their jobs workers must produce a value greater than their wage (surplus value). Thus, a substantial portion of the value created by labor is seized by the owner and becomes the owner's profits. Further, competitive pressures (1) force capitalists to treat their workers as *things*, commodities do be bought and sold like steel ingots or sheets of plywood, and (2) shape many capitalists into predators working against the best interests of the larger society.

It is almost as if two different species of beings were talking about two different worlds. How can such great divisions of opinion exist between economists when they take a look at something as central to capitalism as the profits that fuel it?

POLITICAL ECONOMY: A GENERAL DEFINITION

For our definition of political economy—and we say "our definition" because there are others that refer to schools of thought within the mainstream framework—we will repeat the definition we used in our brief preface to this book:

> Political economy…is more concerned [than mainstream economics] with the relationships of the economic system and its institutions to the rest of society and social development. It is sensitive to the influence of non-economic factors such as political and social institutions, morality, and ideology in determining economic events. It thus has a *much broader focus* than [mainstream] economics (Riddell, Shackelford, and Stamos, *Economics: A Tool for Critically Understanding Society*, 5th Edition, 1998, emphasis supplied).

Two points merit special emphasis. The first is that, as we mentioned above, political economy has a "much broader focus" in the sense that political economists are willing, as one writer put it, "to let more things into the analysis." Second, as we are using the term, it refers rather specifically to the schools of thought that followed in the wake of Karl Marx, Thorstein Veblen, and John Maynard Keynes. Because of the wide influence of their ideas on successive generations, we have separate essays on them in this book, along with an essay on social classes in capitalism and one comparing U.S. capitalism with the Swedish economy, one importantly shaped by Swedish political economists.

We are able to talk in the same breath about differing schools of thought in political economy, even though there are important distinctions among them, because they share the following critical judgments:

1. Although most mainstream economists claim that they are doing "economic science," it fails to explain and predict actual events in the real world.

2. A principal reason for this inability to explain real events is the key assumption of "economic man" in mainstream economics, along with a parallel assumption that human beings by nature have "unlimited wants for consumer goods."

3. Mainstream models are typically not presented in the historical context that shapes all human events; and, furthermore, virtually all mainstream economists are ignorant of the history of economic ideas, and thus unaware that the principal assumptions of their analyses have been under challenge by political economists for over two centuries.

4. Mainstream economists typically presume a separation between economic activity and political power.

5. Graduate economic programs are largely confined to mainstream instruction, and a particularly narrow version of that school of thought.

THE CLAIM THAT MAINSTREAM ECONOMICS IS A "SCIENCE"

The debate about methodology between the mainstream and political economists has been going on for a long time, but it has mostly been an academic affair. However, sometimes it gets aired in public, as in a recent article by the principal *New York Times* economics writer, Louis Uchitelle. We insert that article here in a slightly abridged form because Uchitelle neatly summarizes the overall issues we want to discuss. (And you might note that Uchitelle tends to lump all economists into two or three broad groups. As you read the article, try to keep in mind our earlier discussion of the implicit problems of doing this.)

"A Challenge to Scientific Economics: An Older School Looks at a Broad, More Intuitive Picture While Modernists See Just the Numbers and Facts." *New York Times*, January 23, 1999, p. B7.

Robert L. Heilbroner, [whose] 1953 book, "The Worldly Philosophers," has sold nearly four million copies [and] is a "Profiles in Courage" of the great thinkers who shaped modern economics...is at one end of a growing debate over whether economics, as practiced today, is effective. Sure, economists do a lot of good research, Mr. Heilbroner, now 79, acknowledges. Some of it yields important insights. But their models are too simplistic. They overlook factors that shape the economic and social system and in doing so forfeit the deep understanding achieved by an Adam Smith or a John Maynard Keynes, two of his worldly philosophers.

"The worldly philosophers thought their task was to model all the complexities of an economic system -- the political, the sociological, the psychological, the moral, the historical," Mr. Heilbroner said. "And modern economists, au contraire, do not want so complex a vision. They favor two-dimensional models that in trying to be scientific leave out too much and leave modern economists without a true understanding of how the system works...."

The shift from this way of thinking came after World War II, when economics gradually ceased to be a social science and took on the techniques of a natural science. Mathematics became the language of economics, and computer models of the economy became the chief research tool. These models require assumptions about the way markets and people behave, assumptions that are often unrealistic, although in recent years economists have fed more and more actual data into their equations in an attempt to approximate the real world....

That still falls short of what Mr. Heilbroner has in mind. The modern economists separated out the subjective, often intuitive judgments that earlier economists had considered so important. These were considered not susceptible to scientific inquiry, not measurable.

In the process, economists also squeezed out the word capitalism, the once traditional name for the market system, with its subjective connotation of class struggle between owners or managers and workers and with its suggestion of the privileges that go with various levels of wealth....

Paul Romer, a 43-year-old Stanford University economist, would classify [these suggestive judgments] as political or public policy issues but not part of a scientific explanation of the workings of the economic system...He likens an economist's role to that of a doctor who explains what will happen if a cancer patient is taken off an aggressive program of chemotherapy and radiation. "You can let the pastor, the legislator, the family and the philosopher struggle with the moral question of whether to actually stop the treatment," Mr. Romer said, "but what you want from a doctor is correct scientific statements about what will happen if."

Keynes made no such distinctions. Drawing on intuition, observation and his own broad experience, he concluded that the United States and other nations found themselves stuck in the 1930's Depression in large part because business refused to invest, although the nation offered plenty of savings to finance investment. Keynes' sweeping insight forever changed the way economists think about the way a capitalist system functions. And Keynes, having found the problem, saw no reason to be shy about solutions, calling for enormous Government spending to offset the decline in business investment. "Keynes certainly had a view of what was a good society," said Robert M. Solow, a Nobel laureate in economics at the Massachusetts Institute of Technology. ..And he tried to save society from itself"....

Leaving Politics to the Politicians

[S]cience does not take you far enough, says Mr. Heilbroner, an economics historian at the New School for Social Research. "You have to ask [for example] what is the correlation between high levels of education and high levels of wealth," he said. "Is education in our system a privilege of wealth and a function of the class structure?"

These are questions that science cannot address but economics must, says Mark Blaug, an economics historian. Otherwise, the findings are skewed. "There are so many things going on in the economics world at the same time," he said. "Not just standard economic forces, but all the other elements that shape an economy -- politics, morals, psychology, sociology -- and therefore economics will always be vague and imprecise, more like history than math." Going beyond science sits easier with older economists like Mr. Heilbroner or Mr. Blaug, who is 71, or Mr. Solow, who is 74 and, like Mr. Heilbroner and Mr. Blaug, came of age as an economist in the 1950's, while Keynesianism was still in its heyday and the cold war had not yet helped squeeze value judgments out of economics.

Mr. Solow, however, is a pillar of mainstream economics. His economic growth theory, in which he explained the interactions of capital, labor and technology in generating economic expansion, is a model of economics practiced as a science. He would never, he said, "advise a student to go to work on the nature of the class structure...You are condemning him to failure," he continued. "We do not know if there are applicable rules." And yet in an autobiographical sketch, he argued against thinking of economics as science with a capital S. "That is perfectly consistent," he wrote, "with a strong belief that economics should try very hard to be scientific with a small s. By that I mean only that we should think logically and respect fact." Fact, he said, should be enlarged "to include, say, the opinions and casual generalizations of experts and market participants, attitudinal surveys, institutional regularities, even our judgments of plausibility. My preferred image is the vacuum cleaner, not the microscope."

[Gradually] economics is moving this way...[and the] new approach was on display at the recent annual meeting of the American Economics Association, where economists at one session reviewed their research into today's unusual spectacle of an unemployment rate and an inflation rate falling together instead of moving in opposite directions, as economic theory dictates and as they once did. Drawing on psychology, the researchers have even tried to quantify how people actually behave or feel about work. "Our modeling now is much more flexible," said Lawrence Katz, a Harvard labor economist. "I really think we are seeing a blossoming of a broader social science field, where the core research techniques are maintained but are supplemented with findings from other fields that were once quite separate."

Judging Numbers, Not Just Calculating

And Mr. Heilbroner applauds. But it is not, in his view, enough. The questions that absorb the younger economists are too narrow, he says. From Adam Smith's day, economics has always been an inquiry into the nature of capitalism in its various forms, an inquiry that requires as much history, sociology and ethics as it does science, Mr. Heilbroner says.

Economists, for example, cannot just chronicle the rise of output as an economy grows. There must also be a judgment about the quality of that output: Does it show up as more school construction or warmer clothing in winter or as more channels of bad television programs and higher pay for chief executives. That is how the worldly philosophers would have thought, Mr. Heilbroner suggests in a new chapter added to the seventh edition of "The Worldly Philosophers," to be published in the spring by Simon & Schuster.

"Economics will not, and should not, become a political torch that lights our way into the future," he writes, "but it can and should become the source of an awareness of ways by which a capitalist structure can broaden its motivations, increase its flexibility and develop its social morale."

To summarize this debate, we have Professor Heilbroner expressing the political economy view by arguing that the most serious shortcoming in mainstream economics is its use of "simplistic models," and that "trying to be scientific...leaves modern economists without a true understanding of how the system works." And, on the other side of the debate—the version of mainstream economics that is our focus—Professor Romer argues that we want from economists "correct scientific statements about what will happen *if*." In a middle ground is mainstream economist Robert Solow, who prefers economics "as a vacuum cleaner, rather than a microscope," and wants economics to be a "science with a small s."

But, then, Solow adds a telling point by saying he would not advise his students to study the "class structure" of capitalism because there are no "applicable rules to study it." In making this comment, Solow points to a dimension of mainstream economics that sharply distinguishes it from political economy and that greatly limits it as a potential source of useful knowledge. This dimension is its steadfast refusal to include social class, among other things, as a legitimate category of study, despite the obvious and enormously important fact that we are all fundamentally shaped by the economic class in which we originate, and that most of us will end up in the same class where we started. In eliminating the class system from their analytical purview, mainstream economists bring to the table an exceedingly odd dish.

THE EVOLUTION OF ECONOMICS TOWARD "SCIENCE"

The history of this dispute among economists about economic methodology is a complicated story, only part of which is told in Uchitelle's article, and we need to add a few details. Uchitelle tells us that the "shift" toward mainstream thinking came following World War II, "when economics gradually ceased to be a social science and took on the techniques of a natural science...and mathematics became the language of economics, and computer models the chief research tool." However, the story starts at least as early as the fifteenth and sixteenth century in Europe, when essentially religious explanations of the universe gradually gave way to scientific ones, and with stupendous effects on the world. Columbus's voyage to the New World, Galileo's telescope, Harvey's findings about blood

circulation, and Newton's discovery of certain laws of gravity—along with many similarly astounding discoveries in the seventeenth and eighteenth centuries—made inevitable the declining influence of non-scientific explanations of the world. This scientific assault on alternative explanations of human beings and their universe continued, and of course, continues now.

The horrific conditions for many workers crowding into European cities since the early eighteenth century led to the development of a new practical science, public health. The public health "movement" led governments to promote the habits of healthier living and, especially, to construct systems to protect water systems from sewage. This movement was complemented greatly by the discoveries in the nineteenth century of Louis Pasteur and others unveiling the role of invisible bacteria in the spread of disease. Together, public health and biological science led to a dramatic increase in the life span in industrializing nations after the late nineteenth century. The average life expectancy in the U.S. in 1776 was about 35 years, about 50 years in 1900, and is now about 75 years. Research done by the Museum of Natural History suggests that, "From 1900 to 1990 we have gained about 25 years of life expectancy; nearly equal to what had been obtained in the preceding 5000 years of human history!" (This quote was taken from the MNH web site, *www.amnh.org.*)

Not surprisingly, the success of the natural and physical scientists in actually giving more life to people in industrial countries led others to try to duplicate their methods of making assumptions, especially about things that were regular and could be measured, drawing hypotheses, and testing these hypotheses "in the field." It is true that in the case of the two most influential economists of the eighteenth and nineteenth centuries, Adam Smith and Karl Marx, the former wrote without mathematics, and Marx confined his quantitative analysis to a few simple algebraic notations. However, by the late nineteenth century most economists had adopted some version of the "scientific method" as their approach and, in doing so, marshaled the economics profession toward mathematics and statistics.

Also during the nineteenth century, economists adopted the idea of "equilibrium," borrowed from physics, and it became integral to their analyses. In doing so, economists made an extraordinary leap of faith about their ability to study and predict human activity. When social theorists use the idea of equilibrium in model building they are implying that patterns of human life in a fundamental way are analogous to (say) the equilibrating balance of forces in our solar system that keeps Mars, not to speak of monstrous Jupiter, from ramming us, head on. That is, this idea presumes that the economy is typically *stable*, but when buffeted away from stability, will always return on its own. A critical implication here is that, if the economy is assumed to be stable and self-correcting, it is better to allow it to function on its own, without extensive government interference. These equilibrating systems, whether among the planets or in people's activity, suggested to Adam Smith and to many economists after him, that they were "natural," and this meant they were "God's work." Smith also believed that individuals possessed a natural self-interest that would lead to "the best of all possible worlds," an idea whose modern embodiment we will take up in detail later on.

Alfred Marshall, an especially influential British economist writing in the late nineteenth century, was particularly important in this evolution from imprecise economic language to the precision of quantitative models that incorporated the idea of equilibrium. Though Marshall warned that "economics cannot be compared with the exact physical sciences," he still believed that economics was specially "advantaged" over the other social sciences because:

> …a person's motives—not the motives themselves—can be approximately measured by the sum of money, which he will just give up in order to secure a desired satisfaction; or again by the sum which is just required to induce him to undergo a certain fatigue (As quoted in Riddell, Shackelford and Stamos, p.8).

This means that the prices we pay for products, the amount we invest to try to make profits, and the wage that will induce one of us to go to work, are all *numbers*, that is *quantities* that can be everlastingly manipulated by mathematics and analyzed by economists. Marshall and most of his contemporaries thought that the focus of economists should be the prices that emerge in what he called "the ordinary business of life." This meant, for example, to learn how self-interested individuals formed the prices for products, for labor, and for money (interest rates) in competitive markets. Marshall and his contemporaries

recognized the aggregate economy as cyclical; however they also thought it was actually formed by all the individual markets added together, and essentially behaved no differently than would a single one of them.

Competitive markets were thought to work with equilibrating precision, and in the hands of Marshall supply and demand, acting as if "two blades of the same pair of scissors," were the prime determinants of market price. Complementing Marshall's system, and developing along with it, was the work of economists who saw markets as driven by "marginal" decisions made by producers, consumers, and workers, that is decisions about whether to produce an additional unit of production, to purchase an additional item of consumption, or to work an additional unit of labor time. In this theoretical world, capitalists made decisions by projecting the revenue and cost—thus also the profit—of the next (marginal) unit to be produced; and consumers behaved in terms of the marginal satisfaction anticipated from a product measured against its marginal cost. Some practitioners of this sort of analysis, who were called "marginalists," even imagined a system of mathematical notations incorporating the marginal decisions of all economic actors into one giant quantitative model.

The marginalists, in focusing a microscope on the margin of economic actions, were especially important in prompting economists to think narrowly, an ironic consequence of their desire to explain everything with a single giant model. Their method implied the fateful idea that the institutional structure of capitalism outside individual markets, such as its system of social classes and the distribution of income and power, was not within the scope of economics. Marginal analysis also implied an extremely limited role for government. If the system was the outcome of a limitless number of individual marginal decisions made in self-regulating markets, then the thick fist of the government could not be expected to solve any "economic" problem.

In 1879, Professor Marshall published the prototype for the modern economics textbook, which he called *Industry and Trade*. By 1890, he was calling his book *Principles of Economics*, and in this version the geometric models of supply and demand that all principles students must now learn appeared as footnotes. Though Marshall kept the diagrams in his footnotes, economists who followed with their own principles texts gradually moved the diagrams from the footnotes up to the text where ultimately they would dominate. Thus began the joyful birth, or sad decline, depending on your view, of twentieth century economics.

Further leading to quantification of economics was the theorizing of the British economist, John Maynard Keynes. In his revolutionizing book *The General Theory of Employment, Interest, and Money* (1936) Keynes used geometry, mathematics, and compelling and elegant prose to revolutionize the way that modern economists think about the business cycle. Keynes' work, which our readers will take up in another essay and in economic principles courses, gradually won over most economists in the capitalist world. Actually, Keynes preferred a dense prose to mathematics or geometry as a way to express his economic theories. And he different crucially from the classical school in arguing that capitalism was not a self-equilibrating system (as our readers will learn from reading the earlier essay on Keynes.) Nevertheless, Keynes' followers constructed diagrams and formulae to carry his theories forward, and these "macroeconomic" models, like the market analysis of Alfred Marshall and the marginalists, successfully lured more and more economists into the encapsulating, and, no doubt many economics beginners would say, suffocating, webs of a geometric world.

In 1948, Paul Samuelson of MIT, using his own two-volume mathematical expression of mainstream economics as a model, wrote the first widely used economics textbook. He combined Marshallian analysis, by then called "microeconomics," and Keynesian macroeconomics and called his book *Economics*. This title was, of course, greatly misleading given all the many kinds of economic analysis, most especially political economy, that he simply ignored. Samuelson has, in updating his book over the years, gradually added considerable non-quantitative materials, but the geometric models and other quantitative materials that make up the theoretical core of mainstream economics remain central. Samuelson's amalgamation of microeconomics and macroeconomics has come to be called 'neoclassical" economics, and within the economics profession is the common way to describe mainstream economics.

On this matter of what to call the various schools of economics that we have discussed above, there are several possibilities. John Kenneth Galbraith has called the dominating school of economics, from Adam Smith until our own time,

the "central tradition." We will use that term on occasion. Most typically, we will draw from a fusion of terms used by Marx, Keynes, and Samuelson, as follows: we will refer to the central tradition in economics from Adam Smith until Keynes' *General Theory*, in 1936, as "classical" economics. For economists in the central tradition after 1936, we will continue to use the term "mainstream," or "neoclassical."

ECONOMICS: THE SCIENCE THAT IS NOT SCIENTIFIC

We all know the old saying, "the proof of the pudding is in the eating," a metaphor so compelling it has for a long time become part of the language. It is in the terms of this metaphor that mainstream economists answer such critics as Robert Heilbroner, to whom they say: "Our assumptions might be unrealistic, and our models might be narrowly conceived, but they work better to predict *economic* behavior than the theories of our competitors." That is, "the proof of models is how well they work."

This aspiration to "correct scientific statements," as Paul Romer puts it, implies that mainstream economists are doing science in the same way that natural or physical scientists do it. Yet, in comparison, consider the example of physicists. It is beyond dispute that they know some things, such as the law of gravitational pull, more or less for sure. And, in the case of medical doctors, though often differing on particular diagnoses, they also know countless things with a degree of certainty, such as specific physiological dimensions of, and limitations of, the human body. On the basis of highly predictable outcomes, physicists and other real scientists have enabled human beings to live longer and to transform utterly their natural habitat, perhaps to the edge of ruining it. However, there is nothing similar in the annals of economics, and there probably can never be a set of principles, models, theories, conclusions, or predictions comparable to those in the physical sciences on which economists based their methods of inquiry.

We are not questioning whether mainstream economists work diligently and honestly, as do the real scientists. Nonetheless, economists don't know with any degree of certainty what is going to happen in the next instance with respect *to anything*. And, that is why they always disagree about *everything*. To make the point, we've constructed below a partial list of central questions concerning how the capitalist economy operates, or how it should operate. As you study economics, no matter what version of it, you will discover that *there is not now, nor has there ever been,* universal agreement on the answers to these questions among people calling themselves economists:

- How should we measure the unemployment rate and what will it be next month?

- Will the aggregate economy go up next month? Or down? Or stay the same? What will happen to it if government personal income taxes?

- How do you measure inflation, and how does it affect various people?

- What has caused capitalism to dominate its rivals? Is it economic freedom? Is it greed? Is it imperialism? Is it brilliant entrepreneurship? Is it the surplus value taken from the hands of workers and made into machines?

- Why are people rich or poor in capitalism? Luck? Greed? Connections? Hard work and perseverance?

- Does free-market capitalism generate the kind of competition that forces firms to operate in society's long-run interest, or do firms, unregulated, run roughshod over small rivals, consumers, and needy politicians, and promote environmental degradation?

- Is economic power distinct from political power; and if they are not distinct, how are they meshed; and how do they affect such aspects of the economy as wages, profits, laws regulating the economy, interest rates, prices, exports and imports?

- Is a growth in GDP a good thing, or a bad thing? Is the Federal Reserve System a "neutral monitor" of monetary policy, or primarily concerned with protecting the interests of wealthy bondholders?

- Is a certain amount of unemployment a "good thing" for capitalism?

- Does capitalism "provide economic freedom directly [and] also promote political freedom?" (Milton Friedman, 1962)? Or is advocating capitalism "Like the elephant running through the chicken yard, yelling everyone for himself"? (Lester Pearson, past Prime Minister of Canada, 1962.)

To summarize our point about this list in another way: if you were to choose *at random* any professional economist in the world and ask that person any question on the list above, *there is no way to know in advance of asking what his or her answer will be.* If this were true, for example, of the science of physics, in what shape would the space program be?

THE ECONOMIC MAN IN MAINSTREAM THEORIZING

In the view of political economists, the unrealistic treatment of how people behave in capitalist societies is a critical flaw in mainstream economics. The essential assumption of neoclassical economics is that people are utterly selfish, pleasure-maximizing automatons who respond in predictable ways to all stimuli. This theoretical creature is called "economic man," or sometimes "rational man," and this man is not the kind of human being the rest of us would ever know, want to be, or take home. John K. Galbraith, probably the most famous contemporary American economist, and a long time critic of mainstream economics, has written that the assumption of economic man as a rational maximizer:

> …requires that the ultimately valid propositions of economics be essentially given, like the structure of neutrons, protons, atoms and molecules. Once fully discovered they are known forever. Unchanging also, it is held, is human motivation in a competitive market economy. Such fixed and permanent truths allow economists to view their subject as a science… From this closed intellectual exercise, which is fascinating to its participants, intruders and critics are excluded often by their own choice, as being technically unqualified. And, a more significant matter, so is the reality of economic life, which, alas, is not, in its varied disorder, suitable for mathematical

replication (*Economics in Perspective: A Critical Analysis*, 1987, pp. 284-85).

This quotation carries many layers and meanings worth dwelling on. Along with Galbraith, we are not contesting the idea that most human beings will try to serve their own long term interests as well as they can. It is, therefore, not unreasonable to assume that in capitalist societies most of us will seek some of our rewards from the marketplace, whatever our role in it. Yet, this readily observable fact can not help us to know, simply by looking at another human being, what he or she will do in the market *at the next moment*. It is the central practice of real scientists to experiment with the objects of their study until, in their labs, they come to know with some confidence, what consistently will happen to "y" if they change "x"? This is not what mainstream economists do because their subject is human behavior, something we can never predict with the kind of confidence that makes real science possible. Therefore, while the scientists are doing science, economists are, as John Maynard Keynes argued, engaging in an exercise in logic based on assumptions that can't be proven rather than on countless tests in labs that produce essentially the same result.

We need to make our point carefully here, so repetition is in order. We recognize that there are broad patterns of behavior in capitalist markets that are broadly predictable. In fact, almost all of us order our individual worlds in terms of these patterns of behavior. However, to go from *broadly predictable* patterns of behavior to the assumption that all of us, all the time, have the knowledge, time, and inclination to maximize economic gains, carries us from reasonable observation to basing economic models on a badly distorted mirror of real human activity. For example, in order to predict consumer behavior, neoclassical models usually assume that: all people have perfect information about all of the goods that they might want to buy, they know all of the prices and qualities involved, they know how much satisfaction they will receive from each product if they buy it, and they are completely rational and self-centered. These assumptions imply that when we shop we are not influenced by store displays or other impulses that might interfere with the rational calculation of which good will bring the greatest satisfaction to us per dollar we spend. This view of how human beings shop in modern capitalist cultures is, to put the best light on it, quixotic. More important than what we call it,

mainstream economists necessarily presume it when they talk about "rational" or "economic" man.

There is a further problem here. In mainstream economics, economic man has also long been the idea of "man with unlimited wants." William Rohlf, writer of a popular and typical mainstream introduction, reveals early on a central intellectual foundation of mainstream thinking with the following extremely crucial argument:

> The fundamental problem facing individuals and societies alike is the fact that our wants exceed our capacity for satisfying those wants (*Economic Reasoning*, 4th ed., 1999, p. 4).

What could be wrong with this statement? Most prominently, it is "outside" history and, as such, it bases the economic analysis that will follow in Rohlf's book on a "made-up" human being, one constructed for the sake of that analysis rather than one inferred from what human beings have actually done. Thorstein Veblen saw the assumption of a rational economic man as central to what he called "the hedonistic approach" to economics, his description of the central tradition in his own day. In 1919, Veblen described actual human beings as:

> [P]roducts of…hereditary traits and past experience cumulatively wrought out under a given body of traditions, eventualities, and material circumstances. The economic life history of the individual is a cumulative process of adaptation of means to ends that cumulatively changes as the process goes on, both the agency and his environment being at any point the outcome of the last process. His methods of life today are enforced upon him by his habits of life carried over from yesterday and by the circumstances left as the mechanical residue of the life of yesterday (*The Place of Science in Modern Civilization,* 1919).

What, then, do we think human beings are for the purposes of studying their economic behavior? For an answer from political economy, we extend these comments from Veblen by buttressing them with some evidence from history.

ECONOMIC MAN AND HUMAN HISTORY

One of the most renowned economists of the twentieth century, Joseph Schumpeter, proclaimed, in his *History of Economic Analysis*, that:

> What distinguishes the 'scientific' economist from all other people who think, talk, and write about economic topics is a command of techniques that we class under three heads: history, statistics, and 'theory…Of these fundamental fields, economic history—which issues into and includes present-day facts—is by far the most important…If starting my work in economics afresh, I were told that I could study only one of these three but could have my choice, it would be economic history that I should choose (Schumpeter, 1954, p. 12).

History was an essential part of economic analysis, according to Schumpeter, for three reasons. First, a grounding in economic history allowed the analyst to understand the economy as a process unfolding in historic time. In other words, to understand the present, Schumpeter argued, we need first to understand the past. Second, historical analysis incorporates the important institutional "data" that are often excluded from mainstream economic analysis. Finally, Schumpeter argued that those who fail to examine the historical record are likely to commit "fundamental errors" of analysis.

As we have said, one of the more "fundamental errors" of mainstream economics has been to insist that the "hedonistic" tendencies of human beings were present from the dawn of time. In fact, these habits have been accumulated by people in the relatively short era of world history that is capitalism, mostly by those living after 1500 A.D. in Western Europe and North America. Adam Smith argued persuasively that self-interest and the human propensity to barter and trade were natural (i.e., genetic) traits of human beings. Smith reached his conclusions by observing people in his own time making exchanges based on self-interested behavior, and he subsequently decided that the "propensity to truck, barter and exchange"—to offer a good or service to someone else only in exchange for an equally valued good, service, or the equivalent in dollars—must be a natural instinct. Moreover, the self-interested trader would only trade to become better off, due to the

ubiquitous profit motive. Hence transactions between humans in the capitalist age came to be seen as exchanges between two flinty-eyed, rationally-calculating, self-interested beings who were always looking to profit on any deal. This model left little room in human behavior in the market place for altruism or sentimentality.

Was self-interested exchange a "natural" tendency of humans? When Smith wrote in 1776, he was ignorant of, or ignored, the writings of those historians of the ancient world who had described a very different system of exchange in the ancient economies of Greece and Rome. In these ancient civilizations, exchange most often took the form of elaborate systems of reciprocity or redistribution. Ancient Babylon and Egypt both operated systems of redistribution whereby most of the produce of the nation was collected, recorded, and then placed in centralized storehouses. In lean times (to which these primarily agricultural civilizations were especially susceptible), the stored produce was redistributed to all of the citizens, be they peasant, weaver, or potter, according to their needs, not sold to the highest bidder. These economies were organized along the lines of gigantic households, in which all members of the society were expected to make their contribution to the household and in turn to share in the nation's produce. The Biblical story of Joseph[1] (more recently popularized as the guy with the amazing technicolor dreamcoat) describes just such a redistributive system as well as the rationale for the redistribution based on collective capacities and collective needs, rather than individualistic exchange. Recall that the brothers of Joseph, after selling him into slavery years before, came to Egypt in hopes of asking for some of the stored grains so that they could survive the famine in their native land of Canaan. Joseph, in his capacity as manager of the Pharaoh's stores of grains, gave generously to his brothers, despite their mistreatment of him so many years earlier.

Other exchange often took place for honorific or social purposes, rather than for economic gain. Another Biblical example describes the honorific

---

[1] To construct a pre-capitalist history of trading patterns by human beings, Karl Polanyi used the Bible, along with mythology, literature and the visual arts, and other available written sources. We highly recommend his *The Great Transformation* (1944) because it sought a solution to the puzzle of "what is human nature" in the annals of human history rather than by mistakenly assuming, as do the dominant mainstream economists, that predatory capitalist behavior and compulsive shopping, for example, are representative of all human behavior for all times.

exchange between King Solomon of Israel and King Hiram of Tyre. Hiram offered Solomon all the cedar and fir trees that he needed for the temple he planned to build, and in exchange Solomon offered him wheat and oil. This was not economic exchange but an exchange of tributes (1 Kings, 5). Economic historian, Karl Polanyi, described many such systems of reciprocity—for example, giving gifts of fruit to kinspersons and receiving in return gifts of fish—which existed in pre-capitalist societies present and past. Polanyi argued that this was not barter and trade, but rather a socially-organized system of reciprocity, based on sharing with the rest of the community (Polanyi, 49). To sum up, in *The Great Transformation,* Polanyi argued:

> [A]ll economic systems known to us up to the end of feudalism in Western Europe were organized either on the principles of reciprocity or redistribution, or householding, or some combination of the three….In this framework, the orderly production and distribution of goods was secured through a great variety of individual motives…Among these motives gain was not prominent (p. 55).

The obvious implication of Polanyi's point is that the mainstream argument—that self-interest and the instinct to barter and trade is a *natural* trait of human being—is at odds with the historical evidence. The most we can say is that self-interested behavior came to be rewarded in pecuniary terms during the short span of human history occupied by capitalism, and that five hundred years of capitalism have probably reinforced self-interested behavior in ways that make it difficult to suppress. But the latter is a very different proposition than to argue that self-interest is inherent in human behavior. And, in some societies dominated by private firms—such as in Sweden—public policy is nevertheless based upon such human motivation as generosity and reciprocity, rather than on the assumption that all people are greedy in all their transactions.

Space does not allow us to tell the stories of how the first markets emerged and then became the ubiquitous markets of economic theory, or how the human yearning to be productive and creative came to be twisted into a labor-leisure tradeoff in modern economics. Suffice to say that a careful study of history is an essential part of economic analysis. Keynes argued that "the economist must study the

present in light of the past for the purpose of the future," and to borrow an idea from philosopher, George Santayana, we might say that economists who ignore history are doomed grievously to misinterpret it. Whether using the lessons of history in formulating present-day policies to make a better future, or whether testing the theories of modern economics against all of the learning of historians, history is indeed an essential part of the study of economies.

MAINSTREAM ECONOMICS AND THE HISTORY OF ECONOMIC IDEAS

A related flaw in mainstream economics is that it is gradually eliminating from the discipline the history of economic ideas. Nothing demonstrates more completely the myopic mainstream vision than that it has expunged Veblen and Marx, and put Keynes out on the margin, those economists many twentieth century scholars consider three of the most instructive modern thinkers. There are many costs in doing this. First of all, economists are human beings like the rest of us, and thus their ability to think clearly about the world constantly competes with the Byzantine mix of distorted memories, fantasies, and prejudices that constitute the mind of anyone. This is no small matter, because another aspect of the growing domination of economics by mathematics and abstract geometry is to create the false impression that the models are somehow above memories, fantasies, and prejudices. Nonetheless, even the most abstract models were imagined and constructed by *human beings*, and it is not humanly possible for a person to think any thought that has not been sullied by the myriad waves of stuff that swirl through a mind.

Therefore, our focus on these economists themselves is motivated by two main reasons. The first is the reminder that economics is the study of human culture *by* human beings who, in a vastly complicating part of the mix, live in and have attitudes about that world they are studying. These prejudices arising from the stuff in our heads, and the fact that we are part of the world we are trying to study, are further reasons for disagreements among economists. Such prejudices would, thus, help to explain the story about the alumna who visits her old economics professor a decade after graduating. She notices a final exam on the professor's desk, takes a quick look and blurts out, "Isn't that the same exam I took?" The professor replies smugly, "Yes, but that was ten years ago. Now the answers are different."

Second, we have included articles on Marx, Veblen, and Keynes because they stand out among modern economists in producing political economy of the highest order. As you read about their fiercely independent ideas and see them as grandly confident thinkers, you will likely better understand the wide influence of the worlds they imagined. Keynes founded modern macroeconomics and forever changed the way that economists, and those who listen to them, view the world. Veblen challenged, and his "institutionalist" followers, including John K. Galbraith, continue vigorously to challenge, the central notions of mainstream theory, and particularly its efforts to explain economic activity without regard to the findings of the other branches of knowledge. Veblen continues to have much to tell us about how our economic life is rooted in behavior, such as "shopping 'til we drop," that can likely better be understood by the categories of anthropology, or abnormal psychology, than by those of modern economics. And, of course, Marx remains among the most influential thinkers in the modern world, even after the fall of the communist states, because his ideas remain relevant as a critique of capitalism.

THE MYTHICAL SEPARATION IN THE MAINSTREAM BETWEEN ECONOMICS AND POLITICAL POWER

In addition to concluding that mainstream economics has peopled its models with creatures existing in a historical, psychological, and cultural vacuum, political economists are also highly critical of the mainstream presumption that "economics" is distinct from "politics" or "power." As a typical example from one economic principles text (an example picked at random from a shelf of them), there is the following statement:

How did the very wealthy get that way? Of the 400 people on the Forbes magazine list of the richest people in America (with an average wealth of about $500 million each), about one-fourth got rich through inheritance. The other three-fourths, such as Bill Gates of Microsoft, got rich through working, starting their own businesses, inventing new products, and so on (Alan Stockman, *Introduction to Economics*, 2nd Edition, Dryden Press, 1999, p. 425).

Notice how Stockman avoids mention of government, the legal system, or any other institutions related to political power that might have played a role in helping the Fortune 400 amass their wealth. And this is true, even though about 100 pages earlier, he actually mentions monopoly charges brought against Microsoft Corporation by the U.S. Justice Department. In fact, wealth becomes accumulated in any society, either from inheritance or some other way, *because the laws allow it to happen.* For instance, as recently as 1959 the highest (federal) marginal tax rate was *91%*! Since then, the laws have been changed, and now the highest marginal rate—for income over $271,000—is 39.6%. In other words, today's Fortune 400 are accumulating their wealth faster than in 1959 partly because lawmakers changed the laws on their behalf. For a comparison, Sweden's welfare state provides all citizens, among other benefits, health care and schooling, and to pay for these benefits Swedes pay over *half* their income in the form of taxes. In the United States, this average tax rate is about 30%, meaning that we have a very different set of rules regarding how much wealth and income you get to keep for yourself and how much will be used for broader, social purposes.

As a second example of how government is involved in this process of wealth creation, journalists Donald Bartlett and James Steele (in *America: Who Pays the Taxes?, 1994)* demonstrated the extent to which many of the largest U.S. corporations are subsidized by governments through low, or no, taxes, or by direct subsidy payments. They discovered innumerable examples of this practice, such as bestowing over $100 million a year in total subsidies to McDonalds, M&M/Mars, and other companies marketing their goods abroad. In 1999, *Time Magazine* produced an update on this research, and its reporters concluded that in 1997 corporations received almost $200 *billion* in subsidies from state, local, and federal agencies. Most of this huge flow of government payments exemplifies the power of huge corporations to shape political decisions in their favor, a power that is denied to virtually all citizens except very wealthy ones. When did *you* last press your economic concerns on a U.S. Senator or the U.S. President, as do the owners of large corporations on a daily basis?

One effect of the enormous amounts of "soft" money paid to politicians in the past two decades is a considerably more relaxed enforcement of antimonopoly laws by the anti-trust division of the U.S. Justice Department. Presidents Reagan, Bush, and Clinton, who in succession have directed anti-trust policy for the past twenty years, have thus encouraged the marriage of mammoth corporations, such as the $170 billion merger between Exxon and one of its major rivals, Mobil Oil, and the one now occurring—creating a $350 billion company--between already massive companies, Time/Warner and American Online. Mergers of this order are sold to the public on the grounds that only they can provide the high-quality, low priced goods for which we clamor. Yet, mergers can as often as not mean less competition, higher prices, and a growing challenge to democratic rights in areas where they operate. Our point here is important if we are to distinguish adequately between mainstream economics and political economy. To the former, political power is most often considered part of the background institutional structure which is, as they put it, "taken as a given" and thus is left to political "scientists" or others to worry about. It is this determination to ignore the great concentrations of economic power in capitalism that allows conservative mainstream economists such as Milton Friedman to argue that capitalism always "promotes political freedom." For their part, political economists see capitalism as *intrinsically political*, where the capitalist workplace is a rigid hierarchy of control and where the alleged "neutral" government is disproportionately--as even reasonably alert children now know-- in the service of the rich and powerful.

Karl Marx suggested that the government in modern capitalist countries is "the executive committee of the capitalist class," that is, of the rich and the powerful. As you will likely discover in an economics principles course, income inequality is now greater in the U.S. than in any other advanced capitalist society--and it has consistently been among the most unequal for over two centuries--because our laws allow that consequence. The political economist might explain why Bill Gates is worth $90 *billion*, while at the same time 43 *million* people in the U.S. do not have health insurance coverage, in this way: powerful people and corporations have consistently defeated efforts in the U.S. to provide adequate health care to all citizens, while they have spent lavishly to ensure that lawmakers make rules of the capitalist game that allow individuals to accumulate vast fortunes.

THE MAINSTREAM AND CONTEMPORARY GRADUATE PROGRAMS IN ECONOMICS

Since it is probably not by virtue of divine intervention, and certainly not from success in predicting what will happen in the world, why does the mainstream version—and in this context we are talking specifically about the narrow model building we discussed at the beginning of the essay--dominate economic instruction in the capitalist world? As we have said, the answer lies largely in the kind of graduate programs that now train economists. All but a few of these programs in the U.S. focus on a narrowly conceived foundation of economic theory, statistics, and mathematics. For example, consider aspects of two such programs always ranked among the very best, M.I.T., which has housed Paul Samuelson since the 1930s, and Stanford, where Paul Romer teaches. Here is how Stanford's economics department describes the desirable academic background for prospective graduate students:

> Most of our recent successful applicants have had scores above the 95th percentile on the quantitative GRE, and received excellent grades in economics and math courses. The department requires competence in the calculus of several variables, linear algebra, and probability and statistics as they are used in modern economics. Applicants are not required to have been undergraduate economics majors, but some substantial preparation in economics is desirable (Stanford University web site).

According to the M.I.T. web site, the "core requirements" for its Ph.D. in economics include the following courses:

- Two courses in microeconomic theory
- Two courses of macroeconomic theory
- Two courses in mathematics for economists
- Two courses in econometrics (statistical economics)
- One course in economic history

Perhaps most striking about these two programs is not what is included but what is actually left out. Here's a list of subjects that one does *not* have to study as a graduate student to get a "doctor of philosophy" in economics at Stanford or MIT:

- Philosophy, religion, ethics
- History beyond a single course, literature, classics, foreign languages
- Art, art history, and music
- Natural or physical sciences, psychology
- Political Science, sociology, anthropology, international relations

Without question, when Ph.D. students go beyond the core requirements, and especially when many of them write their theses, they will do research in other disciplines, particularly the other social sciences and history. However, the core of the typical program makes it quite clear that whatever information is taken from outside economics, it will be filtered through the tiny meshed screen of a narrow definition of economics, itself already filtered through the even more narrow screen of mathematics, and statistics. Thus, we have a situation in which, to get a Ph.D., increasingly students need not know anything about the economy, but must understand incredibly complex mathematical manipulations. If it becomes the case that only mathematical economists get Ph.D.s and only Ph.D.s teach economics, the profession will have become self-perpetuating, no matter its failures at being scientific and its exclusivity. This trend would mean, also, that increasingly only the math whiz can succeed in economics, and only those who feel comfortable working within a theoretical world where it is assumed that human behavior can be modeled with equations.

David Collander, in *The Spread of Economic Ideas*, a book co-edited with A.W. Coates (Cambridge, 1998), provides the following evidence of how survival in the economics profession has narrowed the interests of those studying economics:

> Economists readily ferret out the incentive system. In a [1987] study Arjo Klamer and I did of graduate economics education, we asked students what would put them on the fast track. Approximately ninety percent said that knowledge of mathematics and knowledge of modeling was important; only about three percent said that these were unimportant. *Only ten percent said that knowledge of economic literature was very important and only three percent said that knowledge of the*

> *economy was very important. Sixty-eight percent said knowledge of the economy was unimportant.* In my view, these answers suggest that something is terribly wrong in the economics profession and in the incentives that economists perceive (emphasis supplied).

Of course, as we discussed at the beginning of this essay, the mainstream school is broad enough to include a variety of different approaches, including some that are also skeptical about the narrow model building. For example, in 1991, the *American Economic Review*—the most prestigious mainstream journal—invited twelve eminent economists to become the Commission on Graduate Education in Economics. They were asked to study the nature of graduate economics training and to report their findings. In describing the contents of their report, John Cassidy, economics editor of *The New Yorker*, wrote that:

> [The Commission] feared the universities were churning out a generation of "idiots savants, skilled in technique but innocent of real economic issues." The commission described the state of academic economics in damning detail, but five years later little, if anything has changed. "That report took a lot of time and energy on the part of everybody involved," Stanford professor Anne Krueger, who headed the commission, told me. "Yet, basically, if only the report and a pin had dropped at the same time, the pin would have sounded noisy" (*The New Yorker*, December 1996).

As a final comment on this issue, it is not just political economists and a few mainstream economists who are unhappy with the fact that narrowly trained model builders dominate the profession. John Cassidy also quotes two other people who should know what they're talking about. One of them, Joseph Stiglitz, an academic economist who became head of the Council of Economic Advisors to Pres. Bill Clinton, told Cassidy that, "Anybody looking at those [mathematical] models would say they can't provide a good description of the modern world." The other is Laurence Meyer, an economist and currently a member of the Federal Reserve Board. Meyer made the interesting point that the quantitative model builders, who had come to dominate macroeconomics in the 1970s, actually helped him build an economic forecasting business that depended on the older, Keynesian models. His firm profited from the fact that more and more graduating macroeconomists—who could have been his competitors in the forecasting field—were not trained to build models about the real world and thus had a declining value to businesses and to governments. Meyer described to John Cassidy the problems of the mathematical school this way:

> When you close your blinds, you don't look out of your window and you don't care what's happening out there. You don't try to build models which are consistent with the real world. With the blinds closed, it's hard to see anything.

There might be light at the end of this dark tunnel, after all. Michael Weinstein, writing in the *New York Times*, reports on foundation money being spent to help decompress graduate economists from their training. In an article that includes many of the same critical ideas about mainstream economics that we have been making, Weinstein also writes:

> I recently joined several dozen first and second-year students at a conference in Airlie, Va., that was convened to helped them find their way toward applied economics—analyzing problems that real people face. During the weeklong conference, organized by the Social Science Research Council and paid for by the John D. and Catherine T. McArthur Foundation, eminent scholars presented lectures on applied topics ranging from the plight of low-income mothers under the 1996 welfare law to the long-term determinants of innovation....

So has graduate economics training run off the rails? There is another side. Economics professors and graduates from the very schools—Michigan, M.I.T., Columbia, Stanford, Wisconsin, Harvard, Colorado, University of Pennsylvania, New York University—that supplied students for the conference do a great deal of excellent applied work. Compared with 20 or even 10 years ago, there has been an explosion in the number of academics who are consultants to think tanks for policy

analysis, corporations and Government agencies....

[P]erhaps economics has stumbled onto an unwittingly workable life-cycle for many academics. During the first couple of years of training, professors pile on a formidable amount of abstract theory at the only time that students can study uninterrupted at the feet of their masters. But, as Alan Blinder [past vice-chair of the Federal Reserve System and well-known academic economist] observes, as professors age, they turn increasingly to applied subjects. Though graduate programs make it hard for students to follow applied interests early on, many eventually find their way ("Students Seek Some Reality Amid the Math of Economics," *New York Times*, 9-18-99).

There are, then, alternatives voices shouting down the tunnel, and we can only hope that those in the dark, like the many in economics programs that ignore the real world, will listen.

SO, WHAT SHOULD ECONOMISTS DO?

Our position is that the public would do best, if it were to make reasonable economic judgments, to listen to economists from all branches of economics, including those outside the dominating mainstream. This, as we now know, surely does not happen, but what would happen if a hundred flowers did bloom in economics? We would like to answer that question by comparing two ways to look at a currently important social issue, environmental pollution. We will start our comparison with a quotation from a popular textbook, now in its nineteenth edition, written by Roger Leroy Miller. In the chapter about environmental economics, and specifically his discussion of the economist's idea of the "optimal amount of pollution" society should tolerate, Miller makes the following point:

> Recognizing that the optimal quantity of pollution is not zero becomes easier when we realize that it takes scarce resources to reduce pollution. It follows that a trade-off exists between producing a cleaner environment and producing other goods and services. In that sense, nature's ability

to cleanse itself is a resource that can be analyzed like any other resources, and a clean environment must take its place with other societal wants (*Economics Today: The Micro View*, 1997, p. 700).

This fairly straightforward argument contains an important point, and it makes sense in trying to decide what to do about pollution that we weigh the benefits of ending a source of pollution against the costs of doing so. What is unstated here, and it is a telling omission, is the assumption that we can actually know all these costs and benefits and be able to measure them. Concerning the costs of controlling pollution, let's take, for example, the case of managing toxic wastes by incinerating them. It is possible to estimate within a useful range the full costs of building an incinerator, and we can estimate, but only within a much wider range, its long term operating costs. However, and this is the rub, there are many costs of incinerating toxic wastes that are simply not measurable. As a prime example, the scientific community is divided over the health effects of incineration because a by-product of the process is that certain heavy metals, and often the highly toxic dioxin (the chemical in Agent Orange), are spewed from the stacks during incineration. These enter the atmosphere in very small amounts, but no one knows for sure their effects. If you read some of the scientific literature on these pollutants you will come away knowing only that no one knows for sure. What is the cost born by individuals for living next to a possible death machine; and, alternatively, if it turns out not to be such a machine, what is the cost to them, perhaps over decades, of worrying about its effect on themselves and their children? Furthermore, incinerators are almost always located in low income neighborhoods against the wishes of the people living there, and we would need to have some measure of the costs to these poor people of having their neighborhood ruined by the big, ugly, smoking incineration plant that looms over it. Our point is that it is not possible to measure the full costs of toxic waste incineration because many important elements of them are not measurable.

Though we will not go into the details, difficulties in measuring the "benefits" to society of toxic waste incineration are equally daunting. In their case, we would need to compare the benefits to us from incinerating toxic wastes to those from leaving them on the ground where they are produced and not treated at all, or throwing them in

a landfill, or disposing of them in some other way. Thinking about this matter for just a moment will make it clear that any of these methods of "dealing" with toxic wastes will produce outcomes we cannot know in advance, and/or cannot be measured. In other words, economists can give us a model that says, in order to decide rationally about pollution, we should measure the costs and benefits of cleaning up any particular polluting source. But that's about it. We are given a conceptual framework in which to think about pollution control but no way to deal with the insurmountable problems of putting dollar amounts on *all* the material and intangible costs and benefits.

Also missing in the chapter in Miller's book in which the quotation above appears is any mention of several critical aspects of environmental pollution that need to be taken into account. For instance, there is no mention of our point that poor people— and people of color, especially—are most likely to live close to toxic incinerators; and there is no mention of the fact that the pollution control business is a huge industry with substantial political clout at every level of government. Moreover, Miller seems to have no curiosity at all about the relationship between the roughly three to four *thousand* advertisements the typical adult now sees every day, the rampant consumerism this creates, and the fact that toxic wastes are generated and have to be disposed of. He can ignore those aspects of the issue because, like any good mainstream economist, his job is to take the "world as given" and make correct scientific statements about it, despite the fact the consumer wants he is taking as given might, in fact, be leading us toward the destruction of our planet. Miller's analysis of pollution, therefore, is quite typically mainstream in his trust in highly abstract and simple models which promise a good deal more than we think they can deliver.

The political economy world is a far less certain world, one where the political economist works always to push away the fog, hoping, hoping for a fleeting glimpse of real economic forces. From such a view, with uncertainty the ever-present companion and belief that everything remotely relevant *must be given attention*, the political scientist might look at environmental pollution, in general terms, in something like the following way:

We believe that human activities that threaten the environment, or human health, need to be curtailed. And, let's assume—

from a large body of persuasive, though not necessarily conclusive, data accumulated from many branches of science and from reputable literary and journalistic sources—that modern patterns of consumption in wealthy countries currently pose a dire threat to the environment and to human health. Then, let's assume it is possible through education to persuade people that it is in their long-term self interest to learn to live with less instead of giving in the cajoling voices of the advertisers always to try to accumulate as much as possible. Then, let's set as our principal goal trying to imagine ways to reconstruct society so that human beings become gradually less insatiable in the face of the endless swirl of commodities. And, let's plan to do our work with a kind of analysis that will be accessible—and hopefully useful—to others who share our interest in preserving the planet for coming generations.

In this example, we distinguish the political economy approach from the mainstream in four critically different ways:

1. We believe that human nature is pliable and conditional, rather than fixed.

2. We have made explicit value judgments about the way we think the world ought to be.

3. A central basis of our analysis is empirical and historical (and thus inconclusive), rather than theoretical and conclusive.

4. The questions we ask, our method of answering them, and all the other aspects of our investigation, are couched in a language designed for all people who want to build a more reasonable world, rather than symbolic language accessible only to the narrow few.

CONCLUSION

There are, to be sure, a number of other differences that exist between mainstream economics and political economy, as well as disagreements within these groups. Please remember that we have been describing polar

clusters on the great spectrum of economic ideas. In the earlier chapters, we take up more detailed discussions of the voices that have generated the major political economy challenges to the mainstream. After you read about Marx, Veblen, and Keynes, and about social classes in capitalism and the modern Swedish economy, you can compare them to the mainstream explanations that will almost certainly be the focus of your economics courses. Then, perhaps, you can decide for yourselves what version of modern economic analysis—or what mixture of those to which we introduce you—makes the most sense